Here's how readers around the world have
responded to the Internet essays of John Kaminski:

Your critical analysis of the whole miserable mess is
incalculable and has importance beyond measure to all of us,
and it's up to those who read your material to get your
message out to as many people as they can.

— Bob Leslie, Halifax, Nova Scotia

You are becoming the "Paul Revere" of our time. Your
keyboard is your horse and your words the lanterns.

— Duane Evans, Greenville, South Carolina

If his work were in the American and British mainstream
press, Bush and Blair and their neo-mafiosi thugs would
have been deservedly lynched long ago. "The Perfect
Enemy" is where Michael Moore, Noam Chomsky and their
ilk — overrated chicken-shits, the lot of them — fear to
tread.

— Dave Bunford, Swansea, Wales

Kaminski refuses to be misled by either the mainstream press
or by obsessive conspiracy theorists. Readers will go a long
way to find a match for the brilliant disclosures in John's
essays or the clarity of his presentations. They're a wake up
call that we can't afford to ignore.

— Paul Balles, Ph.D., Manama, Bahrain

I feel pity of what is going on the Middle East region,
especially, in Iraq. Your clear-cut vision towards the US
policy in the region in unquestionable. I mull over your

article for a while and could detect that even Arabs don't have your sense of thinking and sincere feelings.

— Abduh Moqbil, Taiz, Yemen

John Kaminski continues to pull back the wool from humanity's eyes. Anyone without the requisite courage to dismantle personal and collective illusions should steer clear of this man. His insight into the charade that masquerades as reality is as relentless as it is liberating. No one can afford not to be a serious student of his work.

— Bob Cinque, Marymount, Washington

How about the cell-phones, which don't work at that altitude — surely this is the most damning evidence. Personally I knew 9/11 was a crock of shit because I dreamt America as a bloated pig about to slit its own throat — days before the incident. The day it occurred I felt punched in the gut by the lies soaking our TV screens. I was alarmed because I felt so ALONE in my conviction it was a crock of shit. Moreover I believed no one would have the courage to speak the truth. Only one man stood out. That man was you, John Kaminski.

— Willow Rainmaker, Navajo reservation

This is feeling so much like Germany in the 30's. Thank you for being a lighthouse in this storm.

— Rusty Miller, Lubbock, Texas

Without a doubt you must have had a past life as a prophet, perhaps, Jeremiah. No one, but no one in the blogosphere, speaks with the moral clarity and sheer, incisive power that you do.

— Don Paulus, New York City

In John Kaminski, I see the greatest and the noblest American patriot who has dedicated his entire life to the presentation of truth to American people regardless of consequences and who, in reality, is the main spokesman for the millions of the ordinary and common human beings coming from all walks of life not only in the United States, but also for the rest of the world.

— Michael M. Djuricich, Indianapolis

Just when I think the whole gang is beginning to succumb to the brainwashing, there stands John K., just like a stone wall. In the nick of time.

— Pete Wagner, Perryville, Maryland

Our government's peace is WAR; their justice is INJUSTICE, and their honesty is DISHONESTY, plain and simple. Your written words speak so loudly they are nearly screaming off the page. But who is listening, who is hearing, and more so, WHO IS BELIEVING? Americans are tragically asleep and smug in their own security of affluenza which is beginning to unravel at the seams. We have a fascist government and the beginnings of a police state. For all who bravely express their wisdom, knowledge and credible information on the Internet, please accept my sincere thanks and be safe. We need you. You are a lifeline.

— Grannie Frann, address unknown

For all those children raped
and mothers murdered
by American, British,
and Israeli butchers
in Iraq, Afghanistan, Palestine,
and elsewhere.

And for
Rachel Corrie
and Tom Hurndall

THE
PERFECT
ENEMY

The internet essays of
John Kaminski
volume 2

Sisyphus

Press

Sisyphus Press
P.O. Box 10495
State College, PA 16805-0495

Kaminski, John: The perfect enemy:
The internet essays of John Kaminski, volume 2
ISBN Number: 0-970-1950-7-9

John's website can be found at: www.johnkaminski.com

Cover design:
Laurent Bompard
VISUALTHINGS.COM, Barcelona, Spain
<laurent@visualthings.com)

Foreword

George Orwell said: "During times of universal deceit, telling the truth becomes a revolutionary act." We live now in a time of universal deceit and John Kaminski is telling us how things really are in this world. And the way they are is something many people would rather not know.

John Kaminski says what needs to be said in these times. He is not polite. He is not diplomatic. He is not careful not to offend. He writes the truth as he sees it, something that many other political and social commentators and journalists are afraid to do, for fear that if they state clearly what they know to be going on in America and the rest of the world, they will lose their jobs. John Kaminski has no job to lose, and writes from the conviction that somehow over the last few decades the United States of America has gone insane and is destroying itself along with the rest of the world. But the situation is not completely hopeless. John Kaminski has a stubborn faith that Americans — if they really knew what their government was doing, and has done, in their name — would be outraged.

He also believes that enough Americans, sufficiently outraged, can save themselves, their descendants, their country, and the rest of the world from the dismal and robotic future into which it is being dragged by a depraved U.S. administration that has shown itself to be completely devoid of morality.

John Kaminski's essays range over many matters and are written from a broad perspective. He feels strongly that people need to hear certain unpalatable truths about their country and their leaders because he believes that people are in great danger, and their only hope is to wake up and understand what threatens them.

He points out that there is a plot to destroy democracy in America, and that the plotters are well-advanced in their plans. The plotters are intent on gaining control of the entire planet and all its resources, and they intend to use the U.S. (especially its military power) to accomplish this aim. But the American people as a whole cannot be relied upon to support an immoral and rapacious America, one that bombs and invades other countries, and imprisons and tortures ordinary citizens of those countries, while allowing big corporations to take up no-bid contracts for "reconstruction", the bills for which are ultimately paid for by U.S. taxpayers.

Since the American people would not allow this kind of thing if they knew, their influence on American foreign policy has to be reduced to zero, and so democracy in America must be eliminated for this plan of global domination to succeed. John Kaminski reveals in his essays that this is the case, and that Americans need to hear this if they are to save their remaining liberties and restore those that have been lost under the Patriot Act and other "anti-terrorist" legislation of the last ten years (not to mention legislation that is intended to be pushed through in the wake of the next big "terrorist attack").

But who are these plotters? John Kaminski regards as the prime suspects the international bankers, those who control the world's money supply.

The social condition that makes the most money for bankers is war. John Kaminski elaborates upon the thesis that the prevalence of war during the 20th century, and in particular in the opening years of the 21st, is due to the influence of the international bankers, seeking, as ever, to maximize their profits at the expense of ordinary people. He writes: "9/11 was devised in Washington, like all those other events [the first WTC bombing and the Oklahoma City bombing], for the purpose of replacing the unpredictable chaos of liberty with the tightly regimented exploitation of sheer totalitarian profit maximization. That's what NAFTA, the Patriot Act, the FCC consolidation were all about. And 9/11. Mission accomplished. The permanent war is on."

The evidence that the official story regarding what happened on 9/11 is a fabrication is now overwhelming, thanks to the research of many intelligent, rational and independent investigators who have published their findings on the web. But most Americans remain unaware of their conclusion because the hundreds of web sites which reveal the falsity of the official story have been ignored by the mainstream media. This is because those who control the corporations which own the mainstream media do not want this knowledge to get out to the general public. The falsity of the official story has also been assiduously ignored by those commentators on the so-called 'Left', such as Noam Chomsky and Amy Goodman, whom we might have expected to be diligent in exposing government lies, but who have shown themselves by their public statements on the subject to be complicit in the 9/11 cover-up.

John Kaminski insists on presenting, again and again in his essays, the facts and the implications of the facts, which show that the U.S. government has lied about 9/11 from the first day. If the mainstream media refuses to present the evidence of the falsity of the official story to the American public, and those who also claim to represent an "alternative" view also refuse to present it, then the only way it can reach Americans is via the web and via those few print publications which manage to see the light of day. John Kaminski's two books of essays (this being the second), and his booklet "The Day America Died", attempt to overcome this conspiracy of silence and to tell Americans what they need to know, namely, that their government does not have their best interests at heart, but rather is involved in a long-term plan to reduce them to the status of peons, with no rights and hardly any freedom. And the same for their children and their children, for ever and ever. This outcome, John Kaminski believes, can only be prevented if Americans wake up and realize what danger they are in.

These days there are an increasing number of critics of the official story regarding 9/11. But some of these critics are actually trying to protect the Bush administration by diverting attention from more serious allegations to less serious ones. To understand where John Kaminski stands in this spectrum of critics one must first understand the distinction between LIHOP and MIHOP.

LIHOP = let it happen on purpose. MIHOP = made it happen on purpose. The Bush administration is not unhappy with rumours of LIHOP because that distracts from MIHOP. Even if a LIHOP case could be established, the Bush cabal can say: Well, WE HAD NO IDEA it would be THAT bad! They can feign ignorance, incompetence, etc., which everyone already knows is endemic in Washington, D.C. But 9/11, as John Kaminski shows, was made-in-America and was MIHOP (it had to have been done by people working within the system). LIHOP is incompetence. MIHOP is murder and treason.

Those who are trying to protect the system ignore evidence of MIHOP. They promote LIHOP so as to make the Bush administration look bad, but only to a limited and manageable extent, thus preparing the way for Bush to be defeated by Kerry in the November election (if there is an election). But replacing Bush with Kerry will leave the system intact, and those who planned and carried out 9/11 will escape exposure and retribution. Those who push LIHOP and ignore MIHOP are protecting the 9/11 mass murderers. John Kaminski is definitely in the MIHOP camp.

John Kaminski is not forgiving of the "misstatements" and errors of our political leaders. To call their actions, decisions and policies "errors" is to excuse them. John Kaminski, rather, accuses them of "offenses against both the citizens of America and people in countries all over the world, include making false statements and perjury; extortion and blackmail; unlawful imprisonment and filing false charges; massive theft and bribery; obstruction of justice on a wide scale; criminal conspiracy in many matters, most especially in the destruction of the U.S. Constitution and the deliberate poisoning of the American people; espionage; treason; and foremost, mass murder of innocent people at home and abroad." To someone unacquainted with what is really going on, or who does not want to know, these charges may seem exaggerated. Unfortunately they are not, and John Kaminski is one of the few writers who is prepared to state these charges publicly and to provide the evidence for them.

When George W. Bush, shortly after 9/11, delivered a speech in which he said, "To the nations of the world — you're either for us or against us", we can now see in hindsight that that was a declaration of war against the rest of the world. He in effect offered the nations of the world a choice: submit to U.S. power, policy and demands, or face "serious consequences", meaning, as we now know, bombing and invasion, or at least the permanent threat thereof.

Bush, Cheney, Rumsfeld and Ashcroft created, in the wake of 9/11, a state of perpetual war for the United States. Cheney and others have admitted this by stating that their "war on terror(ism)" would likely last a generation or two — in effect perpetual war.

John Kaminski asks: Who benefits from this state of perpetual war? He answers that it is a cabal, a network of informal conspiracies if you wish, foremost among whom are prominent banking interests acting in concert with governments and government-established entities (such as the CIA and CIA-funded front groups such as the National Endowment for Democracy) for their own interests at the expense of the common people. One of their tactics has been the maintenance of the common people in a state of ignorance and deception concerning their activities and policies. John Kaminski's work seeks to remedy this condition of ignorance and deception by revealing what is actually going on in this world, who is doing it, and how it affects everyone.

As John Kaminski writes in "The Perfect Enemy": "The harder an enemy is to find and defeat, the better it is for those who seek to destroy that enemy. The CIA's creation of al-Qaeda is the perfect recipe for those billionaires whose objective is endless conflict from which to make more money. This is the new era in which we find ourselves."

John Kaminski believes that most Americans are living within a delusion, a deluded conception of their own country and its place in the world. The "official story" about the U.S.A. is that it is a model society for the world, a democracy, a society which stands for freedom, equality and justice for all, which seeks to bring the benefits of freedom and democracy to all countries.

This is cant. The truth is very different, and John Kaminski has labored mightily to bring this truth to the attention of Americans, because these delusions are not harmless. Indeed, they make possible the enormous harm inflicted by the U.S. and other governments upon their own people and the peoples of the world, because governments can only act with the permission (tacit if not overt) of their people. If enough people are sufficiently outraged by the immoralities perpetrated in their name by their governments, then, John Kaminski believes, they will find a way to stop them.

It is a delusion that America goes to war only in a just cause. In fact the U.S. has involved itself in many wars, not for noble purposes, but mostly to benefit those who run things behind the scenes - the international bankers, the military, and those companies which make the weapons (such as cruise missiles, million-dollar machines, the product of American ingenuity, whose only purpose is to kill).

John Kaminski writes: "American prosperity is based on war. And we, the average citizens, get so little of it. Most of it goes to those who get the Bush tax breaks and no-bid contracts. You know how it goes with addictions: the more you have the more you want. So now with the American economy, the plan is to crash it, eliminate most of the population, and resell the real estate that will be taken by default. Great plan. Superior profit potential. For those who have the guns."

The "conventional wisdom" expressed by respected political commentators such as those whose measured discourse is gladly broadcast by such respected print and online publications as The Nation and Common Dreams, is that the solution to America's problems lies in "working within the system" to remove George W. Bush as president and replacing him with some alternative, any alternative, and it seems the only alternative is John Kerry. John Kaminski sees that this is no solution to America's problem because Kerry is himself a part of the problem, and the system as a whole is rotten. And a rotten system must be replaced.

Americans can save themselves only by returning America

to the republic it once was, with a government based upon the principles and prescriptions of the Constitution, a government in which the checks and balances among the Legislative, Judicial and Executive Branches of the government function as the Founding Fathers intended. This state of affairs has been destroyed by the usurpation of unchecked and arrogant power by a series of administrations, culminating in one whose leaders can properly be characterized as "servants of evil".

One of the other themes running through John Kaminski's writings is that of the pernicious effects of organized religion, whether it be Christian, Jewish, Islamic, Hindu, or any other. It is not that he disparages spirituality, rather that he sees organized religion as another way for people to be enslaved, for people to be prevented from thinking for themselves and experiencing divinity (if such exists) in ways they choose for themselves. Organized religion does not open people to a spiritual dimension but rather closes them off from it. He is particularly critical of those religious sects which foment bigotry and hatred of others, providing support for those who would like to invade and pillage those countries where those "others" live (especially if they live atop large oil, natural gas or mineral reserves).

John Kaminski also has harsh words for the Zionist goal of a "greater Israel", to be achieved partly as a result of the genocide of the Palestinian people. And he has similarly harsh words for the U.S. administrations which over recent decades have provided Israel with many billions of dollars (taken indirectly from the pockets of U.S. taxpayers) used to finance Israel's war machine, including its development of nuclear weapons, with which it can now threaten any country in the world.

In 1859 the philosopher John Stuart Mill, in his essay "On

Liberty", defended freedom of expression of opinion, and his defense remains relevant today, especially when this freedom is under attack by those in the U.S. who see (and would like everyone else to see) dissent from the official line as "unpatriotic".

Mill said that silencing an expression of opinion is a deprivation. If the opinion is right, people are deprived of the opportunity of exchanging error for truth. If it is wrong, then they are deprived of the clear perception of truth as a consequence of its collision with error.

Mental well-being depends on the freedom to express one's opinion. A society in which freedom of expression and opinion is suppressed will develop a collective mental illness, as we see happening in the U.S., and not just because of suppression of information concerning what happened on 9/11.

Mill put forward the following reasons for not silencing the expression of an opinion, however false or unpalatable that opinion may seem to some. (i) The opinion may be true; to deny it without good reason is to assume one's own infallibility. (ii) The opinion may be mostly false but yet be partly true, in which case by silencing the opinion we miss the truth it contains. (iii) The opinion may be false, but only a contest between it and the commonly held opinion will establish that the latter really is true, rather than it's being believed on improper grounds, such as having been uttered by some government spokesman or some talking head on TV.

John Kaminski exercises his right of free expression in these essays, and his motivation is an honest one: to bring people to see what is really there, in contrast to the illusions that they hold about what they think is there. He attempts to expose the hypocrisy which characterizes the claims made by government officials, and to reveal the outright lies that they purvey in an attempt to hoodwink the American people and make the world safe for millionaires to acquire more millions, while the majority of ordinary people lack the basic necessities of a decent life: jobs, health care, and a decent education for their children. In the best American tradition he calls for a rebellion against an immoral and life-destroying tyranny. Will you join the rebellion? Or will you go as sheep to the slaughter? John Kaminski's essays will help you to decide.

Peter Meyer, webmaster, www.serendipity.li/   June 2004

Table of contents

Testimonials
Foreword

Acknowledgments

Chapter One

We are as others see us

We are not who we say we are. To insist we are is to say that the rest of the world doesn't count, that the opinions of our friends don't matter, that their honest attempts at objectivity are not really important to us.

We are not who we think we are, or claim to be. We are what others say we are, which is why in courts and schools and businesses, we don't accept what people claim about themselves; we ask witnesses, teachers and references. We are who others say we are.

If we continue to say that our opinion of ourselves is all that matters and everything that others say is mere envy, we are practicing a demented, paranoid self-centeredness, and will never be good neighbors to anyone, nor legitimate citizens of the world. This behavior is justifiably ostracized and ridiculed — and often treated medically — in what passes for polite society.

Yet this is the course America is on, ignoring all the criticism from people who have proven they're our friends. We follow our own selfish hearts, and because of our behavior, the world is bleeding.

Recently, the august and enigmatic nation of France tried to show us the error of our ways, and to show our gratitude we responded with ethnic slurs and insults. The French have probably been America's most consistent allies over time; they even helped us fight the British on occasion. They are our friends. But now, in our insular and arrogant ignorance, we castigate them for advocating the elementary rules of civil civilization.

Germany, Russia, Turkey, Chile, and even Cameroon have surpassed the United States in the requisites of basic humanity and civilized behavior in recent weeks, but Americans only scoff at their unsophisticated naiveté. How could they dare preach peace when America has its heart set on war, no matter how unjust or predatory? Who do they think they are, Americans demand to know, when the United States has already decided what is best for the entire world?

Then, consider China's recent assessment of the United States, as furnished in a 2003 report from the Xinhua News Agency.

Now you can say China is our adversary, and that everything the Chinese say about us is mere propaganda. Or, you can try to be honest, and accept their observations as the semi-objective facts they are. You tell me — and yourself — as to whether this report has the ring of truth.

• The U.S. always issues reports about the state of democracy around the world but never reports objectively about itself. True or false?

The six-part Xinhua article challenges the myth of "American Democracy," citing such human rights violations in the U. S. as widespread violence, suspicious judicial decisions, a widening gap between rich and the poor, systemic gender and racial discrimination, and pervasive interference and exploitation in the affairs of other nations. Are these assessments untrue?

"Under the pretext of safeguarding this kind of democracy," the report states, "the United States continues to make rash criticisms of other countries and interferes in their internal affairs. Nevertheless," the article noted, "well-informed people know that the so-called democracy has been nothing more than a fairy tale since the United States was founded more than 200 years ago."

Consider the facts this Chinese article uses to critique American society. And ask yourself — without making any defensive judgments about the motives of China to impugn the credibility of what is being said — if these assertions are not true. Then ask yourself why these questions are not being asked by the very people who should be asking them — namely ourselves.

• The 2000 election debacle further exposed the glaring flaws of the so-called democratic election system in the United States. Fifty million voters cast ballots, less than one-fourth of the 205 million eligible voters in the nation, a record low in U.S. election history. Is democracy only a fairy tale, Xinhua asked? True or false?

The reports quote Larry Makinson, executive director of the Center for Responsive Politics, a nonpartisan group that studies money and campaigns. "The depressing thing about American democracy is I can check the fund-raising balances at the Federal Election Commission and tell you what the election results will be before the election."

The article also says the judicial system in the U.S. is extremely unfair: 90 percent of the persons on Death Row have been victims of sexual abuse and assaults. Most who were sentenced to death were too poor to hire their own attorneys. And it quoted a Columbia University study insisting that in 68 percent of death penalty cases in the U.S., the sentence did not fit the crime. Sound familiar?

The Xinhua report also notes that U.S. spending for prisons

far exceeds the budget for education, and that the gap between the rich and poor in the United States has widened at the same pace as overall economic growth.

"Statistics show that the richest which account for 1 percent of the U.S. citizens are in possession of 40 percent of the total property of the country, while over 32 million citizens, or 12.7 percent of the total population of the country, live under the poverty line," Xinhua asserted.

Do we dare ask ourselves if this a real picture of democratic America? Or is China just waxing propagandistic?

Is China correct when it insists that America "stop arrogantly ordering other countries around on the pretext of human rights" that the U.S. itself doesn't really practice? Or are we just going to insist, along with our very religious president, that China merely envies our freedom?

And what do we make of it when someone who is our erstwhile enemy speaks to us more honestly than our own government? What kind of condition are we in when that happens?

When we encounter opinions about ourselves that may not coincide with our own observations, we rightly must ask who is correct: them or us? But we must be objective, or else the question is useless. So we turn to other sources for verification and decision, and in this case, one more favorable to our own need for self-respect, namely that quintessential American newspaper, The New York Times.

The recent report by Roger Morris on how Saddam Hussein first came to power in Iraq is especially enlightening.

He writes: "Forty years ago, the Central Intelligence Agency, under President John F. Kennedy, conducted its own regime change in Baghdad, carried out in collaboration with Saddam Hussein."

In 1963, the tyrant of the day who was seen as a threat to the West was Abdel Karim Kassem, a general who five years earlier had deposed yet another Western-installed monarchy, Morris reported.

The Eisenhower administration's tolerance of Kassem as a counter to Washington's Arab nemesis of the era, Nasser of Egypt, was much like the way Ronald Reagan and George H. W. Bush behaved toward Saddam in the 1980s against their common foe of Iran. By 1961, the Kassem regime began threatening and talked openly of challenging the dominance of America in the Middle East — all steps Saddam was to repeat in some form. Kassem's days, like Saddam's, became numbered.

In 1963, Kassem was overthrown and executed. The U.S.-installed successor was the anti-Communist Baath Party, and a key U.S. liaison in that coup d'etat was Saddam, then a 25-year-old muscleman who figured prominently in the bloodbath that followed. In 1968, in another coup assisted by the U.S., Saddam came to power; by then, a good friend of the CIA.

To knowledgeable people in the Middle East and Europe, this history is well-known. Most Americans have no clue about it. So when America preaches about the nobility of its motives today in Iraq, much of the rest of the world knows what vicious horse-poop it is.

George W. Bush is simply repeating a cynical pattern that the U.S. has followed in Iraq and other Arab countries for decades on end, but most Americans remain, in their trivia-numbed self-centeredness, clueless.

And this is where we are today, as a nation. Will we listen to what the people of the world are telling us about ourselves, or continue to act out our own self-deluded fantasies of messianic and racist superiority?

For God's sake, the key to integrity is admitting our faults, confessing our sins. Everybody in the whole world realizes this. Yet America admits no faults, and by its commitment to megalomaniacal acts, reveals to the world it has no integrity, and is not to be trusted by its neighbors, nor by the people of the world.

Will we risk the future of all life on this planet for the schemes of a few powerful men who are trying to steal money they don't really need from all of the rest of us who genuinely do?

These are men who don't listen to anybody and truly fit the description of both schoolyard bullies and paranoid delusionals. One day, if there is a God in heaven, they'll really get what's coming to them. We can't let them force us to share the same fate that awaits them, and if we'd read a little history and listened to the opinions of our friends, we surely wouldn't.

Chapter Two

Dear American People

We now face a daunting task. An unpleasant and possibly fatal realization now confronts all of us in our daily lives.

Many of our most powerful leaders need to be arrested for numerous and continuing crimes against humanity.

The longer this action is postponed, the more harm will be done to everyone and everything on earth. No redress of our grievances by them is possible in the current situation. Made mad by power illegally stolen from the American people and by successful crimes that have gone un-confronted, they listen to nothing except the homicidal impulses of their own greed.

The imminent threats of the needless deaths of millions of innocent people and the permanent poisoning of large amounts of land by radiation are policies that have already been implemented and executed. Innocent people are dying every day around the world because Americans refuse to pay attention and challenge what their leaders are doing.

The sick men who perpetrate these deeds and lie about the reasons why they do them must be stopped. This is no longer a matter for debate.

The entire world stands stunned as it watches America turn from Dr. Jekyl into Mr. Hyde.

These criminals must be stopped, or the perils to us all are both obvious and staggering.

We can no longer consider that this will not be done. Only how much more devastation we will permit to be inflicted upon us and the world before we do it.

Whether we will do it must be inevitable if we are to survive as a nation and a species. If we don't do this, we all face a future of being impoverished prisoners with no voice, or we face no future at all.

These crimes, offenses against both the citizens of America and people in countries all over the world, include making false statements and perjury; extortion and blackmail; unlawful imprisonment and filing false charges; massive theft and bribery; obstruction of justice on a wide scale; criminal conspiracy in many matters, most especially in the destruction of the U.S. Constitution and the deliberate poisoning of the American people; espionage; treason; and foremost, mass murder of innocent people at home and abroad.

With all the lies President George W. Bush and his demented minions have told about the reasons for wanting to torture the hapless populace of Iraq, there can be no doubt now of the lies that they told about the tragedy of September 11, 2001. Most people already know that those killings were not inflicted by so-called Islamic terrorists, but by the highest levels of our own government using Israeli mercenaries posing as Arabs to advance its evil, police-state agenda. The so-called war on terror is really nothing but a ruse to enrich those invested in the industries of the war machine; it is really a war on freedom, as many people already know.

Our leaders have exhibited no hint of willingness to admit their obvious participation in these crimes, and there is no indication that they are ever going to by a justice system they themselves control. They have been caught in so many lies to the rest of the world that America is now a laughingstock to everyone with ears to hear.

But the laughing stops when Bush deploys his nuclear arsenal and squadrons of mass death.

Suddenly, no one in the world is safe anymore, and America is to blame.

Thinking, feeling, compassionate and humane people have no choice but to oppose this evil agenda and stop these madmen from what they are doing, and are about to do.

How to do it?

Many millions of Americans have during spring 2003 stepped out of their homes and stood on street corners and in parks, eloquently expressing their opposition to the savage and uncivilized actions of the U.S. government.

These gestures of concern for themselves and the rest of the world have been insufficient to deflect the tranquilizer-glazed megalomaniacs in charge from their criminal course of destructive behavior.

The same people who have carried their signs into cities and onto bridges to demonstrate for peace must now take a different tack.

From this date forth, protests must be directed at police agencies and our local elected officials, to enlist their help in ridding the world of this scourge of sinister oil executives who have hijacked and vandalized the government of the American republic.

These new protests must not be violent, though of necessity, they will be angry. But this anger must be polite, articulate, and not deviate from the purpose of the task now at hand.

Large groups of people must meet and talk with local police chiefs, county sheriffs, district attorneys, city council-people, town select-people, ward bosses and aldermen, to explain to them as patiently and convincingly as possible that our nation is in peril, that the democratic system we have grown to love and cherish has been distorted and perverted by corruption, and now is a clear and imminent threat to the health and survival of our country and its people.

We have no choice but to convince them of the rightness of our concern, and the obviousness of the threat. There are enough intelligent people in America right now to be able to do this. It must happen everywhere, in every town and state.

Impeachment of anyone is no longer a realistic course to follow because the level of corporate corruption reaches so deeply into the ranks of our elected representatives. In all but a few instances across the entire country, you have to be corrupt and on the take merely to run for office.

But for a few stellar examples of integrity such as Ron Paul or Dennis Kucinich, there is no purpose in appealing to the better natures of our legislators, because they have been bought off and will never challenge the leadership of the system. Unfortunately, this is exactly who needs to be challenged, and arrested and jailed, tried and convicted.

Articulate spokespeople from large citizen groups must convince local and regional authorities to issue arrest warrants for George W. Bush, members of his Cabinet, and prominent members of the Congress for their criminal failure to protect the American people from the predations of the corporate looters who are actually running the government now, and telling the president and his gang of immoral thugs what to do.

With adequate evidence, these arrest warrants could include CEOs of egregiously criminal corporations such as Enron, Lilly, and HCA Corp., as well as hundreds of others who have either shown great disregard for the health and welfare of the people, or who have clearly been the recipients of illegal federal favoritism. These warrants also could include judges, like the one who allowed Vice President Cheney to keep his criminal conspiracy with the energy companies secret from the American people, or the one who told Fox News it has no legal obligation to tell the truth. These are both clearly crimes that were committed by cynical political functionaries wearing black robes, and betraying their oaths to protect us.

Why we need to do this is obvious.

Because the next level is shooting in the streets; and we don't want to get there.

Even though it may happen, nobody really wants to get to that point, although it IS the point we WILL get to if enough people suddenly realize that local law enforcement is unwilling to protect the people they are sworn to protect from being robbed and/or killed by their own government.

Nobody needs to be fooled by the terminology here. We all know what the next step is after being betrayed by our own cops and soldiers, and it is not going quietly into dissenter camps already being established by Attorney General John Ashcroft.

It's later than you think, people. The militias are already locked and loaded. Unfortunately, they won't stand a chance against tanks and CS gas. Think Waco, nationwide. It's not a fantasy anymore. If we don't take action now, it's inevitable.

One more thing, if you'll indulge me.

I live in a small town where nobody gets too worked up about anything, except occasional zoning issues. Everybody's mostly too busy having fun in the sun to think about serious matters.

Yet last night (3/16/03), two hundred people showed up at the beach carrying candles for the express purpose of participating in a worldwide vigil for peace. There was no real political invective, just quiet prayers. I wanted to say something, but I was too timid, and it seemed like not the proper venue to say what I wanted. Now I realize it was, and I blew it. I promise never to keep my mouth shut again in such a situation.

This is what I wanted to say. America is a Christian nation, or so some people say. We'll let them say it for the moment.

America is a Christian nation. America has killed ONE MILLION children during the last twelve years in Iraq. And now is poised to kill more. Killed a million children. Can any of us understand what that means? America is Christian nation.

George W. Bush is a devout Christian. He prays every day. He was born again. He has given his life to Christ. He killed five thousand (or more) innocent people in Afghanistan, three thousand in New York City. And promises, on the Bible even, to kill many thousands more. George W. Bush is a devout Christian.

To me, this is what it means to be a Christian. To kill people indiscriminately and then lie about the reasons. I thank God every day that I am not a Christian. Because I'd have to kill people and lie about it.

All of which is to say ... leave your Bibles and other holy books at home, people. Keep it to yourself. Nobody needs to know what you have to say about God. Your actions will show who you are a lot more clearly than your empty and insincere parables. If the words of Christians were sincere, those million children in Iraq would not be dead. Save your smarmy holy rhetoric for others who are uncertain about their real motivation.

All people are the same: we all want love, security and friendship. And we especially don't want to live in fear of our leaders, or fear having our conversations wiretapped by lunatics who want to put us in jail for what we think.

For those of us who are certain about our own motivation, and don't selfishly condemn others who do things differently than we do, we have a big job to do. We realize that religious gobbledygook only complicates matters, and excludes many who otherwise could be our friends.

Stay focused on the big task at hand. We have lost our freedom in an unprecedented situation, and we have to get it back. Be truthful, but be careful.

<u>Chapter Three</u>

9/11 was a hoax

The American government killed its own people

(Editor's note: This story is intended for people who have accepted the official version of the 9/11 story. It should be distributed widely to the uninformed few who still believe this tragedy was engineered by Muslim terrorists.

Either by incompetence or by design, George W. Bush allowed the 9/11 attacks to happen, and probably was involved in the planning of them. The American people might stand by and allow him to slaughter every nation in the world, but they will not stand for it when they know he participated the mass killing of his own people. Or will they?)

Opposed by everyone in the world who was not bought off, the illegal invasion of Iraq was undertaken for many reasons — the imminent replacement of the dollar by the euro as the world's primary currency, the tempting lure of untapped oil reserves, the desire to consolidate U.S./Israeli military hegemony over a strategically vital region — but the most important reason was to further obscure questions about the awesome deception staged by the American government that has come to be known as 9/11.

9/11 was a hoax. This is no longer a wild conspiracy assertion; it is a fact, supported by thousands of other verifiable facts, foremost of which are:

• **The attacks of 9/11 COULD NOT HAVE HAPPENED** without the willful failure of the American defense system. In Washington, Air Force pilots demanded to fly but were ordered to stand down. Yet instead of prosecuting the president and military leaders for this unprecedented dereliction of duty, military leaders were promoted and the president was praised for presiding over a defense system that suspiciously failed the most crucial test in its history. None of the deaths would have happened without the deliberate unplugging of America's air defenses.

Planes that lose contact with control towers are usually intercepted by fighter jets in a matter of minutes, as the incident with the golfer's plane a few months earlier so clearly demonstrated. Yet on 9/11, the jetliners that struck New York were allowed to proceed unmolested for more than a half-hour, and the plane that supposedly crashed in Washington was not intercepted for more than an hour and forty minutes after it was widely known that four planes had been hijacked.

• **The twin towers could not have collapsed** as a result of burning jet fuel. Most of that fuel was consumed on impact. In the South Tower, most of the fuel was spilled outside the building. Heat caused by burning jet fuel does not reach temperatures needed to melt steel. What does stand out as particularly suspicious and still unexplained is that fires raged out of control beneath THREE of the collapsed towers for many weeks, clearly indicating the presence of some kind of substance utilized in the demolition of the structures.

The Twin Towers did not fall because of plane impacts or fires. Most likely explosives were placed on structural supports in the towers (as was done in Oklahoma City), and these controlled implosions snuffed out the lives of more than three thousand innocent people.

• **FBI Director Robert Mueller insisted officials had no idea this kind of attack could happen** when in fact the FBI had been investigating the possibility of EXACTLY this kind of attack for almost TEN YEARS. Numerous previous attempts at using planes as weapons, intimate knowledge of terror plans called Project Bojinka, and knowledge of suspicious characters attending flight schools that were being monitored by the FBI make his utterance a clear lie on its face. In the weeks before 9/11, the U.S. received warnings from all over the world that an event just like this was about to happen, but FBI investigations into suspected terrorists were suppressed and those warnings were deliberately disregarded.

• **The names of the alleged hijackers,** all ostensibly Muslims, were released to the public only hours after the attacks, despite Mueller saying we had no knowledge this would happen. This is impossibly twisted logic. If he didn't know of a plan to strike buildings with planes, how would he know the names of the hijackers? Various artifacts were discovered in strategic places to try to confirm the government's story, but these have all been dismissed as suspicious planting of evidence. Since that time eight names on that list have turned up alive and well, living in Arab countries. Yet no attempt has ever been made to update the list. And why were none of these names on the airlines' passenger lists?

• **Much like the invasion of Iraq, the anthrax attacks** were designed to deflect attention from unanswered 9/11 questions in the patriotic pandemonium that followed the tragedy. In addition to making large amounts of money for the president's father and his friends from the hasty sale of inefficient drugs to a panicked populace, the investigation into these killings was abruptly halted when the trail of evidence led straight to the government's door, and has not been reopened. The anthrax attacks also amped-up the climate of fear and deflected attention from the passage of the government's repressive Patriot Act.

• **The Patriot Act** was presented in the days after the tragedy supposedly as a response to it, yet it was clear that this heinous act, drafted to nullify provisions for freedom in the U.S. Constitution, was put together long before 9/11. In addition, testimony by Rep. Ron Paul (R-Texas) revealed that most members of Congress were compelled to vote for the bill without even reading it. This was a vote to eliminate the Constitutional Bill of Rights, which has defined American freedom for 200 years, and it was accomplished when legislators voted for the bill without even reading it.

• **The invasion of Afghanistan** was presented as an attempt to pursue the alleged perpetrators of 9/11, yet it had been discussed for years prior to the tragedy and actually planned in the months before the attacks on New York and Washington. Statements by Zbigniew Brzezinski and the Republican-written Project for a New American Century have stressed that America needed a formidable enemy to accomplish its aggressive geopolitical aims. The supposed enemy we attacked in Afghanistan was a diverse group of men from all over the world who were initially recruited, encouraged, and supported by the American CIA.

• **The hole in the Pentagon** could not have been made by a jumbo jet. Damage to the building was simply not consistent with the size of the hole or the absence of debris. At the supposed point of impact, a whole bank of windows remained unbroken and there were no marks on the lawn. No airplane debris (except what was planted on the lawn) nor remains of passengers were ever found.

• **The president has admitted** that he continued to read a story to schoolchildren in a Florida school for seven minutes after being informed that two planes had struck New York and that the nation was under attack. He has never explained this puzzling behavior, nor how he saw the first plane hit. It was never televised, only recorded by a French crew filming firemen in New York. In that film, the plane in question does not appear to be a passenger airliner.

• **The plane in Pennsylvania** was shot down and broke apart in mid-air. No other explanation can account for the wreckage, which was spread over a six-mile area, or the eyewitness accounts that describe debris falling from the sky.

• **Cell phone calls cannot be made from airliners** in flight that are not close to the ground. As research by Professor A. K. Dewdney has shown, the emotional conversations between hijacked passengers and others would not have been possible under conditions that existed in those chaotic moments. These calls were cynical fabrications, exploiting the distraught emotions of those who lost loved ones, and were meant to deceive the public.

• **Radio communications from firefighters** on the upper floors of the Trade Center towers clearly indicate that fires were under control and the structure was in no danger of collapsing.

These are merely a few of the deliberately false statements made by U.S. officials about 9/11. They provide crystal clear evidence that our president, his staff, and many legislators should be indicted on charges of treason, obstruction of justice and mass murder. Above all, these evil men should be removed from their positions of authority before they implement more of their moneymaking murder schemes like the one they are now perpetrating on the innocent people of Iraq.

Otherwise, we face a future of endless war abroad and merciless repression at home.

Consider just a few more of the other unanswered questions from among the thousands of unexplained loose ends that all point to 9/11 being an inside job.

• **Who benefited** from the suspiciously high numbers of "put" options purchased prior to September 11 for shares in companies whose stock prices subsequently plummeted, on the supposition that whoever was behind the hijacking was also behind most of the purchases of these put options? And what was the role of the new executive director of the CIA, Buzzy Krongard, who handled many of these transactions?

• **Why was the debris from the collapsed Twin Towers removed** from the site with no forensic examination? Why was almost all of it sold to scrap merchants and shipped abroad where it would not be available for scientific analysis?

• **Why does the government refuse to release** any transcripts of communications or any records at all relating to signals of any form transmitted by those jets?

• **Why did so many people,** from San Francisco Mayor Willie Brown to many employees of companies in the World Trade Center who failed to come to work that day, know in advance that something bad was going to happen on September 11, 2001?

• **Why do all the major U.S. media continue to act as if none of these questions is legitimate or relevant?**

Today, millions of people around the world are protesting the criminal destruction of the nation of Iraq. But these protests won't change the number of minds necessary to stop America's criminal madmen from continuing with their genocidal aim of enslaving the entire world.

What WILL stop them is spreading the realization that President George W. Bush and his billionaire accomplices in the oil industry perpetrated 9/11 as an excuse to begin the militarization of America for the purpose of world conquest.

History has shown all too clearly the deceived American people WILL support the destruction of faraway countries on phony pretexts of defending so-called freedom.

Thus the needless wars continue. Right now we watch high-tech weapons slaughter the defenseless people of Iraq. Soon it will be Iran, Syria, Colombia, Venezuela, North Korea, Egypt, Libya, Nigeria, North Korea, Pakistan, Saudi Arabia, and who knows where else. All these misguided atrocities will be possible because of the hoax known as 9/11.

But the American people will not — and cannot — tolerate leaders who kill our own people merely to invent a pretext — the war on terror — to go around killing anyone they dislike. If the American people DO tolerate such an insane strategy, then they clearly do not deserve to survive as a nation or a people.

<u>Chapter Four</u>

All Americans are now war criminals

The only person at the 2003 Oscars with the human decency to mention the "fictions" that American warmongers have used to create the bloodbath in Iraq was of course Michael Moore, the documentary filmmaker who won an award for his searing indictment of American culture, "Bowling for Columbine."

As expected, Moore was booed by the predominantly Jewish Hollywood assemblage of cinema celebrities. Emcee Steve Martin later made a joke about Moore being stuffed in the trunk of his limo by Teamsters, which evoked derisive applause from the well-dressed audience.

Other than Moore's challenge to the possible humanity of the assembled luminaries, the only remark about the current carnage in Iraq came from best actor Oscar winner Adrien Brody, who delivered an emotional plea for peace and for the safe return of the American troops after accepting his trophy.

Apart from those two gestures, the re was virtually no other mention made of the invasion of Iraq at this annual love-fest of the U.S. movie industry. The oddly comfortable omission of talk about bombings in Iraq mirrored the verbal silence about the subject that dominated the Grammy awards for music several weeks ago, in which presenters and performers, supposedly America's creative elite but really just random and noisy advertising vehicles, were warned by CBS network officials not to make any statements regarding America's clumsy push for war, which was then still being debated at the United Nations.

Evaluating the Grammys and the Oscars together, the

combined performance by the most famous musicians, actors and celebrities of the English-speaking world — which have been totally devoid of any utterances of social conscience — is a nauseating indictment of the social indifference and moral bankruptcy of the U.S. entertainment industry, and as well, the consumers of this irrelevant drivel in America and throughout the world.

Where was Bob Dylan? Where was Eminem? Where was any movie star with social concerns? The American entertainment scene is totally devoid of conscience and not deserving of any audience that calls itself human.

Among this lopsided, pro-war ignoring of the current suffering and death of the Iraqi people — and also the needless deaths of American and British soldiers, many of whom have been killed by their own tactical ineptitude — must be mentioned the deliberately slanted performance of the U.S. media talking heads, who trip over their own tongues trying to insist that American generals are taking great care to avoid killing Iraqi civilians, and that the reasons for the U.S. invasion are actually valid and universally accepted.

The rest of the world, however, knows differently. The rest of the world knows that America suddenly cut off the debate at the United Nations when it became obvious that not enough other nations could be bribed to support the unjustifiable U.S. urge to attack Iraq.

The reporting on American television, however, never mentions that, and seldom shows any of the horrendous and heart-wrenching photographs of children with skulls ripped open as a result of American military action.

Some of the most reliable and unbiased reporting, in fact,

appears to come from Russia, a nation which has joined with France, Germany and others to investigate the possibility of charging the U.S. with war crimes for its irresponsible invasion of a country it charged with crimes it has been unable to prove.

To many people in both America and the rest of the world, the irrelevance and moral perversion of the U.S. entertainment industry is well-known and avoided, although to the majority who consume this trash and emulate the inauthentic trends it popularizes, the cultural dangers of this malicious influence to human social health remain unnoticed.

What should be clear to everyone by now is this. The absence of American social conscience in its entertainment industry shows that America itself is morally degenerate. According to both the tenets of basic psychology as well as the rules of honest behavior by ordinary people, America is in no position to tell anybody anything and have it be believed.

The actions of George W. Bush and his bloodthirsty gang of petroleum psychos have demonstrated clearly that America simply does not tell the truth, nor is it going to anytime in the near future.

That the totality of American mainstream media clearly support Bush and his policy of unjustifiable mass murder anywhere he chooses to unleash it, and that the American people by and large support these policies, should furnish a crystal clear message to the entire rest of the world.

All Americans are now war criminals, willing to support any kind of lie, no matter how ridiculous or lethal, to maintain their immoral position of economic dominance over the oppressed people of Planet Earth.

Let there be no doubt about this. This includes those courageous American souls who protest for peace and are willing to admit their complicity in this matter — for it is this segment of the American population that realizes it has been inattentive to the improper and destructive behavior of its own government that has led to this current danger, as the world prepares to be raped and vandalized by a gun-slinging Texan with his shaky, dry-drunk finger on the nuclear trigger.

Worst of all, George W. Bush is a man who does not know how to tell the truth. In fact, he is utterly incapable of it. Everything that comes out of his mouth has one purpose — to justify his dishonest and rapacious policies that are meant to enrich his corrupt associates at the expense of everyone else in the entire world.

He is incapable of telling the truth. Realize this.

He is incapable of expressing actualized human emotions, especially compassion and understanding for the plight of working stiffs like you and me, because he's never had to work a day in his entire life. The son of a rich man, he's gotten a free pass from every scrape he's every created — notably military desertion and drug selling. But enough about him. He's just a moronic tyrant who needs to be arrested and jailed for life without parole along with the thousands of sycophantic quislings who support his anti-human agenda.

What's more important is the welfare of the troops, both American and Iraqi, and the safety of the millions of innocent people who are now in harm's way for no legitimate reason, for no valid psychological or geopolitical reason.

Hundreds of lives already have been needlessly squandered for the American oil companies.

British New Age guru David Icke showed his courage the other day when he came right out with it. "F*** the troops!" he said.

"They have decided to give their minds away to brainless dictators and that is their choice and they must take the consequences. They don't have to go and kill people, they can refuse to if they want. How about the troops "supporting the civilians" they are going to kill?

"Either the war is right or it is wrong. The fact that it is wrong should not be put aside just because Bush and Blair have done the bidding of their masters and sent 'the troops' into a war that has been long planned and was always going to happen no matter what.

"The troops have a choice. What about the people of Baghdad?" Icke asked.

In the same vein, anti-Zionist activist Carol Valentine recently expressed the same sentiment in an even more forceful way. She said she would put a sign in the back window of her car that read: "US Military = Human Filth."

As she wrote in an e-mail widely circulated on the Internet: "Break through this "support our troops" mind-control rubbish. Treat the public to the truth. To support murderers in their acts of murder is unthinkable."

" ... real people are dying, a real civilization is being destroyed."

I am in fundamental agreement with both of these

courageous souls and others who say the same thing, but I want to put it unmistakable, unambiguous terms.

Whether the United States recognizes it or not, when an international court of inquiry is convened at the end of this unjust and illegal invasion of Iraq, American troops will be eligible for war crimes prosecution in the same way that Nazis and Japanese soldiers were tried, convicted and imprisoned for their actions during World War II.

In fact, what we are doing to Iraq is at least the equal of what Japan and Germany did to us, and perhaps worse. There exists no reason that is not a lie that has been told by George W. Bush to invade Iraq and murder its people.

The petro-psychos in Washington have lied about the 2000 election, lied about 9/11 (and completely thwarted any investigation), lied about the anthrax attacks, lied about the invasion of Afghanistan, and now are lying about the invasion of Iraq. In all of these cruel charades, they have been backed to the hilt by a totally prostituted American media propaganda corps, who are themselves eligible for war crimes charges by their dishonest complicity in this corporate conspiracy against the poor people of the world.

German and Japanese soldiers who were tried following World War II were not allowed to use the excuse that they were just following orders. Soldiers are human beings who are expected to exercise their consciences when they are ordered to commit illegal and immoral crimes against humanity.

To claim they were just following orders is not a valid excuse, never has been.

There is an oil filter advertisement familiar to American TV viewers in which an auto mechanic wisely advises a worried car owner to take precautionary measures and change his filter. "Either pay me now, or pay me later," the mechanic says.

In regard to the American war machine now surging across the globe leaving a bloody trail of violence, it is vital this message now by heard and understood by people in every country in the world.

Each day we fail to stop this bloodthirsty American menace, the price we will pay will keep getting higher.

<u>Chapter Five</u>

Trapped in a poison fog

I had the good fortune to attend TWO Easter dinners with sets of family members this year. Like so many of my e-friends who often complain to me that their families think they're crazy because they believe the U.S. government knows a lot more about the 9/11 butchery than it lets on, and that the recent shoot-'em-up in Iraq was a totally illegal and immoral operation that left the blood of innocent babies all over the American flag, I'm stuck in the same boat.

I'm sympathetic to those messages, because I have a family exactly like that, one that regards me as some odd radical and wonders when I'm going to get picked up and locked away by Ashcroft's storm troopers for many statements that they regard as subversive and blasphemous. But as I have often advocated that all of us who KNOW must do the best we can by informing those of us who don't, I felt obliged to do some educating when the opportunity appeared. Call it a feeble attempt to walk some talk, or possibly talk some walk.

The first dinner was mild and cordial, full of presents and small talk, with not a whimper of war, treason, or how Americans are hiding their heads in the sand and ignoring the blooming tidal wave that signals the coming worldwide police state. Just a little moaning about the suspicious unpredictability of the stock market amid jocular enthusiasm about the latest specifications concerning new cars.

The second dinner, however, with a black sheep nephew who has been ostracized from the righteous and respectable side of the family over his penchant for serial girlfriends and loud blues music, was much more laid back and unpretentious, and the conversation soon drifted to war. Actually, the new girlfriend (and in fact, the new fiancée; he's reforming and settling down as he rocks into middle age) brought it up.

"Why do they have to keep killing all those innocent people?"

My ears perked up. What was this? A whiff of consciousness from my very own family?

But I held back, not wanting to too soon lurch into a full-blown soliloquy about the criminal tendencies of America's kill-crazy government. But then the opportunity presented itself when my nephew noted that it was tragic and regrettable that many American soldiers (he's an ex-Marine) had been stricken by illness as a result of their exposure to chemical weapons.

He looked at me for a response, and I was there. "It isn't really chemical weapons that have been the real danger," I said. "Most Americans in the first Gulf War were sickened by the ammunition they were using, which is made from leftover uranium from nuclear plants. And the second leading cause of all these diseases was from the shots they were given, which contained ingredients that to this day no one has ever adequately identified."

His eyes widened. I continued. "Did you know that 255,000 soldiers have filed for VA disability pensions as a result of being in the first Gulf War? Did you know that 10,000 of those people have already died? And they say that the potency of the ordnance they're using now is much greater, so that we can expect the incidence of illness and cancer in these troops who are serving now is going to be much greater that what happened in the first Gulf War?

"You don't want me to talk about the actual diseases these people get, not at the dinner table ... "

With that he rocked forward and took a big slug of beer. I was an avuncular prizefighter looking for a gentle but irrevocable knockout.

"Do you know why we went to war in Iraq?" I asked quietly. His answer was mumbled, garbled, and uncertain. "Well, yeah, that guy (Saddam) was dangerous; he was a menace."

I pushed on. "Is it OK to invade another country if the reason you're using is a lie?" I asked.

"Well, er, no."

"There were two reasons we invaded Iraq," I said. "First was we said he had weapons of mass destruction. We didn't find any. That reason was a lie. Second, we said Saddam was connected with al-Qaeda and 9/11. There IS no connection. Al-Qaeda was invented by the CIA when we recruited Muslims to fight the Russians in Afghanistan 15 years ago. The U.S. has fought side-by-side with al-Qaeda in Bosnia, Kosovo and Macedonia. The connection is not between al-Qaeda and Iraq; it's between al-Qaeda and the U.S. Both reasons we went to war in Iraq are lies, told by our country. We killed all those people for no real reasons at all, or at least, for reasons that are not the ones they're telling us."

I sensed I could push just a little further. "The invasion of Iraq by the U.S. was much worse even than when Hitler invaded Poland back in World War II. The rest of the world now has us in the same category as Nazi Germany when it tried to take over all of Europe. In fact, what we did to Iraq was much worse than anything Germany ever did to Poland.

"What it's like in this country now is exactly like it was in Germany just before World War II started. New laws are being passed to supposedly protect us from foreign enemies. Back then it was the Communists; now it's the Muslims.

"Think about that when you see people waving those flags next time," I said, sensing he would have no comeback for any of this even if he wanted one. "They are waving those flags and cheering for wars that will take over any country they want for any reason at all. They don't even have to tell the truth about why they're doing it anymore. So when you hear someone say 'support the troops,' what they're really saying is that we can kill anybody we want to for no reason at all. This is what America has become."

After a long, thoughtful silence, my nephew's fiancée spoke up again: "I just don't see why they have to kill all those innocent people."

This time, I couldn't resist an answer. "It's because the people who arrange the wars make so much money off them. They want war, all the time. It's too good a scam for them to worry about innocent people. War is the engine that drives the economy. The same people who make the weapons own the newspapers and TV networks, which is why they all keep saying war is a good thing. When wars happen, some people ... some very rich people ... get very, very rich. That's why they keep doing it. That's why they won't stop ... unless we stop them.

"That's why it's very important that each one of us pays attention and must say what we feel. Otherwise, they're going to keep doing it, and it's going to get worse each time ... "

I could sense the moment had passed, that I had achieved my

objective and it was time to let up. Beer, wine, and gwumpkies had taken their toll, and naps all around were looming in the near future. I hadn't even lurched into my 9/11 rap, or that the Congress was all bought off and incapable of doing anything positive for humanity, or that the U.S. Constitution was long buried by new police-state legislation. But I had pushed them further than I ever had, and gave thanks for that.

After leaving for home, I further reflected about the flags I saw flying on people's houses, the patriotic bunting on the fences, and the marquee at the local church that read: Jesus is the Supreme Commander.

We are trapped in a poison fog of patriotism, and don't dare to question the motives and actions of our so-called leaders. America as a country has held us together and given us a good life in which to prosper and relax. The majority of us do not take the time to carefully examine the reasons our military does what it does when it does them.

We have invented enemy targets out of statements that the rest of the world rejects as clumsy lies. But we ignore the rest of the world because we are Americans, point at our high-tech gadgets, and say with horrifying hubris: "Look at what we've got. We must be right! Because you want what we've got!"

As the venerable TV legend Walter Cronkite recently said, the future seems very, very dark. It will continue to be so unless all Americans, each time they see their flag waving in the breeze, realize that this emblem now symbolizes in this year of our Lord 2003 that Americans can kill anybody they want to for any reason we choose, even if that reason is a lie.

Don't bother praying. God would never help people like that, people like us.

Chapter Six

Horror in your own home

Ignore what your children are learning at your peril

This is a note to parents. You could consider it a warning, but it's really just a congratulatory note, reminding you what you have done to your children by not paying sufficient attention to the world around you.

I myself receive many notes from people telling me they can't watch the TV news anymore. It's just too depressing. And confusing. I also especially get this in conversations with many people I consider less politically aware than myself. They know something is wrong with the newspapers, or the stories they hear on the boob tube, but they just don't have time to analyze their own confusion and sort out the wheat from the chaff. It all sounds so much alike, one false claim after another, and besides, who has the time?

And even if we did have the time, what could we — as ordinary individual citizens — actually do about such doubts. Amid all this flag waving and these terror alerts, who would listen?

There are more important things to do, aren't there?

I mean, so what if children are being blown to bits for reasons that are lies in some faraway country! Life must go on, and we don't have to hear about that, do we? As long as we're not forced to see the photographs, a few deaths over some abstract political debate don't really bother us. It's not our problem. Hey, we have a problem with a neighbor's renegade dog that is far more important to us.

I mean, so what if the corrupt and insincere thugs who run for public office have done away with all the laws that made our country a free society. It hasn't really affected our lives, has it? We still have our bills to pay, our obligations to meet, our kids to get to school. So what if the cops can now come into your house without ever telling you? How does that affect us? We obey the law and have nothing to worry about, right? No big deal.

I mean, we have our lives to live, and if the elite billionaires who dominate all our public institutions want to create situations that simply make more money for themselves, what has that to do with us? We still have our jobs (maybe), our friends (if they actually are our friends), clothes to iron, school pictures to pay for, school board meetings to attend, church charity drives to contribute to ... the minutiae of one's life, particularly if there are kids to be considered, are just endless, and in our drive to get the best of what we want for our offspring, we have to focus on the here and now, in our immediate neighborhoods, to make sure they fulfill their obligations and get the best of what is available to set up their futures, right?

News from some far-off land, or partisan ravings from some disgruntled political observer really don't fit into the pragmatic schedules we set for ourselves. And we must stay focused on those, lest our whole lives suddenly veer off course. After all, abstract political arguments don't pay for four years of college. Or braces.

Yet, there are moments, often when our kids are asleep, when we wonder why and what we are doing all this for, all this running around, all this planning and execution of trivial details. Often at these times we often wonder what we

ourselves are doing, and what our kids are actually learning.
Who will they turn out to be?

And when we really think about those things, sometimes the
epiphanies that seize us are shocking indeed.

Consider what kids are learning today by observing the
current public dialogue.

Growing up in America today, our president and our leaders
are teaching our children that it's OK to kill someone if you
suspect them of harboring ideas that the United States of
America is committing crimes in other countries. No more of
this right-to-a-fair-trial, innocent-until-proven-guilty crap.
Just kill them if you suspect them of opposing American
ideas. Just blow up their countries and kill whomever you
like. If you have the weaponry, you really don't need a
reason. Might surely makes right. That's the new reality. Just
listen to all the new presidential candidates. That's what
virtually all of them are saying.

And that's what are kids are learning today, plus the finest
people in our communities — the judges and doctors and
lawyers — are all in agreement that this is the way we
should be behaving. So show your flag and get with the
program. It's how you'll get ahead. America committing
crimes against other countries? How absurd. We would have
heard about it on TV if it happened.

Hey, it's what the American government has done, is doing,
will continue to do. If the American government says
someone is a terrorist, well hell, they are a terrorist, and they
can be put in jail forever with no trial, no lawyer, no appeal,
no visitors, and never get out. They can even be put to death
by a 2-1 vote in a military tribunal. None of this appeal crap,
where convicted killers can hang onto life for years with

tricky legal maneuve rs. Just kill them. Get it over with.

President Bush recently showed us how people on Death Row should be treated, when during a radio interview, he ridiculed a woman who had been condemned for participating in a long-ago crime that had resulted in a killing. "Please don't kill me," Bush squeaked in a falsetto voice, mocking Karla Faye Tucker, who had become a prominent Christian advocate during her many years in jail.

Some people, even some Christian Republicans, criticized the president for behaving so heartlessly, but hey, that's the way it is now. The president was simply showing our kids how they should behave. You're either for us or against us. If you're against, you know what you'll get. Clarity is a good thing.

That's the way it is now, our kids our learning. We shouldn't have compassion for those who have reformed. If they're convicted, we must punish them. Just kill them, and don't think about what they might have become. It's not relevant. Just kill them.

The same with those blown-up kids in Iraq, especially that boy, Ali, who lost not only his whole family but also his arms.

What do they matter? Iraq is far away and we have our lives to live right here. It doesn't matter that our president used lies to justify the invasion of a nation with a pathetic army. They have oil we want. We have power. It's the law of the jungle. We have the right to go and take it. It's just being realistic. It's the way the world is.

That's what we're teaching our children. If you wave the flag and have enough money to operate in the "right" circles, you can steal anything you want (because you can buy a judge to get you off if somebody tries to catch you), or kill anybody you want, regardless of what they might have done. Life is now all image, and you can get away with absolutely anything if you have the right connections. Do something wrong if you like; then just shape the image to make it appear right. In this day and age, that's all that counts.

Long ago, my father told me this is the way the world is. I refused to believe him, and as a result have no valuable possessions in this world except a rather large and cherished circle of noble friends, most of whom are just as poor as I am.

How we view the world all comes down to money, is what my dad said. That's why politicians go corrupt, why people betray their friends, why real stories of what's happening in the world are not shown on TV.

What most people don't realize is who they are and what they do actually is reflected in the world at large. Since a large majority feels they are powerless and have no influence over events in the larger geopolitical sphere, this is exactly the case: they are powerless and have no influence.

Take 9/11. For more than a year, no one has dared to speak about the embarrassing fact that the official pronouncements on those tragic events that took place do not add up. Wars and laws that were planned BEFORE that sad day were blamed ON those horrid events. But it has not been politically correct to ask those questions. To do so has been considered unpatriotic in this time of national emergency, this War on Terror. But what if the official version WAS a lie? How does that affect us? Do you think more of these things will happen if we fail to catch the grand manipulators in their lies?

And does that matter? Heck, life goes on. All the old sayings are relevant. Go along to get along. You can't fight City Hall. All the noble philosophy in the world doesn't mean a thing when your belly isn't full.

So we are raising a generation of kids to whom morality and fairness, as well and truth and honor, are no longer important. They are inconvenient distractions in the lifelong drive toward the acquisition of material wealth. Philosophy is now a superfluous exercise; what really counts is connections. Allegiances to friends and causes are hopelessly out-of-date and quaint but useless relics of a bygone era of civilization.

Now all that counts is leeching onto those in power and getting what one can in the great rip-off that is always taking place — this is what our kids are really learning in school, and the future we can all look forward to.

I am reminded of those long-ago stories about Nazi Germany, when little kids were forced to wear junior SS uniforms and report to authorities on the political activities of their own parents. So what if their parents were taken away: the kids were serving the greater good of the state, and besides, they got extra rations of chocolate to go with their lessons about the glories of the Homeland. More recently, these stories have manifested as incidents of kids who had been put through school-sponsored drug awareness seminars who turned in their own parents for smoking pot, and other affronts to fascist civilization.

So the lesson is — in these times when people ignore what's going on around them, when the greater human values of compassion and understanding have been buried by widespread media conditioning that truth and justice no longer matter, but only adherence to officially approved norms deserve our allegiance — that you better get a grip on what you've done by not paying attention to what has been going on in the world.

The lesson is this: Don't turn your back on your own kids. If they have been absorbing the facile rhetoric they hear every day on TV and beneath the fluttering flags of their own schools, you may no longer know who they really are, or, on this sad day in Soviet America, what they have become.

Chapter Seven

The perfect enemy

Terrorists who can't be caught because they don't really exist or because they're CIA assets

War is a sociological safety valve that cleverly diverts popular hatred for the ruling classes into a happy occasion to mutilate or kill foreign enemies.

— Ernest Becker

War provides the perfect cover for those waging it to commit crimes against not only enemies but also friends. Amid the patriotic flag waving and somber ceremony, the populace is cowed into distraction and for the most part will not see the chicanery and manipulation that not only created the conditions FOR the war, but also will not perceive that the purpose OF it is not to defeat the enemy, but to financially castrate and sociologically neutralize those who are actually helping to wage the war.

Such is the process by which those in power consolidate their advantage among their so-called friends.

The Christian Crusades of millennia past provide an apt example of this deceptive process. With no enemies nearby and a surfeit of armed and affluent noblemen itching for the joy and profit of battle, kings and ministers of past empires dreamed up external threats by which to distract their powerful friends from contemplating revolution. Jerusalem and the dark-skinned Islamic realms have always been a popular target for Western imperialists of any century. The subsequent conflicts not only reaped new riches for the war-making kingdoms, but also depleted the ranks and resources of those sent to fight, thereby lessening the potential political threat to the very people who dreamed up the wars in the first place. Two birds with one stone.

Those innocents killed in such cynical gambits now bear the unfortunate title of collateral damage, regrettable but necessary sacrifices to the selfishness of those in positions of power who seek to maintain it. So this world full of greedy humans continues to turn.

During war, citizens of the war-making state may not question the motives of their leaders, lest they be accused of treason and summarily executed. Therefore, any state seeking permanent obeisance and minimal criticism from its citizenry will logically aspire toward a regimen of permanent war. It is supremely ironic that a majority of these citizens will wholeheartedly support such efforts, without realizing that it is the destruction of their own freedom that they are cheering.

However, real enemies are usually not so accommodating as to wish to engage in battle indefinitely. They are either defeated and disappear as a viable social force, or, they kick butt and thereby ruin the plans of the manipulative attacker forever.

A shrewd superpower kingdom will cleverly avoid picking a fair fight, thereby eliminating, as nearly as possible, the undesirable surprise of an unexpected defeat. It will also defer toward states of relatively equal strength, establish diplomatic relations, and wait for an opportunity to screw them surreptitiously and without obvious penalty.
Since the situation we face now is that one superpower

outstrips in military might the sum of all its potential adversaries combined, the need for it to be diplomatic is at an all-time low. It simply can do what it wants when it wants.

And yet, humans being what they are — wanting to be free, happy, honest and well-fed — even a superpower in this unchallenged position must construct fantasy scenarios to convince its own people — no matter how amateurishly — that they are doing the right thing by supporting endless wars.

Today we hear all sorts of childish scare-mongering about the terrorist threat, even though a cursory examination of recent history would reveal that most of these threats have been deliberately created by the nation doing most of the complaining about these very threats through its undercover intelligence services.

This epiphany leads to a very startling observation about the nature of the world as human civilization enters the 21st century following the appearance of the Divine Messiah most of this civilization pretends to worship.

It seemed to some of us, for a time — two centuries, actually, that the United States of America was a good country, champion of justice, advocate of freedom, that sort of stuff. What was lost in the education of its own citizens, however, was the frequency with which it went to war, against interlopers who were invariably depicted as venomous foes on the wrong side of democratic progress.

A cursory perusal of this murderous resumé will reveal that the U.S. has always been the aggressor in all these big fights, even though the official histories bend the facts to show America was fighting for freedom against one tyrant or another.

But as time passed and the world got smaller, it became obvious that the U.S. was running out of countries that it could call evil, declare war against, and then pulverize, although it recently has chosen two hapless victims — Afghanistan and Iraq — to annihilate.

Even so, once a country had been seriously obliterated, it simply takes too long to rebuild it into a serious enemy again, even though there is much money to be fleeced from one's own supporters by convincing taxpayers these countries must be rebuilt, and then funneling monies budgeted for these tasks into the pockets of these leaders' corrupt cronies, who then don't even do the work they contracted to do.

Clearly, if the same cartel that has essentially been running this country for all of its 227 years was to stay in power, it had to devise a new formula for finding constant enemies to fight, thereby enriching its own coffers and keeping its own citizenry from noticing too much about the way it actually conducts its business.

So it devised a new system of actually creating its own enemies. It sponsored young malcontents to fight battles that served the purposes of the masters, provided them with weapons and support techniques, used them for awhile, and then seemingly cut them loose to develop on their own. Of course, all the while the progress of these young rebels was monitored by American intelligence agencies, for the purpose of determining exactly when they could be considered mature enough to reclassify them from a developing ally fighting for U.S. interests into a nightmare threat fighting against U.S. interests.

The key element in making this process work was fabricating staged terror events that were actually perpetrated against our own citizens but then cleverly blamed on these various foreign provocateurs whom the U.S. had carefully nurtured and brought to maturity.

The U.S. learned this trick from Israel, which had successfully used the technique throughout Europe (principally in Germany) and specifically in Iraq in the 1940s, to convince its own people of the dangers posed by "enemies" it had previously supported, for the purpose of creating a hysteria to compel more Jews to move to Israel.

Of course, now we see how Israel has used this staged terror formula to elicit world support for its illegal occupation of Palestine. And more vividly, we see how the staged terror events in New York City have driven a large part of Western Civilization into a new, crusade-like rage against the peoples of Islamic countries. Serious historians will note this has all been done before, but the general population contains few serious historians, so most people don't notice that the current war against Middle Eastern peoples began some eight hundred years ago, and has never stopped.

And lest you think all this is merely a flight of literary fancy, I bid you consider the careers of Osama bin Laden and Saddam Hussein, both of whom were catapulted into the public eye as fledgling CIA operatives — bin Laden as an Arab counterculture hero (and cheered on by his family) who rode to the rescue (with large amounts of cash) of the Afghani mujahadeen, accompanied by plenty of assistance from Ronald Reagan's CIA wheeler-dealers; and Saddam as one of the triggermen in a 1968 coup in Iraq that was of course fueled by support from the — you-guessed-it — CIA.

So for these folks to develop into threats against the world (and this is not to mention, among many others, Panama's Manuel Noriega, who also followed the same progressive curriculum as a pawn in the South American drug game and good friend of the Bush family, only to later become the target of a massive American invasion), you begin to see the pattern.

The U.S. has really replaced client-state enemies it first builds up with cash bribes and then converts into enemies with client-personality enemies, whom it nurtures with military support, provokes with a no-win decision (whatever did happen to ambassador to Iraq April Gillespie?), and then invades in a profitable fit of righteous retribution.

Are you getting the picture?

It's interesting reading some of the older stories about al-Qaeda, the so-called terror group founded by bin Laden in Afghanistan (and nurtured by Pakistani intelligence, which was covertly funded by the American CIA), and seeing how al-Qaeda fought side by side with American mercenaries in Bosnia, Kosovo, Macedonia and even Chechnya, but when they were conveniently needed as an excuse for going to war somewhere else (Afghanistan and Iraq), they were quickly converted into an enemy.

Clearly, al-Qaeda is connected to the CIA, but for purposes of stealing Iraq's oil reserves, the U.S. connected them to Iraq, and got a major assist from what used to be called the American free press, but now is called something else, something far worse.

I guess you could call al-Qaeda a multi-purpose CIA asset, good for either good or bad activities.

Al-Qaeda are claimed to the boogeymen who perpetrated

9/11 and were supposedly connected to Saddam.

And yet when you go to find out about them, they disappear in a cloud of undercover spy dust, with no leads suddenly unavailable as to where they might have disappeared (except an occasional tangent to Israel). How utterly convenient. The real reason is because their controllers live at the Pentagon and other prestigious Washington addresses, not to mention a few palaces in Saudi Arabia that have ties to many American corporations.

Occasionally, the powers that be throw us a tantalizing bone — like Moussaoui or Richard Reid — just to try to prove there are actual terrorists out there. But how many more so-called terrorists have been allowed to slip away, under cover of CIA assistance? And, as in Yemen, how many more are prevented from being sought, lest they reveal their ties to the government in Washington?

Instead of having countries to blame for our ills, we now have mystical individuals — terrorists — who absolutely can't be found, except for those the U.S. chooses to identify, like Atta and the supposed hijackers who actually received training at U.S. military installations. Sound like a familiar technique?

For endless war, you must have an enemy who cannot be caught, who is completely vaporous, therefore necessitating nonstop aggressive emergency measures, variously colored alerts and tough talk for those who are unable to see the deeper meaning of words.

The perfect enemy for a state that seeks endless war and strives forever to pull the wool over the eyes of its own citizens for purposes of endless robbery and implementing slavery where freedom previously existed would be an enemy who cannot, under any circumstances, ever be caught. Osama and Saddam doubtless know this.

In the literal sense, this perfect enemy does not exist, which makes him perfect for a society determined to make war, because he will never be caught, and the war can continue forever.

The harder an enemy is to find and defeat, the better it is for those who seek to profit from the staged campaign to destroy that enemy. The CIA's creation of al-Qaeda is the perfect recipe for those billionaires whose objective is endless conflict from which to make more money. This is the new era in which we find ourselves pinioned.

It is the ultimate tilting at windmills, by which the elite who have always run America and made their money by funding both sides in the same wars can perpetrate their vicious schemes of slavery, the gullible can continue to have their empty causes to cheer, and legitimate, God-fearing citizens can cower in fear while the very churches they support participate in the cover-up that supports the tyrants who oppress them.

This is the way the world is, and has always been. Only now it's worse, because the enemy is now a fabricated fiction, available for convenient blame in any and all disasters.

And thanks to media shills who don't ask real questions, well-bribed legislators devoid of conscience, law enforcers who help their patrons cover up crimes; and judges who have no interest in real justice, there is no end in sight for this war on freedom.

The perfect enemy is an invisible construct created by those who control the real money, a shape-shifting fantasy bandito who can be used to justify any atrocity against anyone at any time for the purpose of covering up a greater crime that is committed under the cover of responding to the threat. The perfect enemy is al-Qaeda.

Chapter Eight

Solving the enigma
of media manipulation

Beware the Gatekeepers who distract
from discovering the true facts

No mystery in American history is ever solved because the actual facts of each case never reach the public for adequate examination and resolution. I mean, we still haven't solved the questions of who murdered Presidents Zachary Taylor and Abraham Lincoln, never mind who killed the Kennedy brothers or Martin Luther King.

And this likely will be the fate of the investigation into the tragedies of September 11, 2001 — we will never learn who did what: who planned it, who executed it, who made money off it — although we do have a pretty good idea who is covering it up, since the perpetrators regularly embarrass themselves in full public view with their endless expectorations of self-serving statements and lame lies.

The real reason these mysteries are never solved is not because of any cover-up by government officials or rich power brokers. The reason these mysteries are never solved is because of the corrupt state of our news media, which are wholly controlled by the very same men who commit these colossal crimes that injure us all.

Most journalists have never told the truth about politics; they only are allowed to say what their bosses let them say. And almost always, if the newspaper or TV station is a big one, their bosses won't let them tell the truth about practically anything.

This is no idle complaint, no sour grape cocktail.

We are prevented from acquiring the information necessary to live honest and productive lives: prevented by our schools, which limit the spectrum of functional data that shapes the way we think as we grow up; by our hallowed institutions, which exist at the whim of power structures whose real workings we have little cognizance of; and by the public utterances of people we consider heroes, whose words may inspire us at the time they are uttered, but whose achievements, considered from the perspective of history, often do not match the deeds that made them admired in the first place.

Consider for a moment the historical perspectives of George Washington, who eagerly endorsed the slaughter of natives for the purpose of claiming land in the Ohio territory, or of Franklin Roosevelt, who supposedly brought us out of the Great Depression but now is better known for manipulating geopolitics to get us into World War II by creating the conditions that lured the Japanese to attack Pearl Harbor.

Now, as we wring our hands while the image of America morphs from beacon of liberty to the deadly oppressor, we come to another realization — if we are mature and wise enough to understand the USA has always been a savage beast spewing fictional justifications with polite language, first taming a wilderness continent peopled by beings we called savages, now conquering a world occupied by individuals we disparagingly regard as inferior foreigners.

We come to understand that our prosperity is wholly dependent on conquest and exploitation of those less alert than ourselves. That this beastly attitude has been transformed into heroic legends is simply good public relations. Everybody needs to feel good about themselves, no matter what they are doing. Thus America has crafted for itself a history packed with glorious campaigns and noble efforts. The trail of corpses this history has produced is seldom mentioned.

And thus it is with 9/11.

Many high officials of the current United States government clearly know who planned and carried out the murderous attacks of September 11, 2001. The names of the perpetrators are clearly available in the records of those agencies that monitor stock transactions, specifically the "put" options bought by as yet publicly unidentified individuals in the days immediately prior to 9/11, names kept secret by the confidentiality laws of bankers.

The sad fact is that these names are kept secret even though release of them could shed cleansing light on the cynical murders of 3,000 Americans, 5,000 Afghanis and 10,000 Iraqis in the past two years. The secrecy of banking laws trumps the necessity of bringing mass murderers to justice. It always has and it always will. For the world is about money and exploitation, it is not about justice and honor. In America especially, mass murder of innocents is not as serious a crime as betraying financial trust, according to the laws that restrain us.

So, many individuals associated with the U.S. government know full well who is responsible for 9/11. But they will go to their graves with the secret, because too much money has been made from the deception, and there is still a lot more money to be made in the overzealous military response to a tragedy that was devised for that very purpose.

And it's not merely those insider elitists who made money off their timely investments, with full knowledge of the charade that was about to be played, who are the killers.

As researcher Walter Burien has pointed out, the guilty parties are much closer to home, and more well-known than anonymous moneymen protected by secrecy laws of their own creation. Burien's words paint an ominous picture:

"If you look at "WHO" was holding the majority of "SHORT" derivative positions on the domestic and international stock index markets prior to 9-11, and then reaped over a trillion dollars in profits within days from the ensuing collapse of those physical markets, you will find in that group who was responsible for 9-11. There is one problem in finding this out: government controls the release of that information by the SEC and CFTC. A small conflict of interest exists here, being that the results of that study would show the U.S. Federal Government was holding the majority of the international "SHORT" positions! The promoted airline stock option transaction that most people have heard about in the news is truly minuscule chump change in comparison.

"Yes, government is preparing for an uprising in this country. They need to direct the public eye to a faraway enemy so that they can secure control here. Greed has thrived within government circles. The result of that greed has been obscene and the resulting damage to the morals and health of this country in response is sickening.

"The result of this takeover of the American wealth has been done almost exclusively on paper through manipulation of the legislature and the judiciary over the last 60 years with the cooperation of the syndicated news media and education. With the conquest being done by transferring the wealth on paper, the consequences for the "takers" was virtually nonexistent!"

There you have real American history, not reported by any newspapers or TV shows. It comes off a website in Arizona that is about to shut down for lack of money. The foregoing is an excerpt from "Market Reality: Know What is Going On" by Walter J. Burien. Visit his complete website here: http://members.aol.com/_ht_a/cafr1/CAFR.html

(And send him money, if you can, before it's too late. He's one of the last of the real newsmen.)

So we know who perpetrated 9/11. We know the Muslim hijacker rap was just a deception aimed at creating sympathy for Israel, and allowing it to continue its brutal genocide of the Palestinians while the world's attention was distracted. The deception also provided breathing space for the multinational oil giants who seek to carve up the geography of the Middle East for their own advantage. So a few other assorted infidels had to die. That's just the way it is in the real world, I'm sure Dick Cheney would tell you.

• • •

Most intelligent Americans already know you can't trust what you see on the TV news. But it's very important to point that out to your friends and neighbors who think they can. If you base what you believe on what you see on TV, you are guaranteed to be deceived.

From the perspective of the future, I see Tom Brokaw, Dan Rather, Peter Jennings and Wolf Blitzer as stick figure puppets dancing on the strings of their masters, mouthing false words scripted by drooling demons counting their money in advance of their latest robbery.

How else can one explain the total absence of the most important issues to all humanity on the TV news?

• The most critical issue of the continuing massacre of innocents in Iraq — and one tragically close-to-home for deceived Americans — is the impact of radioactive ammunition on those who did not die in the high-tech bloodbath. All who participated in that murderous charade face a guaranteed future of agonizing disease and death from uranium poisoning, the sick legacy of cruel cynics making money off the recycling of carcinogenic nuclear waste into armor-piercing ordnance.

We already know how this story goes from the first Gulf War. Three hundred thousand American veterans sickened, ten thousand already dead. Servicemen's wives with radioactive uteruses, American babies grotesquely deformed. Hundreds of thousands of Iraqis crippled by cancer or born with burned-out brains.

The government and its media whores deny a connection. Uranium poisoning incidence was recently reported much higher in Afghanistan, after the U.S. did its nuclear rain-dance there. And yet to be discovered higher still in Iraq.

And not a single word about it on television. Anywhere. A sickening silence they call American freedom.

• The greatest case of treason in U.S. history is the massive silence of virtually the entire power structure about the inside knowledge of what has come to be known as 9/11, which was quickly followed by the equally treasonous demolition of the U.S. Constitution known as the Patriot Act.

The deliberate stand-down of the air defenses, allowing thousands of Americans to be slaughtered for the crass purpose of abetting the takeover of Middle Eastern oil; the facile lies of leaders who say they didn't know it was coming yet produced the names of the purported perps on a moment's notice; the billions made by those who did know it was coming and who remain smugly satisfied with their poisoned riches like that smirking Texas vampire ...

That 9/11 was an inside job known and planned well in advance of this mind-crushing assault on the world's senses is no longer just a crazed conspiracy theory — it's a whole encyclopedia of provable facts, observable criminal behavior and stonewalled investigations ... it is a certainty.

Yet not a single peep about any of it on TV. Instead, the evil Muslims who "hate our freedom" are blamed, as we psychologically prepare our pampered populace for a protracted invasion of the Arab world.

It is the conversion of the world into an armed prison of masters and slaves, an excuse to steal Islamic treasures on the trumped-up charge that they are the enemies of the West. But don't count your blessings just yet: it's only a matter of time before the plunderers aim their weapons inward toward the conquest of the zombified American citizenry.

For all the tragic epiphanies about how our faith in democracy and American honesty is a completely manipulated illusion, there is something far worse to contemplate. Suddenly, the view down this sociological well of hopelessness is about to get a lot darker.

Because when you realize what's happening, you'll begin to understand that a lot of key people — people you think you admire, seek out for guidance, and try to support — people that you thought were working for us, working for freedom, are actually working for them, and working for something other than freedom.

It is the dark flowering of our worst nightmare, because it takes away our belief in those who we thought were helping us.

The real tragedy of our wholly corrupt news gathering apparatus is that many of those who appear to be helping the cause of human freedom are actually preventing it in a very subtle and deceitful way.

The recent flap between Mike Ruppert, crusading creator of the highly respected From the Wilderness website, and Amy Goodman, ostensibly crusading interviewer of the much-listened-to radio program Democracy Now, is especially revealing as to the subtly of the deception.

Ruppert has consistently complained about harassment from the so-called left media, which claimed he was a hysterical conspiracy theorist because he asked embarrassing yet wholly evidence-based questions about the unanswered mysteries of 9/11.

Let it be known now that Ruppert is one of the more conservative and respected analysts of the 9/11 enigma. He refuses to speculate about what might have been and instead concentrates on what is empirically obvious. Yet he has been the target of ridicule and scorn from virtually all the left commentators, Goodman and Nation columnist David Corn in particular, and the spectrum of all those supposedly progressive magazines like Mother Jones and The Progressive, and supposedly progressive websites like Common Dreams and Alternet, none of whom will touch the 9/11 issue with a ten-foot pole.

Even as mainstream media and the timid alternative press

toss out tidbits of information that acknowledge questions exist about the official 9/11 story (the Bob Graham campaign gambit is the latest, in which the Florida senator, who is up to his ears in the conspiracy himself, is hinting that Bush has something to hide), Ruppert himself has a credibility gap, ever since he went to New York City in the weeks following the attacks and announced with certainty that Israel had nothing to do with them. In his defense, he had no evidence. In his indictment, he overlooked the obvious existence of the not-so-invisible giant of Jewish power over U.S. politics and media.

So there you have the two litmus issues that can help you distinguish whether a particular news source is on the up-and-up, or simply pretending to be progressive or patriotic, but really just distracting people from the real focus of the story with tantalizing bits of evidence that will ultimately lead nowhere, which ultimately deflects the public from perceiving the right questions to ask.

There are two distinct methods by which you can tell if a story is legitimate or not. They are:

1. Does the story admit there is something radically wrong with the whole sorry official explanation about 9/11? If it does, it might be true; if it doesn't it is disinformation, designed to distract you from not only finding the right answers but even asking the right questions.

2. Does the story have a tangent to Israel's role in the deception of the world? If there is no mention of Israel being intimately involved with 9/11 or the invasion of Iraq, the story is probably disinformation; if Israel is at least mentioned, there is a fighting chance the story may be legitimate.

The best discourse on this whole subject of deception among news sources can be found on the quality website questionsquestions.net, which contains a whole series of articles about the Gatekeeper syndrome, and provides a new and valuable perspective of which media outlets are telling the objective truth, and which are likely not (i.e., virtually all of the popular left alternative choices).

Being a nominal leftie, this is hard for me to say. But you can't trust most of the left websites because they treat Israel like an innocent bystander, without beginning to acknowledge the colossal impact Jews (most of whom support Israel's criminal behavior) have on the American systems of media and education, and on America as a whole. Just ask former Georgia representative Cynthia McKinney, the latest honest voice expelled from public discourse by Jewish power.

And in case you haven't noticed these past few years, America's objectives in the world are Israel's. Just take another look at Iraq, please, and the continuing push the U.S. is exerting throughout the Middle East. The chief beneficiary of all this U.S. tax money, as well as the outcry following 9/11, is Israel.

Then take a look at how leftie publications (forget about the mainstream: The New York Times, Boston Globe, Washington Post, and Los Angeles Times are all Zionist operations) neglect, deride or downplay the two key litmus issues that allow you to determine whether a news gathering operation is legit or a Gatekeeper.

The Gatekeeper series on questionsquestions.net, written by Bob Feldman and Brian Salter, is a virtual checklist of how to tell the legit publications from the phonies.

Feldman's "Alternative Media Censorship: Sponsored by the CIA's Ford Foundation," describes the deceptive dilemma millions of Americans face by trusting such leftie icons as Noam Chomsky, Howard Zinn and Norman Solomon, all of whom downplay the 9/11 conspiracy angle and Israel's involvement in it.

"The multi-billion dollar Ford Foundation's historic relationship to the Central Intelligence Agency [CIA] is rarely mentioned on Pacifica's DEMOCRACY NOW / Deep Dish TV show, on FAIR's COUNTERSPIN show, on the WORKING ASSETS RADIO show, on The Nation Institute's RADIO NATION show, on David Barsamian's ALTERNATIVE RADIO show or in the pages of PROGRESSIVE, MOTHER JONES and Z magazine. One reason may be because the Ford Foundation and other Establishment foundations subsidize the Establishment Left's alternative media gatekeepers / censors."

In addition, Feldman asks: "Perhaps Amy Goodman should finally make full disclosure of all foundation grants that either the Pacifica Foundation, WBAI, Democracy Now, WBAI, KPFA, the Indymedia Centers, Free Speech TV, Deep Dish TV, the Pacifica Campaign or the Downtown studio from which she broadcasted in 2000 and/or in 2001 have received since 1992?"

Just from that information alone, you should be starting to perceive a pattern and a reason why these shows and publications aren't treating seriously the very credible notion that 9/11 was an inside job.

In addition, separate stories by Feldman examine Big Oil's connection to PBS and CIA links to Northwestern University (a famous training ground for journalists), Counterpunch and the Nation magazines, as well as Project Censored. All of these operations are suspect because they receive laundered money from corporate giants under the supervision of the CIA.

Feldman also writes: "The FAIR/COUNTERSPIN/Institute for Public Accuracy alternative media gatekeepers/censors — which includes COUNTERSPIN co-hosts/producers Steve Rendall and Janine Jackson, Institute for Public Accuracy/ MAKING CONTACT executive director Norman Solomon, MSNBC/DONAHUE SHOW PRODUCER Jeff Cohen and WORKING ASSETS RADIO show producer Laura Flanders — have also been subsidized by the Ford Foundation and other Establishment foundations in recent years."

Salter concludes the series with a question: "Is it likely that the Ford Foundation would fund the kind of alternative media which would be inclined to look deeply into the long-running control over U.S. foreign policy exerted by the private and secretive Council on Foreign Relations, given the fact that the CFR counts among its funding sources the Ford Foundation and Xerox? Or would the Ford Foundation more likely favor those who could be relied upon to toe the party line that the CFR (and other elite policymaking NGOs like the Trilateral Commission and Bilderberg Group) functions only as a stuffy intellectual debate society, and that anyone who argues otherwise is a "paranoid nut"?

" .... Judging by the journalism being offered (and not offered) by Nation magazine, FAIR, Pacifica, Progressive magazine, IPA, Mother Jones, Alternet, and other recipients of their funding, the big establishment foundations are successfully sponsoring the kind of "opposition" that the US ruling elite can tolerate and live with."

Read the Gatekeeper series closely, and analyze what Walter

Burien has to say as well (while you can).

By noticing who the participants are, what they say, and how they're funded — and what the implications are of that funding — most intelligent people will conclude that two litmus questions exist in determining whether stories are legitimate attempts to ferret out the truth, or sophisticated deceptions designed to distract readers into peripheral issues that will actually lead you away from the truth.

The two questions, again, are:

Is 9/11 being treated as the criminal inside job it really is, and what is the impact of Jewish/Israeli/Zionist manipulation on the whole effort? That is how you tell the real journalists from the Gatekeepers.

I must say one more thing about Jewish influence. There is no part of my warning about Jewish/Israeli/Zionist dominance of American media on the questionsquestions website, and should some wish to bash me with the anti-Semitism brush, this shallow smear should not be extended to the research of Feldman and Salter.

As it is my fervent conviction that the evidence concerning 9/11 (articulated by me elsewhere) clearly points to a high-level conspiracy (as evidenced most recently by efforts to thwart a legitimate investigation into aspects of the tragedy), it is also my sincere belief that Jewish influence on American media in the single greatest obstacle to finding the truth about recent political events, which is why you hear none of it in the mainstream, corporate media.

Since Israel (and to a lesser extent, the multinational but primarily American oil industry) is the chief political beneficiary of both the 9/11 disaster and the immoral invasion of Iraq disaster, it would be disingenuous of me, considering the power the Israeli lobby wields in Washington, to fail to allege that Israel was the country that helped a criminal cabal of American fat-cat industrialists perpetrate a grievous, treasonous crime against the American people in order to continue their staggering plans to rob the entire world of its resources.

And stories that don't recognize this reality are simply not credible, in my mind.

Forewarned is forearmed. We will never find the right answers if we can't ask the relevant questions.

<u>Chapter Nine</u>

The bursting of the dam

A dream is a wish that your heart makes.

— Jiminy Cricket

This is a dream. I am standing in front of a giant dam. The vast expanse of beige concrete stretches across the field of my vision, towers above me. I am dwarfed into utter insignificance. A soft chorus of whispering voices from my past, perched on ledges in the cliffs at the side of the dam, clatters in my ears, telling me to run, urging me to save myself, reminding me of past events. My feet are bolted to the ground. Suddenly a new low rumble begins. The sun glints over the crest of the titanic wall. Then I realize what the voices are saying. The dam is breaking. I am not afraid. I'm not going anywhere.

A huge crack explodes in the middle of the wall. Monstrous torrents of white froth burst through above me. Chunks of concrete and white water in slow motion spew out above me, rain down upon me like a giant hammer, suddenly crush me in their fury as the entire wall collapses and everything around me is swept away. And yet I am still standing there, while the pent up but now freed river races past me, scourging everything in its path. Boulders roll, earth shakes, sirens wail. And still I hear the voices, and remember the awful, awesome sound of the dam first cracking, like an echo in the heart, like Armageddon's song.

In addition to the other voices of my past, I hear the clamor of new voices in the flood, all warning me to flee, to hide, lest I be swept away like them in the torrent of the unleashed river, and destroyed by the fury of once-imprisoned but now liberated natural forces that crushed the dam into pulverized dust and murky mud. But I am still standing there, listening intently to these new voices as they rush past me in the maelstrom. Beneath the water, in a blue green turmoil of washing machine chaos, I see like passing souls tiny bubbles speaking, all with urgency. The first group of bubbles has a golden glow about them.

"Take care for your soul," the first ones seem to say. "Adhere to your holy books, they will get you through and keep you safe. And you will find tranquil glory with your father in heaven."

I smile at their concern, and wonder passively where it exactly is that they are going, and what they will do there.

The second group of talking bubbles, bouncing angularly in the torrent mixed with chunks of concrete, seems less urgent, more benign, less panicked and somewhat placid. "We are passing to where we began," they chant serenely. "We will choose where we return to the sea of life, but at any time we may escape to the light and sing happily in the lovely air forever. Bye bye, farewell, see you again soon," they seem to say.

The third wave of bubbles, muddy colored and arranged in some kind of mathematical order as they flow past, seem to be wearing — wow — neckties! Hey, it's only a dream. Some even wear sunglasses! They speak to me in a low, confidential tone, with an implied threat of certain power. "Don't tell anybody about this," they dictate, "or you could be in real trouble. You will be debriefed at a later time."

I shake my head and chuckle. I should have known this was a government project. But I ponder a riddle: was it the bursting of the dam that was a government project, or the entire dream itself? Neither, I finally decide. No government would ever tell me to resist all the power it could throw at me and just persevere until the crisis was past.

And then I ask: is this a message from God? I wonder for a moment and surmise: certainly not the God talked about by all religions, which try to get you to believe He said something to someone that was supposed to apply to everyone else, and should be followed obediently no matter what the circumstances actually were. The Lockstep God. No, this message wasn't from him, but it might yet have come from the real God who speaks directly to everyone in times of peril without the necessity of intermediary priests.

In fact, that's the real difference between the real god that everybody can talk to at any time (especially on airplanes in bad weather) and the fake god tossed around by fools in vestments who are trying to make big money (and succeeding) off people who need to believe some magical being created them and is always protecting them.

And so the dam let its watery prisoner past. The flood subsided; the bubbles flicked away into the sunny air and liberated the voices from my head. And I stood there, extremely damp but unhurt, having lived through the crisis of my own desire, having heard the messages of everyone I've ever known as well as everyone I ever would know (remember, it's a dream), I remained unchanged, mute, knowing that I was in the right place at the right time, did what I had to do, was proud of it, was proud that I did not take the easy way and accept someone else's version of the truth but instead forged my own, did my best to help others solve the ever-present puzzles, and in the end accepted no one's advice but my own.

The danger of the bursting dam destroying me did not bother me so much as maybe missing the chance to know why it was bursting. It was bursting, as all dams will one day burst, because humans tried to chain Mother Nature, and she will not be chained, no matter what the holy books say. So if that lesson were to have cost me everything, it would not have been too high a price to pay.

It's not that I don't have much to lose, for, after all, I am in love with life and cherish each moment as if it were my last. But if the bursting of the dam would have been my last, I would have known I had been true to myself and those I love, and for those and other reasons, I also have much that can never be taken away.

And then suddenly I awoke, and knew what I had to do, and did it, while there was still time.

<u>Chapter Ten</u>

The lies of our leaders

In America, it's no longer important to tell the truth

President George W. Bush and virtually the entire American power structure lied to the whole planet when they said Iraq possessed weapons of mass destruction that were an imminent threat to the safety of the so-called free world.

Beyond any doubt, these assertions have since been exposed as falsehoods. Still, few Americans really give a damn, and business goes on, in the fore-shadow of a massive worldwide economic and social collapse.

President Bush and virtually the entire American power structure lied when they said we needed to invade Afghanistan to bring to justice the alleged perpetrators of the 9/11 horror. Shortly after the invasion began, Gen. Tommy Franks announced it wasn't important to capture the so-called ringleader, Osama bin Laden, even as the Afghanis' Taliban government offered to furnish him for trial in a neutral country. The real objective, Franks said during the attack, was to subdue the whole country.

With the fictional al-Qaeda network still being used as a pretext for permanent war against the entire world by the United States, and bin Laden still un-captured, it has become obvious to everyone that the reason for obliterating Afghanistan with nuclear weapons and murdering tens of thousands of innocent people was something other than capturing a suspected terrorist, although none of us are quite sure what that reason was. Talk of Enron, oil pipelines, poppy production for the heroin and geopolitical advantages are generally excluded from mainstream television news.

The situation is identical in Iraq. What was the purpose of blasting several thousand innocents into heaven when the situation it produced is actually more of a threat to our security than was the continued dictatorship of Saddam Hussein? None of us are quite sure what that reason was, although we all have our favorite suspicions: oil, Israel, expenditure of military stockpiles and creation of lucrative contracts for corporate supporters of the war machine in a corrupt attempt to revive a decaying American economy.

Those two lies — justifying depraved mass murder in two defenseless countries — now stand as the ranking horrors in American history. In the 227 years of our history, from the smallpox blankets of Colonial days to the inexplicable immolation at Waco, America as an aggressor nation has done nothing worse (although many military adventures, notably the Philippines in 1899 and Vietnam in the 1960s, were almost as bad and unjustifiable).

But the real question as America sinks into the suffocating hell of a totalitarian dictatorship is this. If our leaders have been proved to be liars about the sick and sinful destruction of humanity in Afghanistan and Iraq, why do a majority of Americans still accept what these same lying leaders said about the 9/11 atrocity, that it was the work of foreign terrorists who envied our freedom! As Gerard Holmgren once so aptly said, this is the most ridiculous of all conspiracy theories.

To a special few, responsibility for the 9/11 butchery has always been obvious. Zbigniew Brzezinski wrote about the need for it in a book, and the Republican-dominated Project for a New American Century recommended it as a desirable event for achieving its goals.

But most simpleton Americans are afraid to even contemplate such a frightening possibility. They would prefer to believe the lie, without really realizing what will happen to them if they do.

In the history of the world, there has never been a bigger lie than 9/11, yet most Americans still cling in closed-minded terror to that official story, swallow their pride at airports as minimum-wage fascists probe their private parts, stick flag decals on their cars in hopes they won't be pulled over and jailed for something they don't expect by Ashcroft's new storm-troopers, and watch in numbed banality as the official government investigation begins by saying they already know who did the dastardly 9/11 deed, so there's no sense investigating that.

Americans have swallowed the lie whole-hog that we need to beef up security because there are terrorists in our midst, when the obvious fact is that the terrorists reside in Washington, and are terrorizing the whole world, with the eager help of your neighbors, the corrupt local police and judges, who accept what their superiors order them to do, just as the guards at Auschwitz did.

Let that one roll through your mind: American cops are now just the guards at Auschwitz, participating in the elimination of all those who won't participate in the American master plan of enslaving the world. Can you say death chamber at Guantanamo with no real trial?

How can this possibly be happening? How can Americans have gone brain-dead all at once? It didn't happen overnight, I can tell you. From the Kennedy assassination onward,

Americans have been conditioned to accept phony excuses for political crimes as protests and questions are all blunted in a mind-numbing miasma of bureaucratic mazes. So everyone gave up trying to ask questions, and rationalized their indifference as not critical to my survival. Time to guess again.

Even more disturbing than the murderous plans of Bush and his petro-nazi gang of Zionist manipulators is the silent acquiescence of the so-called opposition. These "liberal" Democrats CREATED the Patriot Act, which castrates our Constitution. These spineless bureaucrats, ever mindful of the need to attract corporate campaign contributions, went along with Bush's invasions for fear of losing the votes of mindless Americans, and the approval of the Zionist bankers who control them.

Consider the Democratic opposition for a moment: Hillary Clinton, Kerry, Lieberman, Gephardt, Edwards, Dean, Mosely-Braun, Sharpton — all but one of the Democratic candidates BACKED the military moves of Bush. And all of them — no exceptions — endorse the lies we have been told about 9/11, as well as the fiction that Israel is a benevolent democracy.

I get a big laugh out of all these calls for petitions on various issues. Ha. And the same goes double for all this talk about the next election. Ha ha. The elections of 2000 proved Americans no longer have elections. It doesn't matter who you vote for. Who they want to win will win, and they have both the technological expertise and the cash on hand to make it happen. Just ask any Supreme Court justice.

Take your presidential candidate and stuff him. The American system of democracy is dead. The presidential campaign is a sideshow to delude the American populace into thinking they still have choice about what happens.

Bulletin: they don't.

No one in Congress is telling the truth (OK, you might find one or two who are telling the truth about SOME things, one less without Paul Wellstone, who was clearly murdered).

No candidate for any office anywhere in the United States is saying that 9/11 was a hoax, a cynical gambit to scare the American people into accepting police state measures. That's why no candidate now running for any office is telling the truth.

No one who thinks of running for public office can seriously entertain the notion they can fix anything. Because to fix anything, you have to dig into the big problems that keep the war machine afloat, principally the cancerous financial influences of Judaism, Zionism, and the Rothschild banking empire, which have fatally infected most of the societies in the world with their manipulative brand of behavioral bribery, and undermined morality everywhere. When morality is relative, evil prevails, because temptation and corruption are the ascendant human penchants.

No one running for public office will begin to address the obvious issue that 9/11 was aimed at defaming Muslims, thereby legitimizing two horrible American crimes: the Israeli genocide of the Palestinians, and the capture of all the oil in the Middle East.

And when the religions themselves have grown corrupt by their own power over people, there is no hope, anarchy follows and chaos triumphs. There is no hope. That is the situation we now face.

Eventually, after thousands of photos of bloodied bodies, after all the uteruses of our soldiers' wives are bleeding from the effects of radioactive contamination, after you realize that one day you are out of money and there's nowhere to get more because the fat cats have stolen it all and surrounded themselves with Wackenhut wackos, you'll come to the realization about blame.

There's no real sense blaming Jews or Catholics, or oil executives or money launderers. We've done all this to ourselves, simply by not paying attention to what's actually happening.

It isn't Bush or Daschle who are the real scumbags, the real killers of innocent people in the pursuit of profit. It's nobody but us, we the intelligent citizens of the world who failed to pay attention, or took a bribe, or looked the other way when we saw somebody doing something wrong, because it was easier that way.

It is we who kept our mouths shut during all those scams, Vietnam, the savings and loan robbery, Waco, 9/11. We were too afraid to ask real questions, and thought we could get by waving our flags and going along with the crowd. But each new government atrocity got worse, right up through 9/11.

And, sadly, the worst has yet to come.

It's too late now. Nothing can be done. They can't be stopped. We waited too long. We waited until they had amassed their armies, their biological identification devices, their roadblocks, their internment camps for protesters, the death penalty in Oregon for protesting, their genetically modified food supply (guaranteeing billions of needless deaths), their aluminization of our atmosphere, their privatization of our water, their shaping of our very brains through Zionist educational philosophies and Zionist entertainment programming until our minds were so zapped out on misleading trivialities that we couldn't even ask the most basic question of all anymore.

Which is this?

Why couldn't we see this would happen because we didn't pay attention to all those other horrors?

Why didn't we know you can't turn your back on the world, and expect the world to still be there when you turn back around?

There is no forgiveness, and no way to put things right without a massive bloodbath now. Which is just what they wanted, just what they practice. They've won. And we've lost.

But don't blame it on the lies of our leaders. Blame it on the lies we told — and are still telling — ourselves.

<u>Chapter Eleven</u>

The road not taken

Thoughts while passing the point of no return

Sometimes when we're traveling, we get so engrossed in our own conversations we fail to see significant things. We hurtle past these emotional landmarks without noticing them. It may be the very thing we've been looking for all our lives, but we miss it for a distracting remark that happens to turn our heads in the wrong direction at the precise moment or relevance.

What constitutes the point of no return? The days that follow unwise decisions are always tainted by grief and remorse. Sometimes, in the uncomprehending distance between the moment where we passed it and the spot where we realize we've passed it, the epiphany dawns on us — there is no turning back, despite all our fondest wishing and hoping, despite all our teary promises to do better next time. Real life has no reset button. Then comes that hollow time, with its aluminized applause of silence, when understanding crashes in on us. Some mistakes, like the death of your mother or your son, simply cannot be corrected. Sometimes in this life there is simply no going back.

So it is with the American dream, lying crushed by the soulless smirks of official lies presented as eternal truths by neatly dressed young people trying in vain to speak English correctly in front of mobile television cameras, saying things like "the American people support what has been done in Iraq" and trying to show their spontaneous sincerity as the scripted epithets slither from their painted lips.

America has been twisted from an example of hope for the world into an armed robber intent on fleecing everyone it meets. Over the years, America has changed the world from a place of hope to a place of fear.

We stroll past these significant events as the newsreel of our memories unfolds before us. We show a perfunctory horror at the mangled bodies of people we never knew, then go on about our business — to the mall for those birthday goodies meant for people we hardly know, to work on time to meet the daily shift quota, or to our homes to retreat from the daily assault of debilitating images that assail us by using whatever substance pleases us at the moment. So many events we try to pass by and forget.

In the days following these events, we try to rationalize that some mistakes can be corrected: we can go to court and demand a recount for an election that has been so obviously stolen; we can catch the perpetrators of a stunningly horrific crime and try them in a court of law in accordance with the finest traditions of democratic justice; we can appeal to the better natures of elected officials who pass laws without even reading what's on the paper; we can take to the streets to protest decisions to drop nuclear weapons on peasants far away; or we can point out to anyone who'll listen that our leaders are lying about everything they say.

But in the days after that, we learn to our shocked dismay that the courts are closed to people without flashy pedigrees, that elected officials seem not to want to catch the villains who perpetrated shocking mass murder, that legislators only really listen to representatives of large companies who can fund their vacation homes, that large protests are really amusing social events that accomplish nothing, and that precious few people really care whether our leaders are lying or not, as long as we have our homes, our paychecks, our cold beer and warm beds.

Most fail to perceive that if you fail to adequately protect what you have now, chances are good that you won't have it for very long. I'm talking about the future here, although you probably didn't realize it. Listen, can you remember that sound you heard when you passed the point of no return. No, of course not. You were busy. Talking about something else. Since the turning of the millennium, we have passed by four events that have changed the consciousness of our nation and the world forever and irrevocably.

1. The stolen election of the year 2000, in which the surreptitious denial of voting rights to tens of thousands of people of color and manipulation of computerized voting systems turned the vote count in favor of fascism, turned America into a police state. Few then were prescient enough to have predicted democracy would soon die, but it has.

Now there's no going back. The deed is done. The Constitution is nullified. Habeas corpus is gone for the first time in 800 years. The police can come into your home at any time for any reason. People can be executed without legitimate trials. All as the result of a fixed vote. We should have seen it coming. But we were talking, and the moment passed. Now, no amount of second-guessing can turn back the clock. Just look at the political opposition, acting as if nothing really serious has happened; that they can fix the difficulties with a few pieces of legislation. And still America slumbers.

But there is no going back. Democracy died when a bill was passed by those who didn't even read it. The new American way. Goose-stepping in silence to well-rehearsed media approval. And all across the political spectrum, the phony functionaries who grovel for our votes (and who will ignore us when they have them) acting as if this shameful occurrence was normal. Perhaps it IS normal in a society of treasonous pigs with no scruples, which is apparently what America has become. Just a gaggle of dishonest accountants who don't really care where the numbers come from, as long as they get their cut.

2. The mass murder of many thousands of people in New York City, Washington, D.C., and western Pennsylvania was blamed on Arab terrorists minutes after it happened, yet all the top officials insisted during those tear-stained days that they had no premonition such a monstrous event could even happen.

Do you understand how those two thoughts do not and cannot coexist in the same logical space? And if they don't, and you do understand, you also understand that your entire sociopolitical paradigm was shattered that day, because you know 9/11 was the handiwork of the rich manipulators who run our society, a hard-hearted ruse with which to plunder Arab treasures to the robotic applause of the drugged-out and brain-dead American populace.

3. America dropped radioactive bunker buster bombs on defenseless innocents in Afghanistan, leaving them to twitch in the dust as their children developed grotesque red tumors on their heads. This was billed a direct attempt to capture the alleged perpetrator of the 9/11 horror. Yet when said alleged perpetrator was offered up for trial in a neutral country, the U.S. ignored the offer and continued bombing. And it turns out the war in Afghanistan was planned long before 9/11. How can you launch a vigilante blitzkrieg that was planned before the crime was committed, and then insist the war was in response to the crime? Did we miss something? Were we talking about something else when all this happened?

4. Now America can bomb anyone it wants to for any reason. The reasons don't have to be the truth, or even grounded in reality. They can be total fantasy. This is the scenario we are now witnessing in Iraq, where even proven presidential lies barely raise eyebrows and most agree that Iraq needed to be bombed because the president and the TV anchors said so. What was it we were doing when this became a logical action? What trip were we taking when we missed that point that honesty was no longer necessary for doing business in the world? And once they decided they could kill all those innocent prisoners at Guantanamo without real trials, where we going then? What was the sound of the Constitution being ridiculed by federal judges and taken away forever? Did you hear it? What did it sound like?

Was it like T. S. Eliot's "not with a bang, but with a whimper"?

Right after all those wonderful millennium fireworks celebrations, we came to a fork in the road, only almost nobody noticed, because we were all too busy having so much fun and congratulating ourselves about what a wonderful world we had.

Since that magical moment, we have been traveling full speed down the wrong road, with most of us still pretending that everything's OK, that when we wake up in the morning, things will be as they always have been, the stock market will rise, certain alluring items at the store will be on sale, that our jobs will be there and we'll always have plenty of gasoline in our cars. What was it we were talking about when these events happened? What did we think about them? What did we do about them?

What will you be talking about when you pass the point of

no return? Baseball? Dietary supplements? Social obligations? We're going full speed down a road of no return. We took a wrong turn at the millennium fork. Plenty of people noticed, but nobody said anything. We were all making too much money, having too much fun.

Had we been a realistic, functional society — one that cast our focus on the health and maintenance of our lives and our world rather than one that seeks to escape from our responsibilities because we are so afraid of death — we could have learned plenty from those four post-millennium events that have so profoundly changed our world for the worse.

Were we not led in the wrong direction by the pathetic prostitutes we see on the TV screens every night, we could have found out that Katherine Harris and Jeb Bush conspired to deprive over 90,000 people of their legitimate right to vote. I'm not saying any of the subsequent events would have changed if Al Gore had been the president (after all, Bill Clinton bombed the hell out of Yugoslavia at the behest of the International Monetary Fund, and the murderous masquerades in Waco and Oklahoma City were not exactly good advertisements for an open, honest government), but it doesn't seem as likely that Gore would have rammed the Patriot Act down our throats, despite the fact that it was written by Democrats, or bombed New York City on the basis of Dick Cheney's think-tank report. Who knows? Maybe he would have. The people in OKC sure think he might have.

The great lesson that has been missed by the stifling of the investigation into the World Trade Center disaster is the opportunity to see a continuity of manipulative aggression in the foreign policy of the United States throughout the 20th Century. I mean, the situation now is not that much different than it was in the 1890s when a stock market crash was engineered by rich industrialists, and then a new grand plan of imperialism was undertaken by U.S. presidents that resulted in major carnage in the Philippines, Cuba, and even Hawaii that rivals in dishonest insincerity what has recently taken place in Afghanistan and Iraq.

Had there been a legitimate and independent investigation into the horror of 9/11, more people could have seen that the land of the free and the home of the brave has been provoking wars for profit around the world throughout the 20th century, and that even the U.S. motivation for participation in World Wars I and II are subject to alternative interpretations that clearly reveal the main cause of them was manipulative profit-seeking from Wall Street and Washington.

A truly legitimate investigation into the grand deception of what is called 9/11 might also have revealed that it doesn't really matter who is president — that the tyranny and the murder goes on no matter who is in the White House, because that's the way it has always been in America.

A real investigation into 9/11 might just have allowed us the opportunity to at least hope for a humane world, and possibly work toward one. A real investigation would have enabled us to see, perhaps, that a worldwide financial monster designed and driven by behind-the-scenes billionaires, funding both the Bolsheviks and Hitler, has caused all the wars of the 20th Century.

But now the cat is out of the bag for the entire world to see - naked and vicious power, with nothing — secular or sacred — able to stand in its way. No reason needed to use it, only an impulse toward gluttony by a sufficient number of godless petro-nazis mouthing religious phrases to keep the evangelical zombies lulled ecstatically in their apocalyptic aspirations.

As one commentator said the other day, the neo-con conspiracy that has grabbed control of the United States and its military might is now much more dangerous than Hitler's Third Reich or the Soviet Union's Red Menace ever were, in part because there is no one to stop America from turning the whole world into a radioactive wasteland like the one that now exists in Iraq, but also because there is no voice of freedom anywhere in the world able to stand up and oppose the American Zionist propaganda machine that trumpets horrid messages that twist the truth and obscure atrocities. Like "freedom is economic slavery" and "democracy is a one-party system where all opposition is treason." The irony is that the rich patricians uttering these sadistic slogans are the ones who are the real traitors to the people of the world, and everything human and holy.

There was a time, not too long ago (I'm thinking '60s or '70s here), when idealism could have prevailed, where the noble nuances of selflessness and concern for others could have determined the future we have chosen for ourselves. But corporate fascism belittled and marginalized such quaint sentiments as inferior to naked profits and sophisticated selfishness, and now we are traveling down a road on which there are no U-turns. Although it happened very recently, we are well past the point of no return, and the road not taken will forever haunt us in our dreams, in each needlessly mangled body we see sacrificed on the evil highway of pure profit.

What was it we were talking about when all this happened, and how important does it seem to us now, now that we can no longer turn back around and make all those needlessly dead people live again?

And we teach our children that stealing money from the dead is all we need to make us feel good. Rejoice, ye faithful, this is the new American way.

Surely, this is the point of no return. We passed it some time ago. What was it you were saying when we passed it?

Chapter Twelve

The unbridgeable chasm of doubt

Why faith and government don't mix

Sometimes, what is obvious to some remains invisible to others. Why this is so usually involves matters of preconceived beliefs.

We all have selective memories. From the relationship between two people to how each of us perceives the whole world, we see what we are able to see and tend to ignore those things we can't comprehend. We choose to see what continues to make us comfortable, and tend to avoid what challenges our world view. Often what we choose not to see turns out to be the most important thing of all, and we suffer for it.

And it just makes it worse when you know you saw it, and didn't do anything about it.

Two people can get together and each insist that one loves the other, but often neither can perceive what the other is saying, because their frames of reference are either too different, or something in the behavior of one sends one a signal that his words are not to be trusted, or she is not being sincere, even though both believe their sincerity is beyond question. From such dilemmas, wars and divorces erupt like poison mushrooms in a darkened yard. This unbridgeable chasm of doubt has been recently made vivid to me on several levels, though in the interests of decorum, I will say no more about this phenomenon as it has affected me on a personal level.

On a larger level, I see a terrible legacy of cruelty reaching new heights and emanating from the inexplicable unwillingness of the American people not to clearly see the true character of events so disastrously unfolding before their eyes. The power of Old Glory waving in the winds of memory, perhaps, keeps so many from seeing so much, from truly believing that those we would venerate and respect could do harm to us — willing, pernicious, lethal harm. And it is precisely this faith in American society — this socially reinforced mythos — that allows rich criminals to get away with what they do, as they hide behind the very trust they exploit.

It is part of a penalty to be paid when you mix faith and government.

People who've worked hard all their lives and enjoyed the modest successes of home and family are not eager to denounce a system that has given them such a good life. And those who aren't paying attention — and today, exclusively relying on TV means you're not getting the information you need — do not fully realize that everything has changed, that the admired American principles that always seemed to be envied by the world are not only no longer in force, but perhaps possibly never even existed at all.

Such is the case with many when you try to tell them that our leaders not only had foreknowledge but also helped arrange some of the most unspeakable crimes this planet has ever witnessed. Go ahead, just try to tell someone you think George W. Bush knew about the 9/11 horror in advance. Their eyes just roll and they sputter, "Go live in another country and see what its like." The facts you can muster to support such an assertion do not really matter to them, because they have chosen not to 'go there.'

It becomes a little less difficult when you talk about Iraq, and easier still for those who have some familiarity with the Internet, because they at least have been exposed to alternative, more authentic viewpoints than those exclusively expressed on the corporate-controlled propaganda TV networks. On TV there are no innocent Iraqi civilians (read: woman and children) being gunned down by panicked American soldiers, and no American soldiers getting sick and preparing to die from the radioactive ammunition and foul vaccinations their government told them was safe.

But 9/11 is one of those things that it is impossible to communicate to those many naive souls who just cannot believe that the leaders of this country would countenance something so repugnant merely to steal a few billion dollars. Many of you have doubtless heard such distressed responses. "Oh, they would never do something like that. They could never get away with it."

Equally, many of you doubtless know that these same leaders have in fact perpetrated these very deeds, and you realize in your heart that their pious phrases of patriotism are just so much smoke to screen the cash they pocketed for participating in the deadly deceptions.

But for most to seriously consider that the terror tragedy of 9/11 was a staged event devised to usher in a new era of corporate plunder throughout the world requires a total reevaluation of everything they've ever known, or thought they knew. It requires changing your life. And most people, no matter how poor or how screwed by corporate downsizing and/or emigration to cheaper foreign labor markets, simply refuse to change. It's just too difficult.

As long as they can keep food and a roof, the possibility that their leaders would do such a thing remains beyond the realm of probability, beyond the reach of their comprehension, beyond their willingness to see.

And you can hit them over the head with evidence — why did the president block an independent investigation? Why was the World Trade Center evidence carted off before it was examined? Why was the report of the official probe a whitewash that didn't ask any of the basic questions? Why did we go to war in Afghanistan and Iraq? Why were there so many lies told about the whole mess?

These are all questions that the government is afraid to answer, and that people are mostly afraid to ask. Because to ask these questions about the suspicions of criminal behavior of their government requires asking the same questions about their own criminal behavior — how their conspicuous consumption of gasoline, electricity, and other resources destroys the lives of other people and other species all over the world.

You don't have to think about it too long before you realize — if you're perceptive enough — that the behavior of American consumers (and consumers in other high-tech countries, too) is responsible for much of the serious raping of the planet that is now taking place, and threatening all our lives.

And that is simply too much for most people to consider, busy as they are with their meaningless trivialities that ultimately mean nothing to anyone.

It seems to me that a great opportunity has been missed in a potential investigation of what actually happened on September 11, 2001.

And I'm not talking about the cover-up, specifically, although that is certainly a great opportunity that has been missed. Now we are realizing that the 9/11 treason and murder probably will remain unsolved for all time, just like the Kennedy assassinations.

When we discovered that the highest officials in the United States not only knew 9/11 was going to happen (and that is a certainty with thousands of footnotes), but profited mightily from that knowledge, this revelation could have offered a tremendous window into the political behavior of the American nation. And in analyzing that political behavior, we could have seen how throughout the 20th century — and for some years before that — it has been the movers and shakers in the banks of London and New York who have engineered all the wars, all for the profit of those cagey industrialists, bankers and investors who saw monstrous rewards to be made by fomenting strife and furnishing the methods and opportunities to reap them.

If we could have blown the lid off the inside job of 9/11, identified the perpetrators and made our charges stick, it would have given us a window to track down those who profited from the military assaults on all the countries we convinced our citizens we invaded to save democracy, or to repel a rebel threat. Perhaps scariest of all, we could have seen how Germany had developed a barter economy prior to World War II that excluded Western banks from their dealings, or that Japan was forced into attacking us because a few bankers cut off their line of credit, and therefore their supply of oil. We could have seen how we killed all those people in all those countries just to make a few bucks, and sacrificed hundreds of thousands of our own sons and daughters in the process.

A legitimate probe of 9/11 — not like the sham that was just

perpetrated that didn't address any of the really major
questions — would have shed light on the corporate powers
that control the media and the White House, and maybe —
just maybe — would have taken that large step to show the
deluded American populace that we are neither a democracy
nor a republic, that we are a corporate-controlled police state
whose leaders are savaging their own citizens simply to
make more money for themselves and the rich friends who
put them in office in the first place.

But in the unbridgeable chasm of doubt, those are questions
Americans remain afraid to ask. No single presidential
candidate has asked a single legitimate question about who
made the money off 9/11, no single presidential candidate is
talking about how depleted uranium and spurious untested
vaccinations are squandering the lives of our own military
personnel, no single presidential candidate is demanding that
America be returned to the people who own her — namely
us.

Most average citizens are simply afraid to contemplate such
a question out of fear of reprisals by authorities (instances of
which are already numerous) or other social repercussions
(such as loss of job).

Patriotism in America is now the province of outright fools
and those who are paid handsomely to mouth the phony
slogans while they fix elections, pander to Israel and keep
feeding the arms-makers while our bridges crumble, our
manufacturing jobs disappear overseas, our food is poisoned,
and our savings are taken by rich power czars who confer
immunity on themselves because they contribute large sums
of cash to those who make our laws.

It's hard to be patriotic in a country that has become
completely corrupt, and an undeniable menace to all life on

this planet. It's hard to be patriotic in a country that cynically kills its own soldiers after lying about the reasons it went to war. It's hard to be patriotic in a country that has exchanged truth for cash, and woe to you if you don't have the latter.

But most Americans have chosen not to see this. Instead, they watch the TV lies, attend the flag-waving rallies, and hope all these crises will blow over and the land they knew will be returned to them. Well, go ask a Palestinian how that strategy works!

Beyond affection between two people, and out past the way one looks at the world, there is a third aspect of the unbridgeable chasm of doubt that affects us all, in one way or another. That, of course, involves matters of faith and spirit.

I sometimes think that because we are asked to believe the unbelievable in matters of religion, and because we tend to venerate the (usually) men who act as intermediaries between us and the divinity, that we sometimes get confused about our attitude toward our secular leaders. Many who practice the various religions feel that their holy men should not be challenged, and some of those doubtless extend that courtesy to their leaders.

That could be another reason why so relatively few are willing to challenge the 9/11 lies, as some who wrap themselves in red, white and blue assert. Certainly leaders of most states never fail to invoke the deity as a reference for the integrity of their proposals. Some of the more extravagant evangelical denominations even insist that our president's cynical invective is holy unto itself.

In our own case here in America, George W. Bush recently embarrassed himself and all Americans by claiming at a forum in Israel that it was God who had commanded him to smite the Afghanis and the Iraqis, and now he was going to do it again (and surely again and again) against various Islamic countries.

Hopefully, anyone who reads this story would realize the insanity about mixing God with world affairs, but unfortunately a majority of the world's populations does not, and Bush's rhetoric sounds too much like political leaders of other faiths who make similar claims about other targets.

You can tell, if you are capable of listening with any degree of skepticism and discernment, that any political speech that is tied to supernatural sanctions is false on its face, although it is a tribute to the degree of decline in the intelligence of the American populace that much political invective is now infused with these approvals of God, not the least of which is all this faith-based chatter that dominates the Bush administration's murderous lies.

You remember our Founding Fathers, the ones so speciously decommissioned by Bush's Patriot Act. Separation of church and state. There was a very good reason for that Constitutional precaution.

While in matters of the heart or of the soul, faith and spirit are indispensable components of the feelings that lead to happiness and love, that lead to a conquering of the unbridgeable chasm of doubt. How else to bridge the unbridgeable but by the great leap of faith and trust?

But in matters of government, faith is a liability, a danger that always leads to deception and discrimination. One need only look at the current headlines about Iraq lies and 9/11 cover-ups to realize that this is an eternal truth.

The unbridgeable chasm of doubt is growing between two forces in the world: those who believe that money is the measure of all things and that caring about the welfare of others is a needless distraction from the true task of accumulating the most toys and the greatest amount of leisure time — and those who believe that love and compassion are the most important elements of our transit through this existence, that humanity and selflessness are the greatest assets of our species, and that stealing from others is only harming yourself.

This dark chasm is growing. War has been the only solution to it. Meanwhile, all around us, the world continues to burn, leaving the concept of love mere dust in the wind, ashes in the gutter of a hollow and pornographic civilization that clearly does not deserve to survive.

And those perched on the precipice of this unbridgeable chasm doubt are fast approaching the time when they will be forced to make the leap.

They are fast reaching the point of realizing that it is too late to do what they should have done back there along the trail when they realized what they should have done, but cash got in the way.

Speak out now. We're running out of time. Don't make your solution some religious fantasy that helps no one but yourself and excludes others from your prayers. It's time to get real. Just look at what the unreal has done and is doing to us all.

Chapter Thirteen

Winking out

Voices of truth drowning beneath tidal wave of trivial sound bites

An astronomy report I read recently — from God knows where; I get so many e-mails I can't tell one from the other after awhile — said the universe is getting darker. Stars are winking out, and not being replaced fast enough by new stars being born. The universe is getting darker. I guess it's that way here on Earth, too. Getting darker by the day.

No one of any consequential reputation, at least in big media's bloodshot eyes, has leapt to the front of the stage and screamed about what a hoax the Iraq war is, what a profound and criminal affront to human decency the United States has perpetrated on the world. No one with any real power, at least. Meanwhile, the vast majority of the brain-dead American citizenry cheers on the Yankee mayhem as soldiers' gun down innocent Iraqi civilians without a second thought while the war machine defends the right of mega-corporations to plunder the world at will.

Hello!? Does anyone remain unclear about how America's reasons for invading Iraq were all lies? That there were no weapons of mass destruction and Iraq had no connection to al-Qaeda (which is a CIA false flag operation to begin with). Even Saddam was a former CIA operative once in business with the current U.S. president's father, until the powers that be determined Hussein should take the fall so America's criminal corporations could go on a looting rampage (and poison everyone with radioactive debris) throughout the Cradle of Civilization in order to abet Israel's plan to expand its borders exponentially.

Shouldn't all conscious people be howling in the streets
about this? In America, the silence is deafening, and way
beyond disheartening. It's as if all Americans have turned
into drugged-out, robotized drones, incapable of expressing
any desire to know that their country has been hijacked by
criminals who no longer even try to hide their crimes. They
know nobody's listening, and damn few even care that the
U.S. now ranks with Pol Pot (you remember, the Cambodian
butcher who killed everybody in his country with a college
education) in the category of all-time dangerous,
unreasonable and pathological social forces which cannot be
reasoned with by principled individuals.

Instead, all the presidential candidates hem and haw and
ponder how to criticize America's leap into an era of war for
no reason. They object to this evil enterprise on matters of
style, but for the substance of the naked aggression against
the Islamic world, they have no objection.

None of them points out how America has broken every law
human and holy, stolen an entire country; butchered its
inhabitants and then made them slaves and starved them, if
not outright murdered them. Even the United Nations has
now approved this satanic venture. Which means there's
nowhere anywhere in the world where anybody can be safe,
and truly know that the authorities have not been bought off
by high-level, deep-cover corporate cash.

The ayatollah was right, you know. America is the Great
Satan (whose twisted helpers are cynical evangelical
Christians flapping their truthless lips in support of their
monstrous Zionist masters), and now the whole world knows
it, even though most people and U.N. delegates keep their
mouths shut about it because tending their geese and golden

eggs is simply far more important to them than things like fairness, justice and human compassion.

As a result, America gets to execute tens of thousands of Iraqis with high-tech weaponry, poison its own soldiers with depleted uranium ammunition, funnel billion dollar contracts to its own chosen stooge conglomerates, indefinitely postpone free and fair elections for the Iraqi people, and run a new oil pipeline from Iraq to Israel ... and nobody of any consequential reputation in the world gets up and starts screaming that this is surely a criminally insane act that continues to be perpetrated on the decent and innocent people of the world.

America has stolen an entire country right in front of everyone's eyes, and no one is saying a thing about it. Doesn't that strike you as odd? No, not that America has stolen a whole country; the U.S. has done that plenty of times. But that no one is saying anything. That it isn't mentioned on TV (the words "depleted uranium" have never once been mentioned on TV; did you know that?). That our respected leaders divert our attention with trivial matters and completely ignore the critical issues.

America has stolen an entire country, and nobody says a word. The U.N. tried to throw up some feeble roadblocks prior to America's unwarranted attack on Iraq, but now that the diabolical deed is done, the U.N. has approved the arrangement. Wasn't that courageous of them?

A dangerous brute is shooting up every town on the planet and, by its silent acquiescence the governing body of the entire world endorses this activity. Getting darker. The universe is getting darker. As for Earth, well, you know the tale ...

After a couple of years on the Internet I have a pretty fair grip on those who are fighting the madness. Paranoid? Maybe a little. But I know the fake ones, those who pretend to working for human decency but really aren't, like Common Dreams, Mother Jones, those leftie bleeding hearts who never mention the 9/11 fix (find out who made the money on the "put" options and the trail will lead to the coordinators of the event) or the Israeli mindlock on U.S. media. Throw Chomsky and Zinn into the mix. What they write will lead you in the wrong direction.

If you haven't read the Gatekeepers series on questionsquestions.net, you are nowhere. Lost in the miasma of misinformation. Stop signing petitions and supporting fake presidential candidates like Howard Dean. Get to the point. Start screaming.

I was supposed to be on the radio last night in my regular gig (moved to Wednesday) on www.lewisnews.com, but Schantz called me and said a virus has taken his system down, and he probably didn't have the money to fix it. Lewis News, many of you know, is an excellent but unheralded news digest that attracts readers and listeners from all over the world to its modest but honest offerings. It may never be back up, although knowing Schantz, he'll get the thing running with some duct tape and bubble gum one of these days.

He is like so many of the great websites and e-mail newsletters trying to circumvent the media mindlock by sheer force of will. Almost all of these operations are incredibly valuable to those who read them, and almost all of them are one-person operations: Tom at informationclearinghouse.info, Jeff at rense.com, Carol at communitycurrency.org, Michael at whatreallyhappened.com, Ken at apfn.org, Paul at worldnewsstand.net, Edna at Earth Heal, Jean at the Earth

Rainbow Network, Peter at serendipity.li, Mark at lovearth.net ... this list could run into the thousands of single individuals who are valiantly standing as bulwarks against the madness perpetrated upon the entire world by big media tyrants that twists the perceptions of people and makes them think that the slaughter in Iraq is actually a good thing.

But the tsunami of meaningless sound-bites, for which people make millions, is overwhelming most of these single-minded solitary sentinels standing strong against the mindless madness.

Single individuals will not last long against the limitless budgets of big networks who have no intention of telling you what's really happening in the world. In my own modest way, I am one of those single individuals standing in the thin and paltry line of resisters to the big media lies. I'm proud to be here, and I'm sinking fast, despite a recent influx of loving largesse from faithful readers. But forget about me; think about those others that I just mentioned, give free speech a boost. Or else.

If you think you can continue to get away with ignoring the real facts as they are happening, well, you have only to look at what's happening. It was the lack of a truly independent media that enabled Bush and his gang to totally abrogate the U.S. Constitution and turn America into an aggressive nation-molester that now threatens the safety of everyone in the world.

And now the bad news. We are headed into the worst winter of any of our lives. The powers that be will stage more terror attacks to consolidate their new tyranny, and very likely, the entire U.S. financial system will collapse (because a severe depression can provide a major windfall for those who control the system). Nobody except the very rich are ready for this collapse, but all the signs are there, especially in the bond and housing markets. Plenty of us will be winking out this winter. Plenty of people you know.

What will you do when your access to your money is cut off? Start thinking about it now. Later will be too late. In the neo-con agenda, you are scheduled to be winked out.

Start thinking about your access to legitimate information. Where are you getting news you can trust? Work to make sure your access is preserved, and support those you can. It has never been more important.

Because once they're gone, all you will have is Fox News and its clones. Imagine Rush Limbaugh as the leader of the left and Karl Rove as the guru of pure patriotism. When that day comes, it will be painfully clear to any with enough gray matter left to perceive it that 1984 has finally arrived.

Many of the independent media sources millions of people rely on as antidotes to mainstream media poison are now hanging by a thread, in danger of winking out, just like those burned-out stars making our universe darker by the day. You can slow the approaching darkness generated out of Washington by the petro-crazies by making sure your preferred independent news sources will survive.

Because if they don't; you won't.

Chapter Fourteen

When The Big Lie prevails, crime pays

The 9/11 murderers were Americans, and they likely won't be caught

When reality becomes too shocking for us to confront, we invent fantasies to keep us from freaking out and going catatonic. Like the fear of our own impending deaths: too scary to comprehend directly, we invent gods and angels and sundry fantasy processes to convince ourselves we don't really die, because that stark inevitability would paralyze us with abject depression if we dwelled on it too long.

So it is with those indelibly etched images of silhouetted matchstick figures falling from skyscrapers on a warm September morning in 2001. You see them, you know it happened, yet you still can't believe they're real. In this waking nightmare that life in America has become, you avert your gaze and return to the mundane reality you have constructed for yourself, and utilize all sorts of fantastic rationalizations to convince yourself that all is well and you'll still wake up in the morning as though nothing has changed.

And thus it is that two years after the single most enigmatic day in American history, we still have no firm answers as to what really happened, and are not likely to ever find them for certain. When people tell you that everything always comes out in the wash, it is a lie, you know. There are many things about this life that we never find out. Simply consider the Kennedy assassination. Or Lincoln's, for that matter. We never found out the real story. And we never will, or won't be able to believe it if by luck we actually should hear it.

Two years after 9/11, the lies that almost immediately were put in place are still in place, unsubstantiated fictions of how a Muslim terror group that has never been able to be tracked down concocted a colossal conspiracy to crash airliners into American landmarks because, as our president said, "they hate our freedoms". The leaders of the Western world, who have been revealed as consistent liars on virtually all other matters, have managed to get away with their lies about 9/11, waxing reverential and righteous in the staggering silence that has comatized America.

But the stark fact remains — the claims that Osama bin Laden bombed the World Trade Center have never been proven. And the people who clamor for his hanging stole the 2000 election by preventing tens of thousands from voting, rigged the entire U.S. election system by using secret computer software, stole billions from people in California by manipulating energy markets, used nuclear weapons on Afghanistan and Iraq, continue to go to war over what are later learned to be complete fabrications, continue to cynically kill their own soldiers with various poisons, and have completely changed the character of their country by imprisoning and killing people without trial and passing sham laws that destroyed the U.S. Constitution. These are the criminals the American people continue to believe when they say that Muslim terrorists perpetrated the attacks of 9/11.

Why does everybody refuse to see?

Persecution of those who would ask questions now reigns supreme throughout the United States while a citizenry that is supposed to own its own country cowers in fear of being labeled unpatriotic for not supporting its government's policies of mass murder and unconcealed grand theft around the globe.

Worse, the most important thing they can't see is that 9/11 is the event that triggered all these other atrocities. They are all constructed on lies, and so was 9/11. Americans have willingly traded their freedom for this false paranoid terror mindset. And for what reason? I don't know. I can't explain it. It's so obvious. Everyone in the world has been somehow drugged. There is no threat from foreign terrorists. The threat is from Washington, which is inventing foreign territories and killing people everywhere to prove these foreign terrorists are a threat.

It's happening everyday in Iraq and Palestine and many other countries. It's even happening in the United States. Just ask Bob Stevens, the reporter killed by anthrax. Or Vieira de Mello, the U.N. envoy bombed to smithereens by American and Israeli spooks. Of course you can't ask them. They're already dead.

But if they could, they'd tell you it all spins back to 9/11, America's Reichstag fire, which gave the petro-nazis their carte blanche excuse to turn the world into an Orwellian police state. And now we're here.

9/11 was the key.

No answer after two years. Little hope of ever finding one.

The recently staged and bogus federal probe into the disasters in New York and Washington began with the statement that we knew who was guilty of the crime, so that was never discussed. That's like having a trial and saying at the outset someone committed the murder and now we must discuss how it happened. And like the future of our world, the verdict is already a foregone conclusion.

The very fact Bush and his cronies tried to obstruct even this rigged and superficial probe should tell you who the guilty parties are.

But the big questions make it even clearer.

Who profited from 9/11? Banking laws have kept this information confidential, but there should be no doubt then when rumors circulate that it was the Carlyle Group, featuring the current president's former president father, that made the big money on the "put" options purchased in the days before the attack, these allegations should be taken seriously, because they could unravel the entire U.S. government, and concomitantly save the world from the continuing destruction this group of criminals continues to wreak. Unfortunately, we have a justice system that allows the rich to commit crimes with impunity while it pillories the poor over petty matters.

Who really profited from 9/11 are the weapons makers, who now have exclusive and noncompetitive rights to rebuilding Iraq after Bush's murderous boondoggle, and who reap billions in defense contract largesse while at the same time the powers that be cut benefits to the American soldiers doing their dirty work.

Why didn't America's air defenses respond? There is simply so much information on the non-performance of the Air Force on 9/11 — query the pilots on alert in Washington, the controllers at NORAD, and the junior officers who carried out the non-orders of their higher ups — that to not investigate it is a crime in itself, obstruction of justice, treason even.

Why did our leaders publicly say they didn't know this could happen when they'd been discussing these very events for ten years and were able to name the so-called hijackers mere hours after the event? How could they name the hijackers, whom they'd been following for months, if they didn't know this could happen? So-called Muslim suicide bombers don't go drinking at a strip club hours before martyring themselves. The whole Arab hijacker thing is a deception, meant to focus your attention in the wrong direction.

It is a lie. A clear, obvious lie. And why do no major presidential candidates or any major media outlet ever point this out? Why do the American people not point this out to anyone who will listen?

The world is being destroyed because America is living a lie.

And what about the hole in Pentagon? It wasn't made by a jumbo jet. The original hole is tiny. Many windows were never even broken, initially, at the point of impact. And what about the specific people who were killed at the Pentagon, a secret group of Naval intelligence operatives. What was that about?

Why did the Twin Towers fall? Jets couldn't have knocked them down. The fires produced did not burn hot enough to melt steel. Even if they had, the buildings wouldn't have fallen in the way they did, straight down, a perfect demolition. And why did the building NOT struck by a plane fall in exactly the same way? Why do seismographs record an explosion before the buildings collapsed to the ground? Why are there all those puffs of white smoke in the pictures of the collapse, clear evidence of planted explosives?

Why was the evidence carted off and made to disappear before it had been forensically examined? To prevent anyone from determining radioactive explosives had been used at the bases of the towers?

Why did Bush read a book about goats for seven minutes after he knew America was under attack?

Why did the firefighters, minutes before the first tower fell, say over the radio the fires were out and the people in the building were in no further danger?

Why did the American people believe the attack on Afghanistan was carried out to pursue Osama bin Laden? It wasn't. And why did they not prevent the immolation of Iraq? It was based on total fantasy and deliberate lies, which have all now been found out, and still, virtually no one in the world protests. Even the United Nations has acceded to the lies.

Most Americans and many people in the world are simply not interested in controlling their own destiny and trying to resist the totalitarian fascism that creeps every day closer to their homes and their loved ones. So if you have doubts about these questions being realistic, or you have questions about the assertions contained herein, I strongly suggest you review the following material: the fantastic compendium about 9/11 compiled by Peter Meyer on his Serendipity website: http://www.serendipity.li/wtc.htm

Pay particular attention to the new speculative version of what really happened on 9/11 constructed by Canadian professor A. K. Dewdney at http://www.physics911.org/911/index.php/articles/2

Not only does he conclude that there were no Arab hijackers on the planes, he also theorizes that all the passengers were herded together on one plane and deliberately murdered by the U.S. government. Don't think this is a big deal though. Those 3,000 people in New York City were also murdered by the U.S. government in the most horrible crime ever committed by a group of leaders against their own people. Too few will read this piece, so make sure you do. Keep asking the questions. There's no one else. In this matter, the fate of the world depends on you. Spread the word.

Recently, several readers — in particular one Canadian friend — have taken me to task for misinterpreting the notorious remarks by Adolf Hitler so often quoted by those attempting to expose The Big Lie.

Here is the führer's actual quote from Mein Kampf:

" ... in the big lie there is always a certain force of credibility; because the broad masses of a nation are always more easily corrupted in the deeper strata of their emotional nature than consciously or voluntarily; and thus in the primitive simplicity of their minds they more readily fall victims to the big lie than the small lie, since they themselves often tell small lies in little matters but would be ashamed to resort to large-scale falsehoods. It would never come into their heads to fabricate colossal untruths, and they would not believe that others could have the impudence to distort the truth so infamously. Even though the facts which prove this to be so may be brought clearly to their minds, they will still doubt and waver and will continue to think that there may be some other explanation.

For the grossly impudent lie always leaves traces behind it, even after it has been nailed down, a fact which is known to all expert liars in this world and to all who conspire together in the art of lying. These people know only too well how to use falsehood for the basest purposes.

"From time immemorial. however, the Jews have known better than any others how falsehood and calumny can be exploited. Is not their very existence founded on one great lie, namely, that they are a religious community, whereas in reality they are a race? And what a race! One of the greatest thinkers that mankind has produced has branded the Jews for all time with a statement which is profoundly and exactly true. He (Schopenhauer) called the Jew "The Great Master of Lies". Those who do not realize the truth of that statement, or do not wish to believe it, will never be able to lend a hand in helping Truth to prevail."

As my Canadian friend surmised, "Obviously Adolf Hitler was not condoning the use of "The Big Lie" and it certainly was not a creation of his own. An astute reader as yourself must realize he was attributing the use of this manipulation to those who currently control today's Western media in its entirety." (Thanks Kent.)

Make what you will of this, the juxtaposition of Hitler uttering a crucially perceptive statement and America committing bloody crimes against humanity. One of the great losses of 9/11 was the failure of the American people to perceive how America has always driven its own foreign policy by fomenting wars from behind the scenes and then cloaking itself in the hero's mantle in front of cheering crowd of bought-off media cheerleaders. The average Joe has never seen through the subterfuge, and perhaps he never will.

While Americans and Jews have become the principal villains in the new 21st century world, perhaps they have only beaten the rest of the species to a position they also would embrace had they gotten there first. Or perhaps not.

The predator species devours everything in its path until — like capitalism — it eventually turns on its own and then consumes itself. Alien archaeologists may one day write this is what happened on Planet Earth.

Chapter Fifteen

The teeth in the smile

America's karma: Happiness for some paid for by the misery of others

There is no light at the end of the tunnel, at least not in this world.

There are those who seek and claim their light by believing in messiahs or philosophies that provide peace no matter what the conditions in the world in which they live. But despite the constant promises of true believers, this type of light is more apt to result in bloody death over semantic differences than it is in world peace when one version of the ultimate truth collides with another.

On the political level, there is simply nowhere to turn. The world is ruled by guns and greased by bribes, and morality and honesty seemingly have no place in it, except as pathetic pleas from the have-nots begging the haves to have mercy on them ... lies which are always ignored without the appropriate gratuity.

The greatest hope of all, democracy, has been revealed to be an alluring but deceptive scam, as persuasive patrician propaganda misguides the hordes like a flock of birds whose natural radar has been somehow scrambled, and the masses cheer for mass murder in the same enthusiastic tones they spew when rooting for their favorite sports team.

Personal corruption — the notion that everyone has a price beyond which they cannot maintain their integrity — dooms even Jesus' brand of communism into an exercise of coercion and cupidity, where the cost of maintaining your honesty can easily be your own life.

And the comfort of that ever-elusive benevolent dictatorship on which so many of the religions are based fails miserably on the political level when doctrinal consistency does the death penalty trip on sensible, individual compassion.

So how do we govern ourselves equitably? Are the choices only fascism or anarchy? Is the only question a matter of liberty vs. security? Will we give up everything merely not to be killed by those who wield more power than we can ever dream of?

So it seems in the world of AD 2004, where the powers of material consumption reign supreme and the wistful melodies of harmony and altruism gather mold like obsolete stock certificates in the trashcan of a fast-buck telephone boiler room.

As a society, and perhaps as a species, we are doomed, condemned by our shortsightedness to rip-off the quick profit and laugh another day despite the clear knowledge that the pie-plate is almost empty, and one day soon there will be nothing left to eat. And knowing that the feast is almost over only makes us eat faster.

I believe this is called "whistling past the graveyard," and I also believe that this is the time in history when this tune can be heard, almost in unison, being whistled all over the world.

The clock is ticking, and seemingly no one has the sense or the discipline to develop and implement a conceptual chemotherapy than can arrest the tragic spread of the cancer known as the rationalization of human avarice. Everybody's too busy stealing.

Lately I've been canvassing my old friends, many of whom do not know about my recent evolution as a writer. I've been asking them how they felt when they learned the disaster called 9/11 was really a political operation engineered by the highest levels of government in Washington.

Because they are my old friends, many of them respond with a genuine fraternal concern. How could you possibly believe such a thing, John?

I ask them if they've read the literature — how the Twin Towers could not possibly have been brought down by airplanes, how Arab hijackers preparing to donate their lives to Allah would not be seen in strip clubs, how no American official was ever penalized for the catastrophic failure of the air defense system, how the incriminating debris was carted away before it could be forensically analyzed, how officials insisted they didn't know such a deed could happen but nevertheless knew the names of the hijackers, how the official probe of the greatest disaster in American history was conducted at one tenth the cost of the probe into Clinton's blowjob ... and other items. I ask them if they know the details of 9/11, if they've bothered to look into it.

They always say no. It's just too depressing to contemplate. And then comes the clincher. They always say, "I just know my country couldn't do something like that to its own people."

Have you ever heard a clearer sign of pervasive brainwashing?

I usually stop trying right at this point. There's simply no sense in mentioning to such people that the great opportunity that has been missed in the 9/11 mystery is the possibility of perceiving how America has raped the world throughout the

20th century, cloaking sophisticated schemes of exploitation and theft in the noble rhetoric of freedom and upward mobility. Actually, the mobility for most of those who come in contact with the forces of American liberation is straight down, into a square hole in a cemetery. And those are the lucky ones. The unlucky ones, like so many recent examples in Iraq, are left where they fall to decompose into rotting detritus and eventually, into dust.

But you can't tell most Americans about this. They shift uncomfortably, and if they're your friends — or those who used to be your friends before you started conversations like this — they merely smile wanly, with a feigned compassion that masks an inner panic and an overwhelming urge to run screaming from the room and straight to the nearest hard liquor location.

They smile meekly, kind of like the smile you get from a salesperson selling a product he knows you don't need, right after you tell him you don't need it. It's a particularly American smile, one that will never evince the cognizance linking American prosperity to dead, dark-skinned peasants.

It is a fake smile that seems to say, "Y'all come back soon." But you know that if you ever do, their door will be locked as tightly as the door to reality is locked for them.

I read somewhere recently that a baby learns to smile by emulating the look on the face of his or her loving parent, and by mimicking that facial expression communicates that their relationship is both satisfactory and safe.

I also read somewhere else lately that the first impulse in every laugh is relief that the fear of death has been avoided for yet another instant.

And I contemplate how someone of little power in a Third World country would view an American smiling during a debate of someone trying to explain how his or her own government would have killed a large number of its own citizens merely to increase the prosperity of its own privileged class.

This person would not mimic the smile indicating mutual satisfaction and safety, nor would they laugh reflexively indicating their fear had been relieved. It would not be the shape of the lips they would see and respond to. It would be the teeth, and what those brightly polished yet clenched teeth of vacuous and insincere American smiles have done and are doing to the rest of the world.

Chapter Sixteen

Why you should not vote

Rigged computers plus corrupt candidates equal no freedom

Here's a simple message vital to the future of the human species that a majority of Americans will have no trouble heeding — Don't vote. Repeat: Do not vote, under any circumstances.

How's that for a counterintuitive proposition? Don't vote and you just might, one day, regain your free country. If you do choose to cast a vote, chances are excellent that you won't ever see freedom again, because by voting, you simply reinforce a system totally polluted by money and corruption that ultimately has nobody's best interests at heart, except for those who print the money, lend it to you a high rates, and then steal it back.

Why would you cast a ballot when fascist controlled electronic voting companies conceal from the public proprietary software that allows them to change vote totals in any way they wish, as the 2002 midterm elections in Minnesota, Georgia, Texas, Alabama and other states so blatantly demonstrated?

Never mind that criminal Katherine Harris gambit in 2000 when she personally disenfranchised more than 90,000 legitimate voters, allowing George W. Bush to embark on his pathological crusade to obliterate the world in order to enrich his friends with lucrative no-bid contracts that destroy the American economy.

The real point is that your vote counts for precisely nothing if some politically motivated computer geek can whimsically change the ballot box totals at the end of the night. Evidence of this activity is now overwhelming. That's what has happened in the last two elections, and that's what will happen in 2004.

So why would you bother to vote?

Then the real question becomes: What if they held an election and nobody voted? What would happen then?

Even if the votes actually were counted honestly, there looms the larger question of whom to vote for?

In this sick dance charitably referred to as the Democratic presidential primary campaign, not a single candidate has even whispered a syllable about any of the three most important issues which should be in the minds and on the lips of every prospective American voter — namely, the 9/11 cover-up which allowed the militaristic maniacs in the White House to start bombing every country they wish to steal something from; the monstrous control of American culture by Zionist media which has twisted the U.S.A. from a well-meaning collection of God-fearing villages into a murderous and pornographic circus; and the deliberate poisoning of America's own soldiers by their own leaders with radioactive ammunition and toxic vaccines.

Not a word about any of that on the Zionist TV stations, or from the so-called liberals and progressives who seek to challenge the tyrant in charge who performs his demented charades in the White House.

Of course the alternative to those posturing, gutless Democrats is our beloved un-elected Republican incumbent, the one for whom was written the popular bumper sticker: "Somewhere in Texas ... a village is missing its idiot." But this is no joke.

How many Americans will actually vote for someone who kills thousands of people based on the lies he tells? Even when the people he kills with those lies are some of America's finest citizens! What kind of twisted monsters have the American people become? Hiding in their decaying homes, ignoring the phony rationales for slaughter, they wave their flags and remain mute, not wishing to hear the truth in foreign newspapers that shatter the hollow lies of their own shameful silence.

Special note to all those parents considering a career for their children in America's armed forces: Uncle Sam is killing your children, even if they don't go to war ... which most likely they will be, lives wasted in meaningless acts of aggression against some innocent Third World country that will be based on lies. These leaders you venerate and grovel in front of are deliberately killing your own children, and you're voting for them!

OK, you can wave your flag now. And stay silent if you like.

What purpose would not voting really accomplish, you ask? Well, when there's nobody to vote for who is really going to address the legitimate problems of the world, and when the votes (it has already been proven) are not counted honestly, what is the point of voting? It's the same point as the presidential primaries: your future has already been planned for you, and you have absolutely no say in the matter.

Of course it's impossible that NO ONE would vote. Diehard political organizations would pay people to cast ballots just to have totals to count. But what if public participation got so low that it became impossible to maintain the fiction that the president had been elected by a majority of the population? As it is now, only 42-44 percent of Americans actually vote. What if that was cut in half, and only 20 percent voted?

What would really guarantee the effectiveness of this idea would be a new law stipulating that a quorum of eligible voters be required to validate an election. Since Bush became president with only 18 percent of the votes of eligible voters, under this law he would not have been able to take office. But that's a pipedream as incumbents in Congress would and will do nothing that might jeopardize their privileged status. Still, all legislative bodies must have a quorum to legally pass legislation. It would be nice if the same basic rule applied to electing the leader of the free world/chief pillager of the planet.

But even without such a law, the consequences of such a mass movement of refusing to vote for corporate stooges who don't act in the best interests of the people would have resonant repercussions and ramifications, and kindle a movement advocating the de-legitimization of the American governmental system, which must happen if humanity is to be rescued from the clutches of this new and growing totalitarian police state menace.

Would things get better, or worse? Some would say worse. But wouldn't such a protest amplify the realization that Americans no longer have a free and untainted election system?

As it stands now, only millionaires can run for national public office, and they must have the support of corporations, the very entities oppressing people everywhere in the world and curtailing individual freedom in the name of profit. So the candidates who run for public office must endorse oppressive policies in order to capture the support of the powerful entities that control the lives of everyone.

This is not freedom, people. This is economic coercion, and directly responsible for America's new trend of subverting all foreign governments through huge loans and huger repayment plans that wind up impoverishing and indenturing every nation that takes the bait.

Anyone who casts a vote for any candidate is endorsing America's stated objective of killing anyone in the world for any reason it chooses.

We need to protest in a serious way that the integrity of America's voting system has been profoundly compromised by electronic voting manipulation, and we also need to demand candidates who can tell some version of the truth that is not totally twisted by the perverse and inhuman influence of corporate financial blackmail.

Until we accomplish these objectives, we will continue to have an America that invades foreign countries based on wholly fictional pretexts and kills its own citizens with impunity, and we will have presidential candidates who cannot address the real issues that threaten our very survival because they are gagged by the financial constraints placed upon them by the very forces that jeopardize our well-being and our survival as a species.

My remedy for this double bind is not to vote. I urge everyone not to vote, under any circumstances.

The honest American people that still remain upright and independent must withdraw their sanction of a criminal and despicable governmental system that is strangling the life out of a majority of its citizens because it has rigged the laws and the courts to assist in the accelerated robbery of the poor by the rich.

What has our system of voting achieved? A Congress-full of lemming traitors who virtually all voted to seriously damage our Constitution without even reading the legislation, and who by a wide margin abdicated their legal responsibility to stop a tyrant who ordered two foreign invasions based on the lies he told.

The eventual objectives of a voting strike by the American people would be to convene Constitutional conventions to restore what rights have been nullified by the Patriot Acts, to outlaw corporate personhood, to recalibrate and detoxify the court system, and to place new restrictions on campaign financing and advertising. All these goals should have the aim of wresting political power from the coffers of huge corporations and returning it to individual citizens.

It's time for real Americans to stand up and be counted. Don't vote. Withdraw your approval of a recklessly criminal governmental system, or share in the guilt of its objective that eventually (and probably sooner than later) will destroy the entire world with its greed.

Don't vote.

Hopelessly warped by the shrill cynicism of men who do not care that real people needlessly die because of their decisions, the American system of governance must be brought down by a massive outcry of moral outrage and sincere shame from every corner of the land. Otherwise no authentic safety exists for anyone anywhere, and the human future cannot evolve with confidence that one day there really will be liberty and justice for all.

What was once the American dream is now the American nightmare.

Only by withdrawing our support for a system terminally fouled by the limitless bank accounts of the patrician plunderers will we have any hope of awakening from it.

Don't vote.

<u>Chapter Seventeen</u>

The cost of the cul de sac
Why we willingly choose to destroy the world

I loved her, and I told her so. Yes, she responded, but you love me the way YOU want to love me, not in the way I want you to love me. So I thought about that.

And then she told me a story she'd learned from Osho, a guru from India notorious to some who didn't really know him but revered by many who did, including her.

It was a story about a cul de sac. Most of us live our lives reliving the same habitual pattern, and keep repeating it over and over again, so that our lives devolve into shallowness, and then pain, and we feel trapped, frustrated, and empty. Osho's lesson, she explained, was to learn all there is to learn about what you like; then finish that dance and move on to the next step to continue to see what life and the world can teach you.

Once the lesson is learned, leap out of the cul de sac, go beyond what you know and learn what you don't. If you don't keep growing, she insisted, you're liable to wither and die, trapped in a blind alley from which you cannot escape. The repetition of what was once pleasure can degenerate into agony if you don't.

I heard what she was saying, at least through my ears and in my brain, but perhaps not in my heart. After all, here was a woman I told myself I loved, an admirable woman, not to mention beautiful, full of integrity, practicality and a social consciousness more realistic than most.

Although I instantly recognized the cul de sac in which I was trapped — sexual pleasure — it has now taken me many months for the logic of Osho's advice to sink in; and I'm still not sure it has. I yearn to leap out of the cul de sac, to go beyond it, yet can't quite bring myself to do it.

But as I begin to discern the fuzzy, confusing border between desire and real love, and how habits and expectations can become objectionable and even destructive if they're not consciously reevaluated on a regular basis, it becomes clear to me that this is not just my problem with an over-imaginative libido I have used to numb my frustrations over my inability to impact this world in a worthwhile and profitable way.

It is also the general problem of the human species and how each of us relates to the world.

We seek to take pleasure from it, and don't furnish the reverence and respect and appreciation necessary to make any love thrive.

Do I really love her enough to forego what gives me pleasure in order to understand who and what it is I love? Do we really love the earth enough to transcend our petty proclivities and try to understand what it is we're all doing here?

Silly stuff, huh? Comparing my love life to the degeneration of the planetary environment that enables us to live in the first place.

Maybe not so silly. Maybe surprisingly germane at a pivotal time in human history.

You need only look at what we have done to the world.

Turned the Garden of Eden into a toxic waste dump. Doesn't that sound a lot like f***ing it instead of loving it? And isn't that what has happened?

At least in America, and perhaps in many locations around the world, we are suffocating in an endless electronic avalanche of prurient images deftly designed to make us covet an alluring array of essentially unnecessary items: toxic creams to keep our skin from wrinkling, automobiles that every year look more and more like penises, drugs that prevent us from remembering we are desperate and depressed from buying all these products that keep us from looking at ourselves.

All of these items are expressly designed to keep us from looking — really looking — at ourselves.

And while we Botox, Lexus and Prozac the scary shadows from our faces in the mirror, in the deafening silence of our distractions we cannot hear the fish screaming in pain as they leap from the caustic ocean preferring suicide to life, or see the dead peasants on the road to Baghdad covered with flies and maggots in the dust, ominous monuments to our refusal to leave the cul de sac of our own preconditioned delusions.

We let the world go by, preferring to hide in our orgasms of distracted delight and misleading ourselves into believing that these will last forever if we can just purchase the right product and find the right situation.

As long as you remain in the cul de sac of your own habits, expectations and desires, the world will not be cured of this manic affliction known as the human rat-race.

Most of us see only two ways out of this existential dilemma: through God or with money.

Some of those who choose God turn their backs on the sweaty, filthy, bleeding world and fantasize that their piety and self-proclaimed purity will protect them from the wrath of Jehovah (or whomever) when their mortal coil inevitably unsprings. It is they who create God as the Evil One, their protector and anesthesiologist who will cuddle their immortal souls while they pretend they don't hear the gunfire in their own neighborhoods, much of it generated by members of their own congregations.

Even those who choose to serve God for the right reasons do a disservice to Him by focusing on their own salvation rather than on the suffering of others, and I'm certain He doesn't like that.

Some of those who choose money insulate themselves from their own guilt by surrounding themselves with luxuries that titillate the senses and forestall self-analysis, reasoning that if they can stay distracted right up to the departure point and then just step in front of a bus, they won't really have to worry about anything else.

But these two avenues both really lead to the same cul de sac, and as the whole world crowds down upon them, seeking sweet security in one form or another, the very conditions of the planet which sustain their lives, and their distractions, continue to disintegrate, and the only purpose of their perfumed escapes becomes a shortcut to self-destruction. Death by suffocation in the cul de sac.

So we endure the mocking lies of George W. Bush and his ill-bred ilk, who dissemble and get away with it because no one has the moral courage to challenge them in a straightforward way. We watch the world burn and the people die and shrug our shoulders, rationalizing that this is all horrible stuff, but that there is nothing we can do about it:

the momentum of the system, all five thousand years of it, is just too powerful for one person to confront.

So we might as well either hide in our self-created depictions of heaven or laugh as long as we can and let the devil take the rest. Well, that is what is happening. The devil is taking the rest.

In the Book of Wisdom, Osho relates: "... unless you go into your suffering, you cannot be released from the imprisonment of it."

Please allow me to redact that down to the present political situation on Planet Earth. "Unless you see that the 9/11 tragedy was unleashed by the very people you pretend to trust most, there is absolutely no hope that you will ever live in a humane or just world, and you might as well shoot your children right now before you give your government the chance to do it for you."

Unless we see our suicidal course as a species as a direct manifestation of the way we are living and seeking material distractions rather than trying to find a worthwhile purpose for our lives, none of the dire situations that threaten our peace of mind and our existence are ever going to be resolved.

On the other hand, if you completely ignore the money situation and let your systems disintegrate while you are preaching about possible paths to peace, as I have, you run the risk of not being able to preach another day.

Perhaps this is my way out of the cul de sac. Sneaking out through the bottom on that day next week when they repossess my car and home, and worse, shut off my computer hookup. But at least I got to say some of what I wanted to say.

Back to Osho: "A new journey has started in your life, you are moving into a new kind of being — because immediately, the moment you accept the pain with no rejection anywhere, its energy and its quality changes. It is no longer pain.

"One cannot believe that suffering can be transformed into ecstasy, that pain can become joy. Whenever anything is total it turns into its opposite.

"This is a great secret to be remembered. Whenever something is total it changes into its opposite, because there is no way to go any further; the cul-de-sac has arrived. Watch an old clock with a pendulum. It goes on and on: the pendulum goes to the left, to the extreme left, and then there is a point beyond which it cannot go, then it starts moving towards the right.

"Opposites are complementaries. If you can suffer your suffering in totality, in great intensity, you will be surprised ... you will not be able to believe it when it happens for the first time, that your own suffering absorbed willingly, welcomingly, becomes a great blessing. The same energy that becomes hate becomes love, the same energy that becomes pain becomes pleasure; the same energy that becomes suffering becomes bliss."

All of which is to say ... we must accept that the world is not what those who manipulate us say it is. And in confronting the continuing horrors that are perpetrated in our names, the recognition of it will lead not only to the cessation of these horrors, but to the knowledge of why we allowed them to happen.

As long as we stay in the cul de sac, we will never know what hit us when the end comes.

So ... did I get the girl? Well ... I don't know yet. My damn pants are caught on the iron-spike picket fence surrounding the cul de sac, and I'm dangling from the top.

I do know she's out of the cul de sac and running free, and I also know that if I'm going to catch her, and really love her, that I have to understand why and where she's running, and not try to corral her into some predictable cul de sac of my own desires.

It's the same with the future of our world. It doesn't look good, but it's too early to tell. One thing's sure: we have to stop trying to shape it into an object of our own desire, and hear what it is telling us, where it is leading us, rather than abusing it by making it a prop to keep us from confronting the shadows in our own faces.

The earth, like the woman I love, is not a product to be used to fulfill our own selfish and ultimately delusional desires. She is a purpose that it is our distinct privilege and honor to try and discover. But if we stay in the cul de sac of desire, distraction, and deception, there's no chance we ever will.

Chapter Eighteen

The real axis of evil

Monsters in our midst — the U.S., Britain, and Israel

Sometimes, after a long storm, the wind eventually blows the clouds away, and the sunlight shines through, revealing a familiar landscape that has never looked so different to us, which comes as a tragic and emotional shock when we realize the time we've squandered refusing to see the beauty right in front of us and the lives we've wasted believing things that in this new light of day we now know for certain were not true.

As I have said many times before in an inarticulate and unformed way, the great tragedy of the 9/11/2001 debacle — in which thousands of Americans lost their lives in a cynical stratagem designed to increase the bloody profits of the weapons makers — was a failure to see how this evil pattern of treason from within was actually the design template of American political behavior throughout the 20th century.

First, by covert financial assistance followed by widespread aspersion and calculated provocation, we create our desired enemy, always with the ultimate aim of reaping fabulous profits from the sale of weapons and the theft of resources down the line.

This design template realizes itself most recently in the creation of Osama bin Laden and the so-called Muslim terror threat, which has now culminated in the disaster in New York City and a schedule of endless wars, now underway, that threatens to destroy the entire planet with its spread of radioactivity and the reduction of all humans everywhere to economic prisoners of this evil game.

Saddam Hussein as well was a creation of the American CIA, which nourished him as a reliable, dual purpose lackey who when the time was right could either be counted on to assist in the repression of those from whom the Western tyrants wanted to steal, or morphed into an evil villain who could then be conveniently destroyed — each course achieving the same objective: total control of the hapless dupes in possession of the coveted resources.

Though it's obvious now to many who realize that American aggression throughout the world is always kindled from the devious minds in Washington, New York and London who put profit before principle, it is not so clear — owing to the multi-layered media mind-lock that forever keeps Americans blocked from seeing objective political reality — how the U.S. has accomplished and perfected this demonic practice of creating conflict as a way to sustain its own affluence.

Again, the great tragedy of 9/11 is that people were afforded the opportunity to look through a window at America's political behavior in real life and in real time, but instead they decided to look the other way.

America's corporate and financial leadership participated in the formulation, execution and cover-up of these fake foreign invaders for the purpose of profit, much in the same way as Vietnam was created out of fiction, as Nicaragua was ravished based on propagandistic fairy tales, and as hundreds of other foreign incursions were triggered by public relations schemes emanating from Washington. This sorry lineage goes all the way back (if not further) to the Spanish American War of 1898, in which an accidental (or perhaps self-inflicted) explosion in Cuba led to the creation and worldwide ejaculation of what we now know as the American war machine.

But the clearest — and most horrifying — glimpse connecting 9/11 to America's past deceptions goes directly to World War II — the so-called good war, which paralyzes the American psyche in a way no other event has before or since.

Like all the other American military interventions overseas, World War II was about reviving the American economy after a devastating depression had reduced the vast majority of U.S. residents to painful poverty.

Today, the object lesson of World War II manifests itself most vividly in the obscene proliferation of Holocaust museums, which constantly remind us that Jews were victims of Aryan genocide. It is a perfect psychological cover for the one thread that connects all the major wars of the 20th century.

Few people today remember the pivotal event of World War I, an event known as the Balfour declaration. President Woodrow Wilson campaigned for re-election in 1914 on a peace platform, and vowed to keep America out of the Great War then consuming the European continent. After he was re-elected however, he changed his mind. Why is a question that can be traced to a single document?

England was losing the war, badly. In a letter to Lord Rothschild, power behind the budding Zionist enterprise, Arthur Balfour promised Britain would look favorably upon a plan to create a homeland in Palestine for the Jews.

Suddenly, Wilson changed his mind. Some say it was because he was blackmailed over a secret lover. Others insist it was his Jewish handlers. Whatever the cause, many tens of thousands of Americans lost their lives in World War I because of a promise by Britain to Zionists to steal Palestine from its Arab inhabitants and create a Jewish homeland.

Few people today remember the seminal causes of World War II, either. After a demonstrably unfair settlement to conclude World War I (some say engineered by Wilson's Jewish adviser, Colonel House) depriving Germany of all its gold, Hitler came to power and resuscitated the German economy at the very moment the entire rest of the world was ravaged by a bank-created economic meltdown, now known as the Great Depression.

Using a barter trade system that completely circumvented control of the Jewish-dominated banking system (and getting help from American banker quislings among whom were the ancestors of George W. Bush), Hitler made Germany into an economic power when the rest of the Western world had been reduced to poverty-stricken chaos.

Because of the unfair treatment Germany had received during the creation of the Treaty of Versailles concluding World War I, and because Jewish bankers engineered that rip-off, Hitler began systematically stripping Jews of the their power in Germany. In 1933, world Jewry declared economic war on Germany, a fact well-documented in the history books. The move did little to curb Germany's economic success, as I say, at the exact time America was suffering the dire consequences of its Great Depression.

Further, Zionists worked out a deal with Hitler to not only fleece Jews in Germany, but to help some of them emigrate to Palestine, but only the Jews who Zionist officials deemed worthy to help start a new Jewish state were eligible. The remainder of the Jews were abandoned by the Zionist enterprise to, in some cases, a fate worse than death.

The epiphany that connects 9/11 to World War II is that there does not exist any non-Jewish written evidence supporting the contention that Hitler had a plan to exterminate Jews. It is true that once Hitler realized in 1942 that the Zionists with whom he had a working arrangement to help colonize Palestine had switched their allegiance to the British that he began rounding up Jews with renewed zeal.

But there is no written evidence among German documents (and Germans were and are notoriously meticulous record-keepers) that there was any plan for what is now known as the Holocaust. Nor is there any hard, non-Jewish evidence of so-called gas chambers. The Jews who did die — certainly not 6 million — perished from either malnutrition or typhus.

Now, in many European countries, there are laws prohibiting anyone from voicing these assertions. Freedom of speech around the world is being killed by Zionist Jews.

In fact, the Holocaust industry (as it is known today) did not really begin to capture the popular imagination until after the first Kennedy assassination, almost 20 years after WW II ended.

Sad to say — and it will horrify many so-called conscious and compassionate observers — but you can't clearly see the horrendous deception force-fed to the world about Arab terror and the Muslim threat without first seeing the colossal hoax of World War Two's so-called Holocaust, which gives the architects of the Jewish homeland a free pass to work their sinister strategies against the entire world.

And when you do see the Holohoax and 9/11 in the same ugly light, you can also see how the Soviet threat was fabricated in the late 1940s to accelerate the profits of the arms makers. And possibly — if you research it — you can understand how Wall Street funded Hitler and the Bolshevik revolution was triggered by a battalion of Jews from Brooklyn.

Hitler, bin Laden, Saddam. Targets created by the Western powers to reap huge profits from the sale of armaments and the robbery of resources. The cost in innocent lives has never been a concern to those who reap those profits, and is of no concern today.

This is what we should have realized two years ago when we watched the rubble in downtown New York City being carted away and dispersed to foreign countries before a proper forensic investigation could be conducted.

Arabs in an Afghani cave (built with CIA money, by the way) could not have dreamed up this complex scheme involving the deliberate stand-down of America's air defenses, the bribery of a plethora of American officials who assisted in a very profitable manipulation of the stock market, and the planting and endless regurgitation of the fantastic fable by the Jewish media.

One fact about the so-called Arab hijackers that is rarely mentioned nowadays is that they were shadowed during their entire flight school follies by a complex network of Israeli "art students" who were quickly spirited out of the country after the dirty deeds were done. Also, many of the "hijackers" have been found alive, living comfortably in other countries, and no attempt has been made by American authorities to rectify this transparent error in the cynical cover story about 9/11.

Now, I am not so naive as to believe that naked power does not rule this world. It has since the Assyrian war machine first massed its phalanxes against the feckless villagers of the Fertile Crescent some five millennia ago.

The sad part is that 5,000 years later, human nature has not evolved one iota, and in the very villages where Sargon and Nabonidus and Xerxes once slaughtered innocent families simply trying to live their lives, now two George Bushes have continued the same primitive practice of killing without mercy in order to steal without conscience.

I am not so naive as to believe that if America, Britain and Israel weren't busily trying to co-opt and prostitute all the nations of the world, then somebody else would be attempting the same stunt. It still doesn't make it right.

From our own so-called modern perspective, it was Britain that first mastered this evil strategy, and built up an empire on which the sun never set by claiming they were bringing civilization to unenlightened regions, but really they were just smuggling drugs – opium - to be precise.

Perhaps to be fair, the British learned this technique from the Spanish, the Dutch, or the French, or the Romans, the Greeks or the Persians. And the Jews.

The Americans simply copied the British model, but there exists strong evidence that the U.S. didn't adopt this model until the Zionists began to enter into the halls of public power at the end of the 19th century.

Since that time, in what has been called the American century, but might better be termed — considering Einstein, Freud, and the New York Times et al — the Jewish century, we have seen the continuation of mass murder covered up by lies, of oppression masked as economic opportunity, and of a so-called civilized society slaughtering innocent indigents for profit, and then sitting back smugly while praising their own humanitarian self-satisfaction.

The real axis of evil (to borrow a phrase from a certain low IQ politician who brays about his religion but has no real concept of its principles, like Thou Shalt Not Kill) is the United States of America, Great Britain, and the Jewish homeland.

The U.S. is the triggerman, which trumpets its hallowed legacy of individual freedom as an excuse for depriving others around the world of that very thing.

Britain is the architect, which perfected its colonial plan and then exported it to America, and retained real wealth in a subterranean way even as it pauperized its own people (something America is doing right now).

Israel, the Jewish homeland, is the tumor that facilitates the cancer's spreading, working its malevolent deceptions so greed triumphs over compassion and survival is everything, even though because of that philosophy the planet is dying, and so is every species on it.

It is wrong to blame Jews for inventing this kind of behavior, because they have only copied it from the other tyrannies of history. But with the sanction of their holy books, particularly the notorious Sanhedrin, which approves of their lying and sanctifies the robbery and killing of non-Jews with no penalty, we can all be sure that this conscienceless behavior will not be corrected as long as Judaism exists.

There are other, lesser accomplices in this great crime, like France, Australia and Japan, feigning fits of conscience while all the while remaining alert for trickle-down largesse, like perverts dawdling outside the brothel door, hoping for glimpses of flesh that will trigger their pathological spasms of voyeuristic satisfaction.

Once upon a time, America had no real enemies, only friends wanting to be just like us, a land of freedom and opportunity where everyone could get a fresh start.

Now it comes to pass that America has no real friends, only embittered former allies, resentful of the exploitation America has made them suffer with its wars and its graft. Now they all want to destroy us, and justifiably too.

In a way it's ironic. Now that America has revealed itself as a killer nation eager to steal and plunder from every other nation on earth, every other nation on earth still wants to be just like us.

This is the world we have wrought, and the dark future we have charted for ourselves, as a result of the shrewd governance of the real axis of evil, which is the U.S., Britain, and Israel.

Chapter Nineteen

The other shoe

America built a prison and put the world on Death Row

My life is like a cage of pain. Oh, I'm healthy enough for my age, though I eat too much junk and don't exercise enough. I talk to the most brilliant people, caring people, the ones most aghast at the way the world has become a slimy cistern of vicious lies, where the truth is what powerful men say it is, and the old values like honor and sacrifice are laughed at by teenage boys boogie-boarding in the surf and trying to figure out a way to live their lives without working. In this still warm November sunshine, trudging aimlessly along a pristine beach, amid shorebirds scurrying for their next meal, I feel like I am on Death Row.

Of course I am embarrassed to say this, with my easy life and convenient contentment all around me. I am shamed by men like Ernst Zundel, who languishes in his tiny prison cell in Canada, abused by callous guards and corrupt judges, who can speak of the noble nature of mankind and how it is time to organize that urge and rise up against the maniacs who enslave us with their jingoistic doublespeak. How can he, who has so little, see so much freedom, and how can I, who have so much, feel so imprisoned?

Sometimes I imagine I am living the life of the world, and try my darnedest to see where it is going, where things are headed. I haven't seen any dolphins this year, all year. Used to be, last year and before, I'd see them every time I looked out to sea. But red tide's been in all summer. Shouldn't swim in it. Get a sore throat. But usually it doesn't smell like it sometimes does, when it makes you cough. The blight doesn't keep the tourists away. They're happy enough to have escaped the snows of New Jersey. But I miss my dolphins. It's not a good sign.

And I miss other things, too. Yes, of course that girl who lit my life but insisted I was lying. That's probably a lump of coal that will never leave my throat. But I miss my country, too, the one I was taught to believe meant liberty and justice for all. What a joke that was, when you finally get around to reading how George Washington slaughtered Indians in Ohio or American soldiers went around executing peasants in Vietnam without anybody ever hearing about it until 40 years later.

Of course, of course, and about American soldiers murdering innocent families in Iraq. Operation Iraqi Freedom, right? Freedom from life, is what.

I miss my country, the one I was taught I had. I think soon too I will miss my planet, given the condition of the fractured ionosphere, the particulated air, the poisoned oceans, and the toxic soil. (A friend put her hands in her garden in a well-heeled Sarasota subdivision recently and came out with chemical burns that took weeks to heel.) This is not to even mention the radioactivity being spread around the planet. You know. It's in the bullets. Oh yes, and also in the sperm of the soldiers who come home in one piece.

In the bright sunshine, dimmed somewhat by those curious chemtrails in the sky, I feel like I am on Death Row. And it's more than the doctrinaire existential dilemma of turning 59. Death from old age would be a comfort to look forward to. It's just that more and more I feel hope is being systematically removed from the world. That a great extermination is about to take place. And, through my inattention to things economic and my willingness to speak about my dreams, I am in the lead phalanx on America's inexorable death march toward Camp Ashcroft.

Others I talk to share my malaise. I hope they have more food in their cupboards than I do. But they too will face this moment.

It was compelling to read the other day of the interview in Cigar Aficionado magazine of retired Gen. Tommy Franks saying one more terrorist attack in this country and all Constitutional guarantees will be terminated. It is one of the great satisfactions of my life that ten minutes after the so-called terrorist attacks of 9/11, I screamed, "This was an inside job!" It's nice to have been proven right, even though a majority of Americans have yet to catch up with the obvious evidence.

Looking forward to that first Red Alert, where nobody will be allowed to leave their homes, and the military will come around, checking out everybody, house by house, no doubt dragging a few away kicking and screaming. Or, maybe they'll sedate you on the spot.

It was somewhat reassuring today to read a letter from a Wyoming newspaper stating that anybody who would work as hard to prevent an investigation into a crime obviously had something to do with the crime itself. This is a revelation that is slowly dawning on all Americans: that all those people in New York and Washington were murdered, not by Arab terrorists, but by rich businessman and contemptuous bankers, who are all still profiting from the business of mass death.

Yet the realization comes too slow, too late. Not one

politician dares even whisper the sentiment. OK, LaRouche.

I am reading increasing signs that the bottom is about to drop out of the American dollar. They're talking bread lines in '05. That will be a great campaign slogan for all those disgusting Democrats who steadfastly refuse to discuss the real issues that are destroying America and the world right before our eyes.

In the meantime, with freedom and the health of the planet precariously hanging in the balance, the needless killing continues: not just in Iraq and Afghanistan, in the Philippines and the Congo ... you know the list — it's long. The needless killing also continues here at home. Did you know that deaths from reactions to properly taken medicines exceed the totals for auto accidents and cancer? Check out those new designer drug ads on TV and imagine how many extra people they're killing. I love that story about how the death rate goes down when doctors go on strike.

That's the place America has come to, and Americans deserve it, too, because of their sheer, selfish inattention to what has been happening, to what has been done in their names. And as with the extermination of 60 million Native Americans that has served as the models for genocides by both Stalin and Sharon, Americans don't really care about who gets killed as long as those sale prices stay low.

It's a sunny day. I feel like I'm on Death Row. I feel like the Earth is on Death Row, and America, George W. Bush in particular, is the executioner.

It feels like the other shoe is about to fall. Will it be an environmental catastrophe, the bursting of the Earth's atmospheric bubble by America's satanic tinkering with the ionosphere, or the collective poison of chloroflourocarbons (or was it fluorochlorocarbons?) denuding our protection from the sun's potentially deadly rays?

Will it be from some designer disease like AIDS or SARS or Ebola suddenly lurching out of control as the American government continues to insist it is tinkering with these poxes only for defensive purposes?

Will chemtrails finally choke the life out of us, or that government-issued bronchitis that everybody seems to have right now? Or will we all die of thirst when all the water supplies are finally privatized and firmly controlled by multinational corporations? Who will make the decision on who will drink and who will not?

Perhaps some new electromagnetic pulse weapon to blow our brains out through our ears in a single, massive moment?

Will we be blown to bits by a suitcase nuke planted by the Mossad and blamed on al-Qaeda? Does everybody know yet that all these explosions all over the world are being carried out by the CIA/Mossad operation known as al-Qaeda? And speaking of that, have you heard anything new out of the official government investigation into 9/11? No, I didn't think so.

Will we be beaten to death, or at least seriously injured like they were on the streets of Miami last week for simply trying to express their First Amendment rights (oops, sorry, we no longer have Constitutional guarantees) and protest the continuing destruction of the American economy?

Will we be spirited away in the middle of the night for pointing out that all those peasants murdered in Afghanistan and Iraq lost their lives for reasons that were demonstrably untrue? Or that the U.S. government prosecutes poor people for misdemeanors committed trying to stay alive, but doesn't prosecute rich people who kill millions and steal millions? That is truly American justice, and maybe should be codified in the Patriot Act. Hell, maybe it already has been.

Will it be the food that will get us, or the Diet Coke? Or will it be our own children who will kill us, recently arrived back from "police action" in Iraq and joining our local constabulary, and eventually treating their own families just like they did those hapless folks in Iraq?

Or will it be starvation, the worst way of all to go. Many already face this problem; many more are sure to in the next few months when prices rise like they did in Argentina and the money is suddenly worth next to nothing.

The other shoe. It's about to drop - the giant leather sole of a combat boot about to press down on our very own faces. Be sure and listen carefully when it does, when you see the last light of day snuffed out by the giant jackboot of corporate America smashing down on your face. You will hear "The Star Spangled Banner" playing smartly in the background.

This is what the storied history of America has evolved into. Liberty and justice are gone, and the phrase "under God" is a meaningless campaign slogan to anesthetize churchgoers who refuse to think or listen. America's penchant for building prisons is now a worldwide operation. There is no one to stop it ... except you. What chance do we have? We are all on Death Row.

Except for a certain, chosen few — those who are willing to lie, cheat, steal and kill, and take the money for doing it — we are all Palestinians now.

Chapter Twenty

Levels of the game

The deeper you go, the darker it gets

Did you know there's a war game played by Air Force types that posits a situation where the United States in the year 2017 conducts a preemptive first strike on China by using a next-generation space shuttle, which swoops down and annihilates strategic targets before booking back up to the Space Station? This is followed by the total destruction of China by a spaced-based laser, which the Pentagon humorously calls the Death Star.

I learned of this gut-wrenching scenario by watching a video entitled "Arsenal of Hypocrisy," a frightening array of future probabilities detailing a shocking portrait of America's militarization of space. This film features the commentary of anti-nuke legend Bruce Gagnon, social critic Noam Chomsky, former astronaut Edgar Mitchell, as well as former president Dwight Eisenhower, and provides such a chilling view of the future that it simply blew all the current news right out of my brain as my jaw dropped open and stayed that way for a few hours.

I mean, what's the point of speculating about what really happened on 9/11 or the sinister butchery of innocents in Iraq when a plan for total domination of the earth through calculated American violence is already in place and inexorably evolving toward its ugly conclusion?

The game is over. Nobody can oppose this war machine. It doesn't matter if we find out that no planes were actually used in the 9/11 deception, that it was all holograms and film. What court, what cop, is going to act on our discovery?

They're all bought and paid for. And so are the "peace-loving" Democrats who are now clamoring to bestow their own version of American totalitarianism on the people of the world.

"Whoever controls space will win all the wars on the earth," says Gagnon in the film. "There is no challenger on this earth able to stand against us."

Gagnon, coordinator of the Global Network Against Nuclear Power and Weapons in Space and organizer of many demonstrations at the Kennedy Space Center, goes on: "We have 7500 nuclear missiles, China has 20. We are going to manage China." He explains that the deployment of U.S. forces in Central Asia is principally about encircling China, including "deploying theater missile defense systems off the coast of China."

He concludes: "They don't want the American people to understand the depth of the plans for moving the arms race into the heavens ... we shouldn't have any illusions anymore about our country ... our democracy is under the control of corporations."

At least watching the film took my mind off the depressing load of e-mails I face every day. These e-mails are certainly just as enlightening as Atkins' film, and one from my pal Hazel the other day got me thinking that even the brightest among the people I have come to know and respect on the Internet are still pretty much in the dark as to what is really going on.

The story, now widely circulated (http://www.rense.com/general45/wh.htm), involved a fellow named Michael Meiring, who happened to blow his legs off last year while constructing a bomb in the Philippines. The theory is that Meiring, operating under the cover of being a "treasure hunter" (a common CIA occupation), was instantly whisked out the country by American agents to presumably a secure and secret location.

Hazel reported he was "a CIA operative and had spent 10 years on assignment associating with Islamic groups, Abu Sayef, MNLF, Moro Islamic Liberation Front, and other Philippine based Islamic groups, supplying them with US counterfeit notes (courtesy of US intelligence) and bomb-making materials so that they may create terrorist mayhem within the Philippines, giving the US a pretext to move in and "help," just like in Indonesia — just like nearly everywhere else these Mafia-like thugs can plant their terror and operate their "protection" racket."

The story set off alarm bells with me. I have long insisted that al-Qaeda is nothing more than a CIA/Mossad strategem, useful in creating havoc when the U.S. military wants to respond to a threat. Got a place you want to invade? Have al-Qaeda blow something up and we'll respond. It's a policy very much on the order of the Israeli formula, which creates terror as a justification to respond to whenever it wants to instill its repression of those whose land it wants to steal.

So now that every time I hear about al-Qaeda doing some dastardly deed, I simply assume it is U.S.-Israeli operatives committing some "false-flag" operation in order to achieve some other devilish purpose, just as we saw in Istanbul, Turkey the other day.

I wrote about this earlier in a piece called "The perfect enemy," which was widely circulated. The point being, an enemy under your complete control which you can deploy at your own whim is the perfect vehicle to keep the war machine making money, and Meiring is one of the best examples of that formula.

The so-called Muslim insurgency in the Philippines (and in a gaggle of other countries) is nothing more than a false-flag operation provoked by the CIA/Mossad construction named al-Qaeda in order to provide a justification for further military action and expenditures on armaments, not to mention that new cash cow - rebuilding countries the U.S. has destroyed, using American corporations with close ties to the Bush Administration. That's really the growth industry you should be investing in, if you're a murderous pig with absolutely no conscience about who you kill and what you destroy.

Madrid was a recent example of one of these false flag operations, as was Riyadh in Saudi Arabia, and, a little while back, the explosion in Bali, meant to exacerbate tensions and repression against Muslims in Indonesia.
Of course the granddaddy of all these provocations was 9/11, where the money men blasted the most famous American corporate landmark, made billions on savvy stock transactions and insurance claims, and created for themselves the perfect pretext to spread their population-reducing and profit-producing mayhem all around the globe, not to mention put all the American people in prison by means of Patriot Act and other repressive legislation.

And speaking of 9/11, I have been involved in the most fascinating round-robin conversation among absolutely the best, most conscientious researchers in the world. I would like to share some of this debate (but not all) with you, to maybe get your opinions on an apparent schism among the group, and also alert you to some very portentous developments.

This debate was essentially triggered by the curious

revelations of Mike Ruppert, certainly the most well-known of those proposing an alternative view of what happened on 9/11. I term the revelations curious because what should have been page 1 news among the 9/11 research community was buried near the bottom of an otherwise pedestrian column about old JFK news and the issue of when the world's oil supplies will run out.

Ruppert admitted as a person that he believed the WTC towers were not brought down by the jetliners that crashed into them, that he believed the buildings were destroyed by demolition charges. He also said he believed no airliner hit the Pentagon, and that something else was responsible for the death and damage there.

This was a change in his basic policy of reporting, and the curious part of it was that he published his admission so unobtrusively. The admission, however, sent shockwaves through the 9/11 research community, and opened up whole new areas for renewed debate.

Because ... if the so-called top 9/11 researcher anywhere had revised his opinion, and now believed that the towers in New York were NOT felled by airliners, and that the Pentagon was NOT really hit by an airliner, it not only gives all those websites and researchers who have been insisting these very things all along a lot more credibility in the public eye, but it also astronomically increases the chances that the general public will begin to believe that George W. Bush's official version of what happened on 9/11 is an absolute lie, and that our country and the world are in much bigger trouble than most people have been willing to believe.

Ruppert's admission significantly increases the likelihood, in the public mind, that 9/11 was an inside job, meant to create a police state atmosphere within the United States, and also meant to create a pretext for bombing any country Bush says is harboring the terrorists who did 9/11.

BUT ... if the Twin Towers were demolished, and the Pentagon was hit by something other than a hijacked airliner ... well, you have to ask: how could Arabs in a cave in Afghanistan have pulled that off? Hmm? Wouldn't you agree?

And if Arabs in a cave in Afghanistan didn't do the dirty deed, who did?

Of course, the shocking part of contemplating that question is that it can't help but shatter the whole world view of whoever has the courage to confront it. I mean, we're talking about the president of the United States condoning the killing of American citizens, a lot of them, right in the middle of America's biggest city.

It's not an easy assertion to consider, for any of us. Because it means that everything this country has stood for, and been built upon, has been a lie, or at least is now a lie. It means that our leaders were willing to sacrifice thousands of its own citizens simply to facilitate a more aggressive and lucrative geopolitical agenda.

It is perfectly understandable to all how the mind of a loyal American would recoil at that idea, declare it preposterous, and consign advocates of such a theory to the loony bin.

And yet one of the top researchers of 9/11 in the world, Mike Ruppert, has admitted that he has been convinced of the truth that the WTC towers were demolished, and that the Pentagon was not hit by an airliner.

And now the choices are clear for every American. You can

either hide your head in the sand and continue to believe that the government of the good old USA would never do such a thing to its own people, or you can confront the evidence. I think now the choice has come down to confronting the evidence or not taking care of your own life.

Which leads me to the little matter of the schism among 9/11 researchers, precious few of whom (and those who do now fall under a glaring spotlight of suspicion as to their motivations) believe that jetliners felled the WTC towers or that a jetliner hit the Pentagon.

The schism is a matter of what constitutes political realism. Of what is possible under the circumstances.

I have long advocated the immediate arrest, on the basis of probable cause for obstruction of justice, of the president and all his staff and cabinet. I'd prefer this order extend to most members of Congress as well. More detailed charges of conspiracy to commit mass murder, and conspiracy to commit treason, could be developed after the suspects were incarcerated and not able to do any more damage to innocent people all over the world.

Among 9/11 researchers, I am not in the majority, clearly. Though I'm not alone, either.

What is happening now is that several high-profile investigators want to make a movie about 9/11 and the sham that the official government probe has become. When this was announced, a number of us worried that the film could become another layer of the cover-up if the right questions weren't asked.

We seem split into two camps: those who believe the crime must be punished and the perpetrators — whomever they may be — arrested and prosecuted, and those who believe (as Ruppert and others do) that the American government must be maintained, that we must go through channels, work within the system, and achieve the best results we can given the political realities we confront.

So what's your call? Should we let the killers slide in the interest of maintaining the decorous, storied infrastructure of the American hierarchy, or should we really go after the real murderers of all those innocent people with everything we have in our guts?

Next time you read anything about 9/11, or the Patriot Act, or the exterminations now ongoing in Iraq, or government scientists developing the famous 1918 strain of Spanish flu, or white-haired Americans being clubbed by Miami police, try to keep this question in mind.

You do know, my friends, which side I'm on.

Chapter Twenty-One

They got the wrong guy

Bush is the real criminal, not Saddam

War is peace, Orwell said. It has never been clearer than now.

The theatrical apprehension of fallen Iraqi dictator Saddam Hussein from his pathetic hole in the dirt is a prima facie example of how the American vision of life and the world has become totally twisted. It was the culmination of an unjust war against a defenseless people, this ritual roughing up of a tired old man who was never more than a puppet following the orders of the master manipulators who always planned to do him in when it became advantageous.

Saddam was never a danger to America, despite all the pre-war rhetoric that has all been proven false.

George W. Bush — and Bill Clinton and the elder Bush before him — have killed many times more Iraqis than Saddam ever did. The 20,000 or so Iraqi innocents who have perished in the ceaseless bombing of the Cradle of Civilization is at least ten times more than the number of political malcontents who ran afoul of the murderous machismo of Saddam's inflexible rule, and the utter obliteration of this functioning nation-state was certainly something Hussein never contemplated.

What the United States has done to Iraq is something far worse than Saddam Hussein ever would or could have done. Saddam was never a danger to his neighbors; that was all

Zionist media spin. The only country in that region that was worried about him was Israel, because he represented an inflexible stumbling block to the expansionist aims of the demonic Jewish state.

Americans refuse to confront the ugly facts about this. They refuse to acknowledge that America has become the real evil empire.

The reasons for invading Iraq have been proven beyond any doubt to have been lies. Iraq had no weapons of mass destruction, nor did it have any connection to 9/11, the two reasons America used to unleash its murderous military might. These have been debunked beyond question; yet Americans continue to send their sons and daughters to slaughter and be sacrificed for the ugly perpetuation of these lies.

How Americans could continue to support these amateurish fictions is something for the historians to contemplate. When you use obvious lies to go to war, then you are the criminals, you are the evil ones. But Americans simply choose not to admit this.

Bush's decision to go to war based on lies have already cost 1,000 American lives, with more than 12,000 additional casualties, and thousands more stricken with a variety of diseases related to vaccines and radioactive weaponry. Plus there's the nearly $200 billion expended from the Treasury that has not gone to pay our military for such hazardous duty nor rebuild the country we have destroyed.

This money is literally a highway robbery of the American people directed by favored American corporations who have reaped billions virtually without lifting a finger. American corporations who have contributed mightily to George Bush and his fascist associates are overseeing the greatest robbery in history (eclipsing the previous record set by Bush the Elder in his plundering of American banks in the late 1980s).

But the American criminal behavior, you must remember, goes much deeper. For 12 years, America and Britain have bombed Iraq constantly, destroyed its civilian infrastructure, and caused the deaths of a half million children who were deprived adequate medical care and nutrition, all this after more than 200,000 were killed in the first Gulf War, all this after a century of exploitation and mass murder by — who else? — America and Britain.

Americans refuse to see that the war against the Muslim world has been going on for more than a thousand years, and nothing has basically changed. We install leaders who do our bidding, and then when we find a more lucrative way to fleece that part of the world, we do away with them, just like the Shah of Iran.

Either Americans remain oblivious to the pain we inflict on this part of the world, or worse, we know what we are doing, which makes us sadistic killers in order to maintain our posh (though rapidly deteriorating) lifestyles. This is the real American way — mass murder for money.

War is peace. America is creating a hell on earth. This mission has been accomplished in Iraq and Afghanistan and many other places. And now the criminals who engineer these inhuman scams seem to want to make America itself into the same kind of place, using arrest without trial, poisoned medicines and medical care you can't trust, the imprisonment of citizens who challenge the banks' warped fictions, and even the end of an authentic voting system.

Even in the obvious onslaught of all these atrocities, most

Americans — perhaps brain-damaged by long-term exposure to fluoride, radioactivity, food additives and other debilitators — prefer to believe the obvious lies spewed out by TV PR types (there are no legitimate journalists remaining in mainstream media, only paid shills) that America is still the world's last bastion of freedom.

Well, that's a lie, just like war is peace. In reality, America is the new totalitarian state, goose-stepping around the world.

Americans are now like what they call "trusties" in the prison of the world. They are like favored lackeys on the plantation of the planet. But soon, as capitalism continues to self-destruct around the world, they too will be tossed into the slave quarters, treated like Iraqis, and consigned to caves like Saddam was found, hiding from the mindless might that has been unleashed in order to further the fortunes of the elite, and pound and poison cannon fodder like us into nonexistence.

Saddam is not the real criminal here. He didn't destroy his own country. He only offed some political opponents, something that happens frequently right here in America.

The real mass murderer is Bush. The corporate TV stations continue to treat Bush as, if not a hero, at least someone who is operating the righteous machinery of democracy.

Democracy is as much of a lie as war is peace. Democracy is the new buzzword for tyranny. There is a robbery going on here which may be too late to stop. The siphoning of money, resources, and even water from the people who rightfully own them to the military-backed corporations who wrongfully control them signals a new dark era in human history, a new totalitarianism frequently predicted in the literature of visionaries like Orwell and Huxley, but never actually witnessed, at least on American soil.

Now with all these free-speaking people put in prison for merely trying to accurately describe what is happening — Leonard Peltier, Ernst Zundel, Charles Sell, Rick Stanley, the list has always been endless — we are witnessing the dawn of a new Dark Ages in which you must believe what you hear on television or you will ultimately lose everything you have.

Stay tuned for "red alert," during which you won't be able to leave your houses so they can come around and take you away one by one.

The American dream is now a nightmare from which there is no escape.

Chapter Twenty-Two

9/11 cover-up falling apart

Even phony Kean commission concedes something wrong with official story

"If what I say is right, the whole U.S. government should end up behind bars."

— Andreas von Buelow, former German defense minister

To many Americans, gulled into silence by fear and terror, the first inkling that something was wrong with the official story of the 9/11 catastrophe occurred about a year after the event, when President Bush resisted setting up a panel to investigate the events of that dark day.

Why would he not want to investigate the greatest crime in American history, many wondered? Then he badly under-funded it. Then he tried to name infamous war criminal Henry Kissinger to head it. Since then, Bush has stonewalled a committee of his own choosing, one stacked with political functionaries that is ill-equipped to conduct either a police or forensic investigation — and, perhaps most revealing, one that accepted the government's version of who the guilty parties were before they examined any evidence!

To date, there has never been anything indisputably authentic revealed to the public about how the U.S. government KNOWS that Osama bin Laden and al-Qaeda were the actual perpetrators of 9/11, though there have been many contrived pieces of evidence presented long after the fact that all have been questioned by those with discerning eyes.

Today, millions of Americans realize — simply from watching thousands of cop shows on TV — that the one most interested in covering up a crime is the one most likely to have committed it. Many more millions also realize that the foremost beneficiaries of the attacks and mass killings of 9/11 are the same people who are now waging wars that are based on some very suspicious rationalizations, most of which since have been exposed as outright lies.

Shockingly enough, even Thomas Kean, chairman of the committee constructed to cover up this greatest crime in American history, blew the whistle the other day that the attacks could have been prevented. It is clear now that Kean's remarks were nothing more than what is called "a limited hangout." But his comment was evidence that a much larger percentage of the American people is beginning to sense that the "they hate our freedom" rationale uttered by the president is clearly bogus, and there is much more than meets the media eye happening about 9/11.

To a far smaller number of Americans, the official 9/11 story began to smell much earlier than when Bush tried to stall the official investigation.

When top Bush administration officials immediately and in unison denied knowing that jetliners could be used to attack American landmarks right after 9/11, a number of alert reporters immediately pointed out that this very subject had been the subject of government scrutiny for almost a decade. And when U.S. officials immediately released a list of the alleged hijackers, the lie was immediately visible to those with eyes to see: how could they deny knowing this possibility of a massive jetliner attack existed, yet be able to name the alleged hijackers almost instantly because these individuals had been under surveillance for months?

If they could name the alleged hijackers, then they couldn't deny knowing the possibility of using planes as weapons existed, could they?

As astonishing events unfolded after the tragedy — the hasty passage of the Patriot Act (approved by Congress despite virtually no one in Congress reading it before voting for it), which nullified large portions of the U.S. Constitution; constant "terror alerts" for which no evidence was ever produced; the war against Afghanistan which was claimed to be a response to 9/11 yet was planned long before 9/11; and the war against Iraq, which was waged because that nation supposedly threatened America with weapons of mass destruction (which have never and will never be found, unless planted) and had ties to that mystery terror group called al-Qaeda (since proven to be lies) — many more millions of Americans began to understand that the new peril we are in is not from some shadowy worldwide terror group, but from unscrupulous demagogues in Washington who will invent any story — and kill any number of people — in order to improve the fortunes of the very military/industrial power brokers who illegally brought them to power in the first place.

In the mind of these many more millions of Americans, a new syllogism began to take shape: if they lied about why they went to war in Afghanistan and they lied about why they went to war in Iraq, how stupid would Americans have to be to believe what they said about 9/11?

And yet, through two years of intense flag waving, during which most Americans were too terrified to say anything critical of those who were ostensibly protecting us from this new wave of worldwide terror, the lies hardened. The media, owned by the same shameful specimens who own the weapons making companies, refused to even entertain the notion that the U.S. government could tell blatant lies to its own people, never mind murder thousands of them in one day.

Worse, what passed for the political opposition was afraid to even whisper what was becoming obvious in the minds of so many Americans with functioning brains — that the initial signs of a deliberate air defense stand-down, the phony mythology about Muslim hijackers, the funny way all those buildings in New York happened to fall, the tiny hole in the Pentagon that was supposedly caused by a giant airliner, and the curiously comatose behavior of our president when the nation he was supposed to be leading was under dire attack — that 9/11 bore a multitude of evidential suggestions that it was an inside job, executed to give right-wing crazies a better shot at looting the treasury of their own country in a variety of ways. This scenario has now obviously come to pass.

And that is really where we stand today. Shockingly, while millions around the country and billions more around the world are certain that this is what happened, not a single major politician now chirping about irrelevant subjects in order to be permitted to run for the office of president against the world's top mass murderer has uttered even a single syllable that these millions of Americans who believe something is very wrong with the official 9/11 story just might be right.

And in the so-called American free press, our prostituted media continue a total blackout on the subject, as evidenced by the total silence that accompanied the recent filing of a lawsuit by 9/11 widow Ellen Mariani against President Bush for obstruction of justice and treason.

This is a travesty of unprecedented proportions. Like the

entire Congress that goose-stepped late at night while it knocked over the U.S. Constitution, here we have the complete political spectrum — every single rich man who has declared his intention to run for president — not daring to admit what millions of Americans know beyond doubt in the sincerest depths of their hearts — that 9/11 was conceived, devised, planned and carried out from the offices of power in the United States, principally Washington, but also New York and Langley, Virginia, and quite possibly Tel Aviv.

You have only to look at the psychologically palsied and putrescent behavior of the official 9/11 investigative body, the Kean commission — as well as the insane and demonic actions of every single functionary in the Bush Administration — to know in your heart that it's true.

And realize the jeopardy we are all in.

Fortunately, there are many scrupulous personalities who haven't bought the shallow lies and who have worked doggedly since that dark day to bring the cynical deceptions to light.

They have analyzed the fall of the WTC towers and concluded they were most likely demolished. Why else would so much of the rubble have turned to powder and the towers themselves exploded at both the top and bottom? Why else would WTC7 have fallen in the same manner of the others when it was not hit by a plane?

They have talked the Pentagon scenario to death and concluded there was no legitimate trace of jetliner rubble to be found, written that a hole of that small type was most likely made by a missile or small remote controlled aircraft, and concluded that reports of identifying the DNA of every passenger on Flight 77 in that rubble was simply an impossible lie if the fires were hot enough to have melted virtually every trace of the crashed airliner.

They have concluded beyond doubt that the alleged maneuvers of the Pentagon jet could never have been accomplished by someone who did not do well in a small plane at a jerkwater flight school.

Many people have asked me, what are the best 9/11 sites? This is a sampling of some of them. Study them. Hone your arguments. Talk to people.

http://physics911.org/net/modules/
http://www.serendipity.li/wtc.html#what_actually_happened
http://www.serendipity.li/wot/anti-war.htm)
http://serendipity.ptpi.net/wot/holmgren/11.htm
http://911research.wtc7.net
http://wtc7.net
http://911research.wtc7.net/talks/wtc7>
http://nyc.indymedia.org/front.php3?article_id=82574&group=webcast
http://www.informationclearinghouse.info/article4582.htm
http://www.radiofreeamerica.tv/video/2003-12-12/911-group.swf
http://news.globalfreepress.com/
http://www.911-strike.com/
http://www.libertypost.org/cgi-bin/readart.cgi?ArtNum=22004
http://home.comcast.net/~skydrifter/exp.htm
http://whatreallyhappened.com/blackmail.html
http://disc.server.com/discussion.cgi?disc=149495;article=45885;title=APFN
http://www.wsws.org/articles/2001/oct2001/bond-o05.shtml
http://www.cooperativeresearch.org/timeline/main/dayof911.html

http://www.media-
criticism.com/Baltimore_Sun_911_Letter_09_2003.html
http://portland.indymedia.org/front.php3?article_id=44629&
group=webcast

(Apologies to the many good ones excluded; I'm only one
guy. These are just a few of the ones I happened to have
used.)

When you read through these and understand their contents,
you will understand beyond question that everything you
hear from the mouths of presidential candidates, government
officials and TV commentators is a lie. That there is so much
evidence to convince you that 9/11 was an inside job, that
our leading officials are criminals and mass murderers, that
you, as a functioning human being on this earth, have no
choice but to try to convince your neighbor that something
must done if we are not to go quietly into this police state
prison that has been prepared for us.

And yet, with all the comprehensive and inspired research
that has been done (really, the Kean commission only needs
to read the Internet before recommending mass arrests for
virtually all of the American government's leadership) there
are two glaring areas that continue to delay the search for
justice about 9/11.

The first involves the suspicious investments prior to 9/11 in
which millions of dollars were made by betting the price of
certain airline stocks (and other companies, some of which
were located in the WTC towers) would go down. Financial
laws guarantee a degree of confidentiality in these
transactions, even though these laws principally protect
crooks with large amounts of money who are often doing
something the law does not permit. Nevertheless, the laws
are set up to protect these identities.

Had America a great and honest leader, he (or she) would suspend these laws and name the beneficiaries of these suspicious transactions, reasoning that the greater good was served by tracking down the real perpetrators of the 9/11 mass murder instead of protecting the identities who clearly knew that 9/11 was going to happen before it did happen. Could there be any clearer path to uncovering the real criminals who killed all those people in New York and Washington (and later in Afghanistan and Iraq)? No, there couldn't. Any genuine investigation into the crimes of 9/11 would start (and very possibly finish) right here.

In addition to releasing the contents of the black boxes that were found in the wreckages of the three disaster venues of 9/11, as well as the contents of the footage taken by the confiscated security cameras near the Pentagon (which could clearly reveal what actually did hit the Pentagon), the names of the investors who profited from insider trading in the days prior to 9/11 would give us a clear look at who the actual perpetrators of this unspeakable crime actually were.

It is a way to solve the crime, and it is clear. Logical people must assume that those who would prevent this method of solving this crime clearly have some involvement in it. This is beyond debate.

The second area most researchers have failed to make any real headway in is the involvement of Israel and its intelligence agency the Mossad in the planning and carrying out of the 9/11 attacks. Sure, Israel was one of those many countries that gave advance warning to the U.S. that something like this was about to happen (you remember, those warnings that Bush and his thugs insist they never got, but fortunately were reliably recorded by the other countries themselves).

The facts are that the evidence for Israeli involvement is substantial. Two workers in an Israeli company located in New York got advance warnings by e-mail two hours before the attacks. Israeli "art students" were shadowing the alleged hijackers for many months during their sojourns in flight schools around the United States. Five Israelis were arrested for dancing in celebration shortly after the planes hit the towers; two had connections to the Mossad. And, perhaps foremost, in the city with the largest Jewish population in the entire world, virtually no Israelis were killed in the 9/11 attacks.

In addition, the men who assumed control of World Trade Center management, Larry Silverstein and Frank Lowy (owner of all those Westfield malls), undertook all sorts of odd security breaches shortly before 9/11 and are connected to the highest levels of the Israeli government.

Taken all together, these coincidences are too astonishing to ignore. And given Israel's history of "false flag" operations (conducting terror and getting the blame shifted to another country), its involvement throughout history in attacks on its own citizens and Jews around the world to get them to behave in a certain way, its ponderous influence on the American congress and the American media, and the words of former Israeli prime minister Netanyahu, who immediately after the attacks said they were a very good thing for Israel, many millions of people believe that Israel was really the driving force behind 9/11, simply to get the Americans to continue to do their bidding in the Middle East, which as you can see by subsequent events, clearly is continuing to happen.

The withholding of information by the U.S. Securities and Exchange Commission of the names of the men who profited from the suspicious trades in the days before 9/11, and the hidden role of Israeli intelligence in a caper in the biggest Jewish city in the world in a complex owned by Jewish businessmen continue to be the two most significant uninvestigated aspects of 9/11, and the ones most likely to lead to a genuine finding of fact about what really happened.

Unfortunately, the powers that be are doing everything they can to impede investigation into these two areas, as well as into all other areas of information about 9/11.

Thus, it stands to reason, just on the basis of rules established in all those TV detective shows, that the powers that be are the ones who committed these heinous crimes, for the purpose of regimenting society more to their liking, because a regimented society is more profitable, and those under the thumb of a totalitarian capitalist dictatorship, as we are now, are far less likely to solve crimes and discover the perpetrators of the horror of 9/11 that changed the fundamental nature of the nation and the world in which we live.

It's not too much to demand honesty and accountability. Insist your favorite presidential candidate tell you about what he knows about 9/11, the insider trading, and Israel's influence. The answers you receive will tell you exactly what kind of candidate you're supporting.

Chapter Twenty-Three

What do we do?

It's not just rhetoric — we need a revolution to survive!

These are impossible questions, ones which I cannot answer. Perhaps you can.

What do we do when the very people supposed to be protecting us are actually harming us? Robbing us, poisoning us, deliberately asphyxiating us, putting things in our water that make us docile, giving us foods and medicines that make us sick, and in general preventing us from living our lives in what we believe is a normal manner.

What do we do when the society in which we live prevents us from being moral? Or from telling the truth as we see it? What do we do when our leaders encourage us not to question statements that we know in our hearts to be lies?

What do we do when our TV and newspapers tell us lies but insist we should regard this information as truth? What do we do when the vast majority of people in our society accepts these lies as truths and ridicules us when we call these statements untrue?

What do we do when we have a legitimate grievance and can't get it redressed without bribing someone? What do we do when we can't trust our courts? How are we to respond when we learn that a private company controls all of our money? Or that the government has the right to poison your baby before you take her home from the hospital?

What do we do when the leader of our country, the occupant of the most prestigious office in the world, is a pill-popping psychopath with no discernible personality whose favorite hobby is killing large numbers of people, either by signing death warrants to execute mentally defective miscreants or ordering air-strikes against innocent women and children tens of thousands of miles away?

What do we do when all those around him, including the so-called political opposition, seem to agree with everything he says and does, and otherwise act as if this demented demagogue pathologically predisposed to obliterating the whole world is actually a normal human being?

It used to be the American way allowed that if you didn't like the way the government worked, you could go to the polls and vote for an opposition candidate who promised to change things. What do we do when all the candidates who are running for every office are all basically saying the same thing and endorsing all the harmful things being done?

What do we do when the concept of one person/one vote has been completely destroyed by computerized voting machines whose totals no one can verify, except the companies that own them, which are themselves owned by rich white men who support the man who got the votes that no independent agency is able to authenticate?

What do we do we when can't trust the food we eat, the air we breathe, the water we drink, or the medicines we take to make us well? How are we to regard these efforts to criminalize vitamins and other health foods when the doctors we go to prescribe medicines that are less effective than those beneficial substances they are working so hard to ban?

What do we do when our nation decides to go into a state of

permanent war, choosing hapless countries to attack and then obliterating them, then fleeces its own citizens with devious legislation that funnels billions of dollars to companies to reconstruct what we've just destroyed for reasons we later learn were transparent lies? How are we to regard such a country, such a group of men who would do such a thing to their fellow human beings?

And how are we to regard ourselves for believing and supporting such insane and inhuman policies?

What do we do when the vast majority of American citizens refuse to even recognize that anything is out of whack?

What do we do when government employees tinker with diseases in a laboratory, and then suddenly the whole country is stricken with a new kind of flu, one that kills children in Colorado and keeps everyone coughing indefinitely all across the nation? Why is it when you look up epidemics in history, you find that most of the recent ones occurred after vaccination campaigns? Why do you feel so uneasy when they tell you to get a flu shot? Or if you're in the military, when they tell you to get an anthrax shot? Or if your wife has just given birth, when the government wants to give your baby all manner of shots, and threatens to take your child if you don't comply?

Why does the American government seem so intent on destroying the lives of its own soldiers? Why do American soldiers seem so willing to shoot innocent women and children? Iraq or Afghanistan were never threats to America. Why do our children so eagerly shoot those people down like dogs? Is that what we really taught them to do in our humble homes? Is it? Are you absolutely sure we didn't? If we didn't, why do they?

What do we do when you can't get any public officials to comment on why there are all these strange cloud markings in the sky — some call them chemtrails — and so many people are sick with respiratory problems? Or perhaps it's the soot in the air, in increased amounts these days because air quality rules have been rolled back by the President who was elected on the basis of votes we were not allowed to recount.

What do we do when they tell us we have to rearrange our lives because of the threat of "terror"? These rearrangements, at least these days, are primarily based on the precedents set by the "terror" attacks of Sept. 11, 2001, in which many thousands lost their lives in New York City and Washington, D.C. These "terrorists" have "terrorized" the world ever since, causing us to go to war in Afghanistan, Iraq and elsewhere.

Who are these "terrorists?" Why has no evidence ever been presented linking them to 9/11? Why was the Afghanistan war planned before 9/11 if it was blamed on 9/11? Why was the war in Iraq blamed on weapons of mass destruction and connection to 9/11 when it was planned long before 9/11? Why didn't the government ever catch those responsible for the anthrax attacks, especially after the trail of suspicion led right back to government offices? Why didn't anybody in Congress read the legislation before voting for the initial Patriot Act?

Why has nobody protested the nullification of our Constitutional rights, especially when the so-called "terror" threatening our security is clearly a behind-the-scenes construction of our own intelligence agencies?

What do we do when the Vice President brings all the top oilmen in the country to his office to create a new energy policy, then they all fleece the citizens of California of billions of dollars in energy overcharges, the principal energy broker presides over the biggest bankruptcy in U.S. history and is not prosecuted, a well-connected actor is elected governor of California to stop efforts to recover this stolen energy money, and the Vice President continues to draw a salary from the same company that receives billions of dollars in lucrative reconstruction contracts for rebuilding Iraq, which is the country we bombed on the basis of lies that were based on the "terror" that caused 9/11, for which they refuse to provide the evidence?

When you wave your American flag today, do you realize it means you are endorsing mass murder and exploitation all over the world? Do you realize the reasons for this demonic behavior are all lies? Do you realize America creates wars to stimulate profits, and has done this consistently for more than a hundred years?

How come so many of our own military service-people are returning from Iraq to America with really strange diseases? How come we use radioactive ammunition when we know it has made thousands sick? How come we give soldiers shots to prevent diseases but we won't tell them what is in those shots? How come the military doesn't desert when they learn all these things, and how come parents can be proud when they bury their children who died in a war that was fought for reasons we now know to have been lies? What's up with that?

What do we do when America moves all its best jobs overseas because of the cheaper labor? What are Americans supposed to do about that? Start their own businesses and keep their products here at home? Hmmm.

What do we do when we can't trust the cops? Whom do we call for help then? When we see our president committing obvious moral and legal crimes and then lying about them, whom do we call to have him arrested? What do we do when we mention this to opposition candidates and they don't answer us?

We can no longer afford to support a government that does not support its people! But what do we do?

We need to begin meeting with small groups of like-minded people who are as aghast as we are to find out how to begin processes of how to arrest and prosecute our criminal leaders. This will be very difficult.

It's not just a matter of canvassing social clubs and political parties. Both categories are largely brain dead and irrelevant, mindless flag-wavers interested more in eating and drinking than in actual freedom. Nor is it productive to stage mass rallies with fractured focuses, where the main message of fading freedom is lost amid a confusing welter of conflicting passions.

No, this requires the creation of new groups, ones devoted to real education and not co-opted. Pay particularly attention to the word "co-opted," and maybe extend it to "infiltrated." This is a situation that applies to militias and politically oriented environmental groups. Both are now under extreme scrutiny by the feds, who are armed with draconian new laws that permit them to throw you in jail for the most trivial reasons.

But the need to be very careful should not stop you from trying to discern and organize people who are genuinely interested in the principles of freedom, in maintaining the attitudes that could make America what we always hoped it would be, and ending this criminal caricature that it has become.

At some point very soon, we all need to address our public officials and determine if they are going to side with the people who are being oppressed or with the oppressors who are being bribed to fleece and shackle the people.

These are the questions we need to ask them:

• Why are there two sets of laws in this country, one for the poor that guarantees they will continue to live in poverty, and one for the rich, which assures they can get away anything as long as they pay off the right person? Why is it that our Attorney General approves of the indefinite incarceration of innocent foreigners without having to present any evidence, yet refuses to investigate charges of treason, obstruction of justice, mega grand theft and mass murder against the rich and powerful men who have seized control of what was once a free country? Who will investigate law enforcement when the law enforcers have turned criminal? Why was Dick Cheney allowed to keep secret the master plan for robbing Californians of $11 billion?

• Why have all laws protecting the environment been repealed when we know the infusion of poisons into products is needlessly killing large numbers of people? Why are we deliberately fouling our air with poisonous chemtrails, and why is it no government official will say a thing about this?

• Why is there a deliberate obstruction created by Ashcroft to prevent ordinary people from finding out what their government is doing to them? Why are ingredients like fluoride and aspartame permitted in what we consume when everyone knows they are poisoning us?

• Why are our schools turning out children who can't spell or think for themselves? And why does our government seek to take away money for those schools and give it to self-serving, thought-limiting religious schools, especially when the Constitution that used to be in force expressly prohibits such transparent favoritism?

The police state is here. Your rights have been taken away, one by one. It is now illegal to think for yourself. Just try to examine evidence showing the Germans never willingly gassed anyone during World War II. You can be thrown in jail just for trying. And knowing that, what does that tell you about the original question? Do you see anything wrong with outlawing certain thoughts? If you don't, then you probably don't have any questions about where you went to school, or what church you go to, and you also probably don't see any purpose in any of this I've just written.

Our reliance on mass media has dulled our minds, our reliance on pre-packaged foods has anesthetized our senses and atrophied our bodies, and our reliance on establishment religion has shackled our spirits, and made us cogs in a mindless machine rather than the sensitive seeds in the soil we need to be to fulfill our human birthright.

We need to grow our own food, make our own clothes, and live in our own houses. We need to break the backs of the bankers who control us with things we don't really need. What do we do with all this time our modern conveniences give us? We seek out more distractions to keep us separate from those we love. All these consumables we covet just make us hate ourselves more, because, deep down, we all know we're not doing what we're supposed to be doing.

What we're supposed to be doing is making a better world, making sure people are not suffering, making sure that we're not destroying the very things that keep us alive. We are not supposed to be increasingly alienating ourselves with false styles and transitory titillations that prevent us from nourishing the very things that nourish us. We are not supposed to be taking pills to make us feel better; we are supposed to be living lives that make us feel better.

The existing political structure in America is rotten to the core, fatally polluted by a private money supply that enables perverted patricians to retain their aristocratic power across the generations. Until this injustice is eliminated, and the power over money is returned to the people, nothing will be fixed, and the unjust wars will proliferate.

Instead of leading a more humane world into a new era of enlightenment, understanding and technological diversity, America is dragging the world backwards into a new Dark Ages where brute force annihilates legitimate efforts toward reciprocal respect and cooperation.

Under present circumstances, there is no alternative to the mass dismissal and prosecution of the entire American government — the administration, the congress, and the judiciary all must be indicted for criminal corruption. To do this, a massive campaign of recalibration needs to be undertaken. Starting at the local level, delegates to form a new government need to be chosen, preferably without political campaigns (and certainly without funded campaigns). These local delegates need to congeal at the state level, and begin the arduous task of reconstituting the federal government without political campaigns, and devoid of the political poison of corporate control.

Once a temporary U.S. Senate is chosen by the states, new elections can be held for the House of Representatives, which then would choose a new Senate as a precondition for being able to hold a nationwide election for higher leadership positions. In the interim, a temporary administrative transition team would coordinate the operations of the federal government, once all the Cabinet-level leaders had been jailed. Who would be named to this team, and how it would be named, remain to be seen. Certainly political parties, military and religious leaders, unions, newspapers, bankers, lawyers and doctors should not be involved in this selection process. Or perhaps they all should. The one thing to be avoided is the dominance of any one segment of society over the entire government, as it is now by lawyers masquerading as professional politicians.

The only way to get a truly representative and functional government is to severely regulate the use of mass media in campaigning, enforce strict term limits for all offices, and to radically revise all laws governing banks. Usury must be abolished, and upper limits on income established, now that we are all certain unregulated capitalism is the cause of most of the world's problems.

All the budgets of the world can be balanced by the simple confiscations of most of the fortunes of the world's wealthiest people, like the Rothschild, Bush and Windsor families. Relax, patricians, you'll still be able to buy your way out of trouble. We won't take it all, just most of it. Besides, many members of these families won't need their money if they're all living at Guantanamo, which should probably be renamed Camp Bush.

No more is it a question of trying to get ahead in this society. This society is broken. It is time to forge a new world, not based on domination, exploitation and war. We must stop regarding the idea of revolution as merely an abstract concept, and realize that a functioning, purposeful revolution is the only way most of us are going to survive. Otherwise, the certainty of slavery for 90 percent of the world's population is unavoidable, and that will only perpetuate the same problems that continue to afflict us.

How we can effect these necessary changes absolutely vital to our collective survival are questions that you, dear reader, must now answer. It is essential that you share your conclusions with others, and not just keep them to yourselves.

If you don't see the need for any of these questions I've just posed, let me ask you this: What will you do when they come for you?

Chapter Twenty-Four

The understanding

America teaching its children to lie, steal — and kill

How you treat a stranger determines how you treat the ones you love.

At first you can't see the connection. After all, how many doors have you slammed in the face of some single-minded Jehovah's Witness, or screamed into the phone at some gentle grandpa trying to raise money for the local fire department? Or, best example of all, how many times have you cussed out a homeless panhandler bugging you for spare change without contemplating the ragged family he may have squirreled away behind some nearby dumpster?

Most of us are too busy to care.

In the self-centered savvy of our synthetic 21st century American lives, we are taught not to realize that how we treat our enemies — or in our haste, those we would categorize as superfluous to our hectic agendas — has a direct and debilitating impact on those who we say are important to us. Our parochial perspectives teach others in our family how to be cruel. We are taught that some people are less deserving than others; that our way of life depends on recognizing and perpetuating these distinctions, and that's the way most of us live.

What happens when those distinctions become blurred? If we hate others on the basis of propaganda lies, how do we decide who we'll love and know the reasons are true?

Most obviously, it is beginning to dawn on many of us that the way America abuses the luckless inhabitants of less-developed lands is beginning to unmistakably resemble the way the U.S. government now roughs up its own citizens, without regard to their rights or their humanity or whatever noble motives they may have, in favor of how big their bank accounts are, and how much they'll pony up to participate in this sleazy scam of corporate conquest and bottom-line tyranny that is now sweeping the planet.

It's as if there's a colossal rush by everyone to buy their way into hell.

Consider, just for a moment, groups of Palestinian children gunned down for sport by bored Israeli storm-troopers, or Afghani families bombed from the sky by hopped-up American airmen, murdered just for shooting celebratory rifle shots into the air during a festive wedding. Compare them to white-haired retirees and principled college students assaulted with truncheons and pepper spray by masked Miami police thugs just for protesting the destruction of American prosperity by rich men who give allegiance to no country.

What's the difference? We are all citizens of the world now — all eligible to be jailed without trial, killed without warning by those who have deemed us excess baggage.

It's much like the way we see that vagabond on the west side of Manhattan trying to clean our windshield. Chances are good, in this raging age, that you'll have a chance to experience that as the American economy continues to be propped up by lies, as more families lose their homes and livelihoods. Then you too will see the ugliness of that temporarily affluent man inside the car, racing off to fulfill his endless commitments without seeing his own future waving that squeegee in desperate frustration receding in his rearview mirror.

But beyond the visible parallel of pauperized Americans more and more resembling gang-raped Iraqis as the herding of humans into categories and camps accelerates, there lies the truly nauseating specter of the behavior of contemporary American leaders and its poisonous effects on America's children.

Contemporary political events and the lies that are told to justify them are turning America's children into monsters without consciences willing to kill anyone for cash. Anyone!

Have you noticed the number of kids going to school dressed in military fatigues? The number of video games where the object is simply to kill without reason? Is this why we had children in the first place?

Most parents do their best in leading their children through the labyrinth of regimens and requirements to give them a decent shot at a functional and productive adulthood. But think of what that involves now.

It requires teaching a willingness to believe in the flag-waving lies our leaders tell us. What kind of adults do you suspect that will produce? You are looking at the future of America and the world, and you ought to be scared.

It requires explaining to them how it's OK that America's Secretary of State — Colin Powell, one of the most respected men in the country — can go before representatives of the entire world and deliver a totally fictional scenario, simply so that his bosses — the men who make the weapons — can obliterate an entire country and enable their companies to pull one of the greatest financial scams in history — the robbery of the American people to rebuild a country that they themselves have destroyed. Amid continuing flag-waving, that plan is scheduled to be inflicted on many more countries which can't defend themselves.

It requires explaining to children why American soldiers who come home in a box are to be venerated as having done something good, as having given their lives for a noble purpose. And that requires lying to your children, and overlooking some serious lies that we told to create the situation in the first place. Because the soldiers who are dying in Iraq are dying for lies that so many Americans try to overlook. Pity those parents who give away their children's lives for lies about weapons of mass destruction.

To most of the rest of the world and especially Iraqis, it is Americans who are the terrorists.

The choice left to surviving children whose siblings have squandered their lives in a war based on lies is to support their parents and believe the lies, or go mad.

Our children learn what we teach them. For a majority of American parents, we are teaching our children to overlook the truth; that real justice doesn't really matter if there is a quick profit to be made. As American soldiers come home and become policemen, and treat us in the same way they treated Iraqis, so our children will grow up and behave in the same duplicitous, immoral way our leaders do now. Why? Because that's what we have taught them.

I wonder how many parents are naming their new babies after George Walker Bush or Richard Cheney? And if any are, I wonder what kind of adults those children will turn out to be?

Will they be children who learn how to steal elections? How to destroy the Constitution by bribing their friends to support their lies? To drop diabolical nuclear weapons on innocent foreigners because there is a moneymaking scheme to be carried out that will make them billions of dollars? Will they be men and women who will destroy buildings in their own big cities and kill innumerable numbers of their own countrymen simply to achieve their political objectives?

And perhaps more importantly, how will these children — grown up with the lies of the present political machinery indelibly etched in their own heads — treat the ones they are supposed to love? Perhaps we can see that now. Perhaps we can see, in the behavior of those who return from Iraq, how we treat the ones they love — or used to.

Is this why we raised our children? To believe in lies? To give their lives for lies?

We are teaching our children that it's OK to kill large numbers of innocent people if those people have some valuable commodity that we covet. Just pick up any newspaper. Listen to your president, the man who laughs about people he is about to execute. That's what it's all about.

How we treat strangers determines how we treat the ones we love. If we abuse strangers, we can't help but abuse the ones we love. Not enough people realize this, or don't realize until they're older, after a few divorces, perhaps.

Need proof? Consider this snippet of conversation between that crusading Idaho dentist Len Horowitz and an interviewer about why it seems everyone in America is sick right now with a bronchial infection no one seems to be able to get rid of.

Horowitz explained: " ... in the contemporary warfare arena, where experts in biological chemical warfare convene and discuss the ways that are ideal to conduct warfare today, to really take an enemy out, you don't want to kill the people. You want to produce people who are chronically ill and become dependent on the state and totally sap the resources of the country. And then you can move in further with your military-medical-industrial complex, your international medical-pharmaceutical cartel. And then you sell these beleaguered and defeated countries all of the pharmaceuticals and chemicals that they need to maintain any semblance of healthy function."

Interviewer: "So you've got a work force that can work, but they're too tired after they finish working to .... "

"That's exactly it," Horowitz exclaimed. "They're completely depleted. They can't put together a military, you create dependence, and thereby you weaken the population, and weakened populations are easier to control. So you've got population control, and you make vast fortunes doing it, versus just blowing up a nuclear weapon and devastating the infrastructure that you own. You and your colleagues own that infrastructure. You want to get rid of the people. You don't want to get rid of infrastructure."

So much for the "why" of this bio-warfare now going on that everyone's overlooking. How about for the "who" and the "how," according to Horowitz.

"What you're looking at with this upper respiratory infection is that it is a multi-factorial illness. It's associated with a variety of chemical and biological co-factors. Just like with AIDS, it's not the AIDS virus that ultimately kills, it's cofactor microbes such as the micoplasma ....

"What you have could be described as an ideal Russian biological cocktail. And I suppose it's called Russian biological cocktail because the Americans likely invented it. What they determined would be the best biological-chemical warfare approach was a combination of chemicals and biologicals so that it would be very difficult to diagnose and then treat the illnesses. Moreover, it would be very difficult to trace where they came from.

"If you've got, say, ethylene dibromide coming out of the jet fuels that is causing immune suppression and weakening your immune system, and then you've got a micoplasma microbe or a fungus that causes an upper respiratory illness, suddenly you develop a secondary bacterial infection. Now you get hit with antibiotics, and the antibiotics cause your body chemistry to go acidic, so now you get rashes and other things, your liver gets full of toxins and comes out through your skin in rashes and they get hyperallergenic reactions associated with the other chemicals.

"So all of a sudden now, you realize that you've got a human being who is completely out of balance and infected by two, three, or four microbial co-factors as well as intoxicated by a variety of different chemicals."

There's your human weather forecast from one of the world's foremost medical detectives.

How are you going to teach your children about that — a diabolical conspiracy devised to poison the Russians that has now been turned on the American people themselves?

And are your children, dressed stylishly in their military fatigues, going to think that's a groovy idea, very patriotic?

When we are with our families, we like to assume that everything we do and everything that they do is based on mutual love. Of course, it doesn't always work out that way, but surely that's what we'd like it to be.

We have an understanding that family comes first, that I would do anything to protect and nurture my child under any circumstances, and that my children, if I brought them up right, would feel the same way about me, as I most certainly felt about my parents.

It is an understanding most families reach. I don't know that it holds up, for those families who still support what America's leaders say and do these days, when you have to teach your children that lying, stealing other people's countries and killing large numbers of people for reasons that are lies are OK. Just the way the world works.

In which case, many of these parents could realistically expect their children to kill them for money, because that's what their country taught them. And sometimes that happens.

And after 9/11, in which America's leaders betrayed their people by complicity in an attack on their own country, followed by wars that were blamed on that phony event, the understanding of mutual protection, respect and allegiance between a nation and its people has been shattered. Honest people are very afraid of their dishonest government.

Also shattered has been the trust between fathers and sons and mothers and daughters, because some insist on believing the lies that it's OK to kill people you don't know for money, while others — still trying to believe the words of holy men who urge us to love others — won't accept those lies that have torn so many families apart.

The understanding that once was between those who care for each other is no longer what it was. The blame can be squarely placed on an America that has become perverted by its own power, and now threatens the lives, livelihoods and love of every person on Earth.

How long will it be, under this present trend, until we look into the eyes of our children and not know them anymore? Or has it already happened?

<u>Chapter Twenty-Five</u>

The race to the rainbow bridge

The choices are clear: either tyranny or enlightenment

My first instinct is to tell you this has nothing to do with current events, politics or religion, but in fact it has everything to do with all three.

My second instinct is to say the most important principle in human politics is separation of church and state — not to prevent the timeless principles of all religions from benefiting humanity, but simply to preclude the bickering over terminology that diverts all arguments about what will enable the human race to survive its own nasty habits and avoid frivolous sectarian hairsplitting.

As a species, we are on the brink of a passage toward a new way of living, of existing, of organizing human society on our planet. The old way has failed, demonstrably. Power accrued to the hands of a greedy few does not result in trickle-down benificence, as the inbred rich continue to insist. And we have no knowledge that a genuine democracy could achieve a greater degree of justice because no actual democracy has ever been in place. But we do know that the old system produces endless wars and toxic graveyards, so wouldn't it be worth at least a try to attempt genuine democracy just once, if it were possible?

Humans are unable to resist material corruption; everyone seems to have a price beyond which their morality fails. We have, by and large, abandoned the exhortations of Jesus to love our neighbors in favor of the bogus belief that money can immunize us from mortality.

Can we devise new mechanisms to mentally vaccinate our minds against the temptation of corruption on a social level? As the human species races toward a future of uncertain outcome, these mechanisms must doubtless center on the nature of money. Rather than continue on our present course toward a more definitive master/slave society in which military force is the defining commodity, we need to find a way to amplify the psychological priority of morality and correspondingly lessen the attraction of first-person greed.

I know it sounds like some kind of hare-brained rationale of Mao Tse Tung (or I guess today that's spelled Mao Zedong), but can't we re-channel our goals for happiness toward our relationships with others rather than toys for ourselves?

It could well be that a merger of banks and churches will one day evolve into a universal currency based dually on morality and the welfare of the system in addition to material worth related solely to survival/comfort of the individual.

Capitalism has failed because it relies on slums in which to dump its failed products, as well as an unregulated fluidity at the top with which to constantly bail us out of our busted budgets. A socialist system has never failed to overcome the temptations of privilege and authority, and tyrannical corruption has always evolved out of noble intentions for the masses in the administrative processes of collectivized wealth disbursal.

No system of government ever devised on this planet has ever truly placed control of its resources in the hands of its community. Corruption has always prevailed, and quicker minds have always managed to make off with the loot and let the masses starve. Real wealth always remains in the hands of the privileged few. There is no clearer example of how our religions have failed us. They have all been bought off by secular authorities in exchange for the state-protected right to fleece their flocks.

We cannot authentically aspire to real freedom as long as the money supply remains in the hands of a few rich men. As long as it does, we have zero power over the events and processes that control our lives.

Of course, currency is a neutral commodity. It has no intrinsic value unto itself. It's obvious worth is what it represents, or the material wealth that it can be traded for, or converted into.

It may be impossible to attach a moral quotient to money, because the very act that would link its use to the consensus precepts of a society trying to be moral would necessarily place limits on freedom of choice that probably most of us could not abide.

So in improving the nature of money as a possible way to creating a more humane and less cutthroat society, we would probably have to limit our goals to examining the practice of usury, and then more assiduously identify those who actually control the money, which will probably be two of the most difficult and elusive tasks humanity has ever undertaken.

That glittering technological marvel called Western Civilization has been built entirely upon usury. Without capital speculation, no skyscraper would ever have been constructed. When will the day come, I wonder, when we ask ourselves this question: Are skyscrapers what we want to express excellence in our civilization? What good are skyscrapers? They are dazzling monuments to greed that serve no purpose other than impress and inspire those who are on the path to exploitation and deception at the expense of others who are merely trying to live their lives.

Could it be that one day we will willingly trade our skyscrapers and our usury for a system that produces happy, self-reliant communities of modest means and virtues, rather than dazzling megalopolises that impress from a distance because you can't see the bodies of the homeless moldering and dying in its windswept alleyways?

Then there comes the question of who actually controls the money supply, and why is it the same people generation after generation? Why have 34 of America's 43 presidents descended from Charlemagne, and why is it every election the masters of finance get to name both alternative candidates? If you think you live in a free country and possess the right of free speech, you are sadly mistaken.

Money rules the world. As long it does, we can never truly rule ourselves.

But money is only a small part of the human transition to a more humane and functional future. It's kind of like the quality of motor oil for the collective engine of humanity. What if riches were really accrued based on the kind of people we could be, rather than they are now, on the kind of material and procedural hegemony individuals can exercise on a given commodity or process? For one thing, this kind of monetary system would solve all our environmental problems almost immediately.

And the principal mode of profit during the five thousand years of organized human society — making war — would certainly decline.

If I may continue with the engine metaphor ... if money is the

motor oil, then religion is the fuel. The performance of the
engine — humans doing what they need to survive, prosper
and be happy — can be judged by the quality of the fumes
cascading out of humanity's collective tailpipe. In most
cases, it's very toxic.

Not only is it toxic, it's quite likely that it's so harmful
because we are using the wrong fuel to produce it. I'm not so
much talking about food here (although surely the future will
allow us to radically restructure our diets into something a
lot more sensible) as much as I am referring to the ideas that
religion imbues in our minds.

Perhaps the image of the American cowboy is the perfect
contemporary metaphor for human beings (or maybe that's
because I spent much of my early childhood with a plastic
gun and holster strapped to my waist terrorizing
neighborhood grocery stores, all the time clinging to the little
finger of my mother).

With that gun in our hands (a symbol of human potency
merged with technological prowess), we can conquer the
wilderness, subdue scary wild animals, and eliminate those
beings we consider inimical to our own interests, specifically
those indigenous savages whose cultural upbringing we have
deemed to be inferior to our own.

We get these ideas directly from religion, specifically the
Old Testament, in which a wrathful God time and again
urges his faithful followers to wipe out the heinous infidels
simply because they worship other gods, or in many cases
simply did not speak the same language as the person with
the more powerful "gun" (though back in the olden days, that
could have been a lance, or a sword).

But now, in a world crowded to the attics with superfluous

souls, the gun-toting cowboy motif just doesn't cut it. The cowboy must necessarily be replaced. But with what?

Individual rights will never disappear, no matter how they may be tailored by the perceived requirements of the state. The principal cornerstone of social life is individual liberty, the conscious choice of one's own fate.

No matter how crowded this planet gets, that will never be bred out of us, because it's instinctual. We each possess our own individual dreamscapes.

No matter now hard the state tries to erase this desire in individuals, it will not succeed. The recognition that each human being is a part of a much larger animal consciousness — call it the Ummah, if you like — must be voluntary. Otherwise, it is tyranny, and by definition, not individual freedom.

Yet, this realization will come one day to everyone. It is written in all the holy books, though by a myriad of different names. And yet, in one certain, very important context, religions have steered us in the wrong direction. Else, otherwise, why all these wars?

Let me explain. I've noticed when I speak with a person who insists she is religious, the sense of what I am actually saying can never get through to that other person's brain, because that other person always interprets my words, not empirically and taken at face value, but in the context of her own belief system. Thus, communication is generally impeded when the receiver of a thought from someone else translates it into the terminology of her own religious outlook. As evidenced by the amount of strife in the world, this usually means mistranslation, misunderstanding and conflict.

In addition, the tendency of most religions to dangle some kind of comfortable afterlife concept as a carrot in front of its potential adherents makes it easier to mobilize these same lemmings as cannon-fodder in wars of a church's choice. Heck, if you die, you just go to heaven, or come back as somebody else. These concepts increase the propensity for killing, not the other way around, as all the holy men insist.

To me, these two reasons are stark evidence of the necessity to separate church and state.

Central to this unfortunate tendency toward confusion and hard feelings in any society is the role of the dominant medium of information, which today would be the corporate-controlled reporters, but in the past would have been the church or the monarch that had defined the type of society in which the people lived.

As the needs of the people at large and the aristocracy that rules would necessarily differ (the latter being the exploiter who collects and the former being the victims who pay), so too would the information they impart, and the perception of their existence would diverge.

Example: the peasantry would refer to their masters as thieves who unjustly steal, and the masters would regard their serfs as mere zits on the complexion of their otherwise rosy-cheeked society. As a result, the measures taken by those in power unfailingly offend those without power; and the response of the poor and victimized undoubtedly produce the same feelings in those who imagine themselves aristocracy.

I rolled out of bed this morning with the word "bifurcation" on the tip of my tongue, as I was thinking about these two divergent trains of thought — the perspectives of the rich and the poor, the haves and have nots — within the current context of creeping tyranny that seems to be about to engulf the entire world. Maybe it was because I watched too much of the superficial political celebrations following the results of the Iowa Caucuses on TV yesterday, too many scenes of forced gaiety by partisans of many candidates all claiming portentous victory in this quirky little political ritual.

What has galled me to no end this political season is the utter and shameful failure of the political opposition to correctly and courageously define the colossal criminality of the present administration in Washington, particularly the failures to notify all Americans that the U.S. is waging wars and squandering the lives of its own children in unjustifiable attacks on innocent people in faraway lands.

Worse, and what seems even farther away from happening, is recognition by the American public that its own leaders engineered the tragedy known as 9/11 in order to profit from the frenzied fear these deceitful attacks produced.

"Bifurcation" is the act of splitting something into two branches. Collective human thought has always been split into two branches: dominator vs. powerless. What I see now, and why this word has relevance to me, is that the truth is not getting through to the people. The picture of the world that is presented by the news media all over the world is simply not factually correct. The bifurcation is growing in the United States, where everything presented over mass media is predicated not only on an enemy that doesn't even exist as a separate entity from the government that is supposedly fighting it. Yet this rationale is presented daily as the justification for permanent violence and continuing robbery.

In 21st century America, we are making war on the ghosts of our own lies, and killing ourselves because of it.

Believe it or not, this clumsy attempt to wrap money, media, and religion into the same thought has a purpose. The purpose is to tell you that the bifurcation — this difference of published perception between ordinary people and the money masters who manipulate our lives — is about to destroy the world as we know it.

Think about the major political events of the last 15 years, just for comprehension's sake. In 1990 we staged the Gulf War after first luring Saddam Hussein, our former ally and CIA lackey, into invading Kuwait. Washington honchos actually hired a public relations firm to concoct shocking stories about the viciousness of Iraq's intentions as a way to justify our immoral aggression.

The mass media stormed on about how the U.S. was defending democracy in the Persian Gulf, but people with actual brains realized we were only defending the right of rich elitists to control more oil.

A couple of years later we had an explosion at the World Trade Center. It was later revealed, but never widely publicized — and certainly never widely known among the American public — that an FBI informant attempted to stop the actual 1993 explosion, but that his "handlers" allowed the operation to continue, for the public relations purpose of casting aspersions on the Arab dupes recruited by the CIA for this lame plot.

Shortly after that came Waco, where almost a hundred people were burned to death in a Texas farmhouse by our country's armed forces. Later stories, read by too few, revealed that a number of those people had been shot to death. The reasons for such rash behavior have never been revealed, but people began to think twice about splinter religious groups.

And then right after that, the Oklahoma City Federal Building came tumbling down, with the onus placed on a truck bomb that didn't even knock down a tree right next to the truck. Yet this obliterated building and 168 dead was used as a pretext to curtail our civil liberties and make those hardy individuals who advocate self-reliance appear as criminals for talking about personal freedom.

And Oklahoma City, of course, was the test run for World Trade Center II, 3,000 Americans were murdered in the heart of our biggest city, with the dirty deed blamed once again on dark-skinned foreigners, and the event triggering a massive war against the whole world as well as the most serious crackdown on the individual liberties of U.S. citizens in American history.

Can you see the bifurcation? Can you perceive the difference between what is actually happening, and the tailored facts that are presented to us by the predatory dominators who control our money and our thought processes?

To me, this is the great opportunity of examining the 9/11 question. In realizing that this astonishing tragedy was engineered by our own leaders, it opens up a window to see how American foreign policy has always been predatory. Lies have been crafted as justification for conquest and plunder, and the American people have smugly bought into them, all the while preaching freedom and manifest destiny. It is the same reason we used to slaughter all those Indians.

Now, I said all that to say this. We are racing toward a turning point. Events such as the degradation of the biosphere, the centralization of food production and prescription drug use, the disintegration of capitalism, and the increasingly sophisticated evolution of weapons are all leading us toward a point of no return where something really bad is going to happen that we will not be able to undo. And it is happening because of this bifurcation in public perception, where the journalists who profess to be objective are either unable or unwilling to confess they have covered up the true facts about so many things that it is no longer possible to recover any consensually authentic vision of what is actually happening to us.

We stand now at a momentous fork in the path of human history. One road, the one we are on, is paved with gold. To proceed down it means more of the murder, tyranny and exploitation that have become the hallmarks of the history of our species. The other path is pure dirt, and believe it or not, leads to ourselves, and a renewed understanding and appreciation of the relationship between ourselves and the planet that sustains us. The choice is clear: it is either tyranny or enlightenment. Pick the gold or pick the dirt. It's the classic devil's bargain.

Norse mythology tells the tale of Ragnarok, in which Loki the Trickster God, representing ordinary people of ancient lineage, meets Heimdall the Priest, representing all the pious and corrupt religions in the world, in a final battle on the Rainbow Bridge, after which the entire world is destroyed. Typically, redactions of this myth manhandled down to us by religious transcribers through the ages have depicted Loki as the evildoer and Heimdall as the pious upholder of tradition. Even from the mists of prehistory we see this deceptive bifurcation of thought, and misrepresentation of intent in pursuit of profit and power stifling the innate human quest for self-knowledge.

If we are to avoid our own Ragnarok, whose specter is imminent in a world besieged by depleted uranium ammunition, genetically engineered food, and psychosis-

producing medicines, we must perceive the bifurcation —
we must see that what our masters are telling us is meant to
kill us, not enrich us.

We stand on the brink of Armageddon. It's no exaggeration.
Curing the disease of money and recognizing that the
master's information is nothing but sweet poison are the two
main obstacle s to what could be a fortunate and fruitful
future for all of us, if we could but recognize and detoxify
those obstacles blocking our path.

Otherwise, one day soon the two ancient protagonists will
meet; certain in their duty, on that fateful Rainbow Bridge.
Right now the best guess is that the Rainbow Bridge is
located between Jerusalem and Ramallah. And as at
Ragnarok, a spark will ignite that will consume the world in
flame.

Chapter Twenty-Six

Spiritual gangsters

Which is more important: somebody's name or the eternal truth?

It's not the creed that's important, it's the integrity.

It's not the name that we give to the thing we worship, it's recognizing the essence of that thing as the highest truth, the thing worth being worshipped, so that the name we put on it doesn't really matter, as long as we recognize the thing for what it is.

We're too caught up in names, in identity, in rituals and holiness. Piety makes me sick. Rituals bore me. What we're looking for is truth, and that can come in many guises, derive from many places, and certainly possess an infinite number of different names.

Do you understand what I'm saying?

Let me make it clearer.

Those spiritual gangsters who were run out of Egypt all those years ago have led us in the wrong direction. And they've been abetted by holy men of all persuasions who have betrayed those who have sought sanctuary with them, solace from them. The maintenance of their own churchly profits has become more important to them then the souls they're supposed to be putting at ease, to be trying to save. It's a problem with every church, synagogue and mosque that ever existed. Some of them lose their souls over it.

Spiritual gangsters, that's the right name for them. They saw the people's need. And they took advantage of it. We have to have that home to go to, that place of rest. If we don't have it, we can't function. Sure, you can call it repression of fear of death. But it's the human condition. We can't deal with it without some help. Otherwise, we'll get sick, or worse, weird. And maybe that's what happened to them. It's the story of the first holy man, and every single one since.

People need to have things explained. Why am I here? What is it all for? And most importantly, where am I going? If it's not explained and then tucked safely away in your brain like some kind of paid fuel bill, you're going to worry. And worry keeps you from seeing, from being able to do all those other wonderful thing that makes life the joy it can be.

But problems arise when you get two different versions of the truth. It's the same truth. But it's two businessmen, each describing it differently, each trying to survive, each trying to make a profit (no, that's too harsh, at this level) ... each trying to make his creed survive to serve the people it was intended to serve. And eventually going to war over their two different versions of the same story. Really sick. It's the story of the stupid human race.

Here in this Westernized world we live in, we all derive our spiritual heritage from the same bunch of Old Testament hooligans who were thrown out of Egypt for nasty, usurious practices that many of them still exhibit today. Then they were kicked out of Babylon and set up shop near the Dead Sea.

Put any kind of name on them you want: thugs with yarmulkes or perverts with crosses, or perhaps worst of all, smug businessmen with clerical collars telling you they can save your soul when they're really thinking about building theme parks in South Carolina. They've bet their eternal souls on their bank accounts, and made people believe that the name was more important than the thing that the name was trying to describe.

And that's how we lost our way.

Which leads us to the present day.

These same certain thugs are acting like any holy men trying to set up an advantage for themselves in order to gain more money to stash in their particular houses of worship. And because they're so subtle, so intelligent, and so rich, they've managed to create laws in a lot of places that forbid people from talking about certain events of history.

Without going into this particularly freighted event, let's just examine what it means to prohibit people from talking about certain events. I think they call it, in some European countries, "profaning the memory of the dead," and they're putting plenty of people in jail for just bringing the subject up.

You'd think, in this supposedly enlightened day and age, that people were intelligent enough and open-minded enough to talk about anything, discuss it rationally, and then come to some sort of consensus about what was the objective truth. But no. It hasn't turned out that way.

The guys with the yarmulkes say you can't talk about it, what we say is true, it may not be challenged, and we'll put you in jail if you continue this conversation.

Well, you have to take it seriously, because there are people in jail because of it. Just look at old Ernst Zundel, kidnapped out of his house in Tennessee and now having spent a year in solitary confinement in Canada without any formal charges, just because he feels the need to point out that those gas chambers you can see on the Auschwitz tour weren't really there in that particular form during World War II. They've been reconstructed, and some people quibble about the reconstruction. But there's a law that you can't talk about, and he's in jail.

It's a classic example of the maxim: it's not the creed, it's the integrity. In this case, integrity is the big loser. Not to mention Freedom of Speech. It's definitely a religious issue. But it has nothing to do with God. Only the version (or perversion) of what one group of supposedly holy men wants to cram down the throats of everybody else.

Now, remember that we have to be careful about who we're criticizing, because all too often we'll discover we're only criticizing ourselves. Such is the case with all this palaver about Jews. Sure, the behavior of Israelis — calling their neighbors vermin and trying to exterminate them as such — brings a lot of needless heat down upon themselves, as do their traditions of usurious banking, constantly claiming they're discriminated against while they're the richest ethnic group on the planet, and also their open sexuality (to put it politely). This last talent causes problems but also makes a lot of money from those who don't like talking about sex in public but sure do in private.

Considering from where the Jewish tradition derives, the very people who criticize it most better take a lot harder look at where their own traditions come from, and realize that the very basis of Christianity and Islam derive from ideas and rules Jews invented. In fact, if you want to get a little paranoid about it, you could wonder if the Jews didn't invent those two spiritual paths in order to gain a little privacy for themselves. Or some other advantage, like yoking people with moral restraints while keeping their own rules more flexible in order to gain a couple of extra points on the rate, if you know what I mean.

Lately I was privileged to receive an interesting post from Rumor Mill News titled "Shock: Secret Identity of Israel's Yahweh Revealed!" I had this feeling I was reading "Weekly World News" in the 7th century B.C.

The point the story tried to make was that if Israel tried to claim some kind of divine right to that land it stole from the Palestinians, it better take a harder look at its own actual history, and realize the basis for this claim rests on extremely shaky ground.

Recently, in a speech to visiting Christian Zionists, Israeli Prime Minister Ariel Sharon asserted, "This land is ours... God gave us the title deeds..." However, recent scholarly research, including discoveries by an archaeological team from the University of Tel Aviv, not only deconstruct the Biblical Old Testament and Torah stories upon which this claim rests, but grant previously unthinkable credence to an ancient historian's claim that the Israelites of Exodus were actually the Hyksos, and therefore of Asiatic origin.

So wrote a cryptic fellow who goes by the name of M-theory. Briefly told, he wrote that the Israelites were never in Egypt and that the Jewish god YHWH had a girlfriend, the goddess Asherah. (Is there a law against saying this?)

He cited evidence that indicates Solomon and David are absent from the archeological record. Holy screaming Pentateuch! Does this mean they didn't exist? Well, the same thing could be said about Jesus. You can't find him in the empirical history books, either.

As far as the modern day Israelis being descended from the Mongol hordes from Asia, well, we already knew that, from Arthur Koestler's famous book "The Thirteenth Tribe" which revealed that most of the present-day inhabitants of Israel are really expatriate Russians, and not Semites (which means there's nothing to be anti- about). Crooks are crooks regardless of their DNA.

Other nuggets from Mr. M-Theory include: "Asherah, (whose name means "she who walks in the sea") supposed consort of the supreme god El, was also referred to as Elath (the goddess). According to Ugaritic tradition, whose clay tablets contain the earliest known alphabet, she was consort of El, and mother of seventy gods. She is also associated with Baal and is supposed to have interceded with her husband, the supreme god, on Baal's behalf, for the building of a palace in order to grant him equal status with other gods. In the cuneiform tablets of Ras Shamrah (Circa 1400 BCE) the head of the Pantheon was El; his wife was Asherat-of-the-sea (Asherah). After El, the greatest god was Baal, son of El and Asherah. Curiously, Baal's consort is his mother, Asherah. In the Lebanon traditions Baal is equated with Jupiter."

Yeeowww! This means that Yahweh, whom Jewish scholars now say redacts back to Baal, had sex with his mother! Holy screaming Sophocles! There must be a law against saying that! Maybe there will be soon.

"According to biblical scholars who focus on the "P Source" for the Old Testament," M-Theory writes, "Yahweh as a name is first used with Moses in Exodus, and is indicative of monolatory (exclusive worship of one of many Gods) rather than monotheism. The name Yahweh can also be translated as "I am who I am", literally a way of saying "mind your own business", a way of disguising his true identity. Yahweh does not appear until Exodus and, strangely, the god Baal is entirely absent in Genesis."

And, the mysterious author adds, in a perfect consistency with the vicious tone of the Old Testament, "This Yahweh is prone to violence and seems to despise his chosen people."

Lest I give away M-Theory's entire game, let me just quote one other segment of his fascinating exploration of pre-Christian mythology.

"The Hebrews living in Canaan were therefore under Egyptian rule. It is also here in Canaan that we can make a comparison between Yahweh and the Canaanite Moloch (Baal) and extrapolate a polemic inversion of the story of Pharaoh ordering the death of all the "first born" in Exodus.

"The worshippers of Moloch sacrificed their first born children to their deity through immolation. Worshippers of Yahweh in Canaan were also known to carry out child sacrifice on occasion, especially in times of hardship, although immolation (holocaust) was supposedly frowned upon. Slitting the child's throat, however, was acceptable."

This information dovetails perfectly with what I've been reading lately in my Talmudic studies on Carol Valentine's eye-opening website Come and Hear <http://www.come-and-hear.com> (a must-read compendium if there ever was one) where the preferred method of execution for innumerable offenses by the goyim (surely you know who they are — they're us, dummy) is decapitation.

So the danger becomes: if Christians and Muslims try to impugn the Jewish faith and declare their god is some minor mountain deity from the hinterlands of Ugarit, they're only going to bring themselves down with it. Because the whole legend of Jesus, which was constructed of equally spurious and un-rigorous chicanery, is cobbled together with the same inconsistency, carelessness and manipulation.

Religion is essentially crowd control, devised by Constantinian-type governments to keep the people from rising up against their leaders. It had to be a very rich person, probably a holy man counting his money, who said "the meek shall inherit the earth."

Anyway, the whole piece — "Shock: Secret Identity of Israel's Yahweh Revealed!" — is well worth reading for its astonishing Old Testament gossip. Click http://www.rumormillnews.com/cgibin/forum.cgi?read=42815

All this folderol goes to show the wisdom on the ancient proscription of trying to give that ineffable and majestic spirit that animates the universe any kind of name whatsoever. You're only asking for trouble if you do, thanks to priests (and ministers and rabbis and whatever kind of guruistic occupational title you want to apply) who value the profitability of the tale they wish to tell higher than the needs of those who need to be reassured that their future is something more than the ignominious dust they will one day surely become.

If you want to go looking for the essence of the spirit that animates everything, don't go searching through ossified parchments in rancid temples. Find the spark you need to mobilize yourself in the diamond's eye in the rain, or in the teardrop of your lonely child. And don't let the spiritual gangsters tell you otherwise.

Chapter Twenty-Seven

Uncle Sam wants you ... dead!

Only a desperate idiot would join today's U.S. armed forces

Do you remember how many U.S. soldiers died in the first Gulf War? On television at the time, they told you it was around 64. Later, as news agencies recalculated the total from a variety of sources, it became 146. But now, some 13 years later, according to the Veterans Administration itself, the first Gulf War death toll among U.S. troops who served there stands at 8,013! And this is a figure from a 2002 report.

I was reminded of this hideous numerical progression recently when I read the Pentagon's report listing 534 American military fatalities as of Feb. 1, 2004. Almost immediately after seeing that, I read the story by Australian investigator Joe Vialls saying the American combat death toll from Iraq was actually 1,188.

So what is going on? As if we didn't know.

Today's Army recruitment jingle is "Be all that you can be." But given the news these days, and the ominous spectrum of options and consequences that confront today's enlistees, it seems like all you can be is dead, or at best, severely messed up for the rest of your life.

It seems like the real choices when you join the U.S. military are somewhere between missing limbs, lifelong cancer from toxic substances, and learning how to murder innocent women and children on the diabolical say-so of those who avoided military service themselves.

If dubious combat in some out of the way place doesn't get you with a roadside bomb planted by courageous souls who resent your invading their country, then the aftereffects of radioactive ammunition vapor, poisonous vaccines, bad equipment, substandard medical care, inadequate training, and, if you're a woman, being raped by your own American comrades, is likely your foreseeable future, as a recent story in the Denver Post so starkly exposed. Soberly considered, these realizations might possibly dissuade you from signing up.

Private e-mail communications I have had with some enlisted men in the military have painted a really grim picture. Americans are now in a minority in the U.S. Army, according to these messages. A majority of our troops are now green card soldiers, foreign nationals who have immigrated to the states and joined the military in order to get their citizenship, if they can survive the experience. And they are not especially eager to uphold esprit de corps, or fulfill any mission they might be given, only to get that piece of paper.

But even worse that that — and what ordinary soldiers and sailors would consider the worst possible fate to befall them — is that many career military personnel who have served their 20 years in order to get their pensions with which to live out their days with a comfortable financial anchor are now prevented from going home because top military officials insist they can't afford to lose them.

Just imagine — joining the military and never being able to get out! It's a tale out of ancient Rome.

And all this isn't even to mention — so far — the phony

rationalizations used by the fake human beings in Washington to throw away the lives of America's younger generation.

Those contemplating joining the military — and parents who are trying to counsel their children with this decision — should contemplate the following choices.

First of all you have wars popping up everywhere, with the Pentagon petrogurus and pharma-psychotics intent on creating new conflicts as fast as they can. But the bottom line is this. Based on what the leaders of our country and the people in charge of our military are saying, they are not telling the truth.

The leaders of our military are not only not telling the truth about why they are going to war, as clearly demonstrated by this ongoing caper in Iraq, where the stated reasons for initially starting this "preemptive" war have been demolished six ways from Sunday.

But they are lying about everything else, as well. They are lying about the number of people killed (they don't even bother to count the Iraqis or Afghanis or Colombians or Filipinos they kill), they are lying about how Americans are dying, or getting their limbs shot off, or dropping dead on the spot from some kind of mysterious pneumonia.

Soldiers going to Iraq were ordered to take an antidote to biological weapons called pyrisdostigmine bromide (PB). They also received a vaccine against botulinum and a drug to protect against anthrax. Some 250 thousand troops took PB, 8,000 received botulinum vaccinations, and 150 thousand took the anthrax medicine.

An investigation in response to the deaths of two soldiers

and the hospitalization of approximately 100 with what was diagnosed as pneumonia has revealed that 10 of the 19 most severe cases, including the two fatalities, had the condition eosinophilia—a higher than normal level of the white blood cell eosinophil. Eosinophilia is commonly associated with an allergic reaction to either toxins or parasitic infection. In these cases, the military claims there is no evidence of toxins or an infectious variant of pneumonia. An Army spokesman blamed the problem on excessive cigarette smoking.

The World Health Organization has specifically warned that "brief accidental exposure to high concentrations of uranium hexafluoride has caused acute respiratory illness, which may be fatal". The WHO report notes that "pulmonary edema [fluid in the lungs], hemorrhages, inflammation and emphysema" were observed in rats, mice and guinea pigs after 30 days of inhaling DU. Fatal kidney damage has also been induced in animals by several days of high exposure. DU, or depleted uranium, in case you don't know this (where have you been?!) is what America's bullets and bombs are made of. And likely what is to account for the continued increase in the Gulf War I death toll over the past decade.

And when the troops come home in a box, they're preventing the news media from even seeing them. And when they're not in a box but all shot up, they're putting them into warehouses because they don't have the medical personnel (or the commitment to treat with decency those defending America) to deal with the injured.

But it's not only that. The current push to refresh overstressed troops now involves thrusting poorly trained reservists and National Guard personnel into situations that are almost too much to bear for the military's most hardened units. Just imagine what these weekend warriors — pharmacists and factory workers from small town middle

America — are up against being tossed into the middle of a guerrilla war where the whole country of Iraq is booby-trapped and the whole population hates your guts and is out to kill you. Care to sign up for that?

Still, when you join the military you must accept the possibility you might get killed. That's why the military exists, so you can't complain too much about that. You can complain about the choices of the leaders that put your dumb butt in that position, but when you join the military, you pretty much give up that right, too. But many troops are complaining that their equipment often doesn't work, the food is barely edible, the medical care (at least in the field) is pretty substandard, and when these injured troops get home, well, that's when it gets dicey ... and shameful.

You've no doubt heard of the debacle of injured troops brought back and left to molder in un-air-conditioned barracks at Fort Stewart, Georgia for up to six weeks without any medical care at all. Or the shot-up zombies wandering around the corridors of Walter Reed Army Hospital in Washington unable to get adequate treatment because there just aren't enough medical personnel to care for them. Soldiers at Fort Stewart described clusters of strange ailments, like heart and lung problems, among previously healthy troops. They said the Army has tried to refuse them benefits, claiming the injuries and illnesses were due to a "pre-existing condition," prior to military service, even though their pre-combat physicals turned up nothing of the sort.

Most soldiers in medical hold at Fort Stewart stay in rows of rectangular, gray, single-story cinder block barracks without bathrooms or air conditioning. The latrine smells of urine and is full of bugs, because many windows have no screens. Soldiers say they have to buy their own toilet paper.

Having to take a pay cut in the middle of combat in Iraq, and then having to pay for their own meals, was a real slap in the face recently.

But the topper — and the one that chilled me to the bones recently — was the recent Pentagon decision to not let people go home when they'd served their 20 years and were due to retire. The Army said they were short of qualified personnel, and those folks scheduled to retire would just have to wait a little longer. Well, that's involuntary servitude, friends. A violation of the Constitution. That reveals that the U.S. government is imprisoning these people who have served our country the best and the longest, and it's absolutely unforgivable, a betrayal of these people's loyalty and devotion to their country.

But it's nothing new. America has always treated its veterans like crap. Oh, the public relations folks in Washington are always full of glowing terms to lure youngsters into serving their country, throwing around words like "honor" and "duty" like they are promising immortality in some patriotic hall of fame. But ask the veterans who come home and have their benefits cut what those words eventually mean. They'll sing a very different tune. And this is nothing new. It has always been this way.

Not many people today remember the Hoovervilles.

At the end of World War One, as the American Expeditionary Force was being demobilized, a grateful U.S. government passed legislation that authorized the payment of cash bonuses to war veterans, adjusted for length of service; a bond that matured 20 years later, in 1945.

However, the Crash of 1929 wiped out many veterans' savings and jobs, forcing them out into the streets. Groups of veterans began to organize and petition the government to pay them their cash bonus immediately.

In the spring of 1932, more than 3,000 veterans and their families converged on Washington. Most of them lived in a collection of makeshift huts and tents outside the city limits. Similar encampments could be found sheltering the migrant unemployed and poor outside any large city in the United States and were called 'Hoovervilles'. By July, 25,000 people had gathered on the outskirts of our nation's capital.

Congress debated but eventually rejected paying the bonuses and the Army, led by Gen. Douglas MacArthur, evicted the protesters and burned their encampment. More than four years later, some veterans got small stipends, but President Hoover was not re-elected.

"We were heroes in 1917," said one veteran bitterly at the time, "but we're bums now." This is exactly what today's U.S. military have to look forward to, and many have already experienced it.

Notwithstanding the immense bureaucracy that the Veterans Administration has become today (and I have no complaints about the VA, seeing as how they saved my life on one occasion), it is ill-equipped and too under-funded to deal with the walking wounded that their nonmilitary bosses with delusions of petrochemical grandeur are producing today.

And this is no bad rant against the people who serve in the military. The vast majority of them, in my experience, are dedicated individuals who believe in serving their country, even if they don't ask the higher philosophical questions of what the military was created for. Because in fact, it was created to kill people. But you can't ask 18-year-olds to be philosophically sound when they're only trying to find a way to pay for college, or, these days, to get a paycheck.

People in the military are just like anybody else. Only these days the frightening trend is they're being taught how to kill, and allowed to murder innocent foreigners in their beds without fear of censure. It's frightening to think how many of these folks will come home and eventually join our local police forces still possessed of that same attitude that it's OK to gun down innocent people without fear of consequences.

All of this might be easy to dismiss were it not for talk of the military draft being re-instituted sometime next year. Because of that, America's parents need to take a much harder look at all these wars that are being created for dubious reasons, and also at the way the military will actually treat their children.

And all this is not just to focus on what America's misguided leaders are doing to their own troops. What are we teaching our children to become, and our citizens to accept?

Did you know more than 5 million children have died in Iraq in the last 12 years? This is what Dr. Jawad Al-Ali, director of an oncology center in Basra, Iraq, said at a peace conference recently held in Okinawa.

Have you heard all the stories of innocent Iraqi civilians being summarily gunned down at checkpoints merely because American military personnel are so terrified for their own safety? So terrified that a significant number of them commit suicide rather than continuing to serve.

Have you noticed that Americans who are dying in Iraq are not the children of affluent families? The class composition of those being killed was pointed out in a comment by Cynthia Tucker in the Atlanta Journal-Constitution: "The all-volunteer military is disproportionately drawn from blue-collar homes." The family median income of recruits into the US military is between $32,000 and $34,000. Military sociologist Charles Moskos told Tucker: "People are forgetting, we're not losing the sons and daughters of America's leaders, but basically minorities and working class whites."

It almost seems like Uncle Sam is trying to kill his own soldiers. But there is even a more sinister and dangerous tangent that follows from that thought.

With all the troops posted outside the borders of the U.S.A., one has to wonder just who is defending us from a possible invasion? Invasion by whom is not the question. Preventing invasion by anyone has always been the top priority of the U.S. military. If not, what is it for? To steal other people's countries so our billionaire oil executives can claim more territory for themselves? That's the way it seems, doesn't it?

If so, what honor does one accrue when joining the U.S. military when it's not for the purpose of defending one's homeland? And why undertake such a risk when the reward is certain disease or dismemberment, and then to be treated with incompetence and indifference upon your return, if you return?

And more than that, how will we defend ourselves with a majority of our troops stationed overseas in search of commodity control, and half of them returning to the states with serious illnesses and injuries, only to be treated badly?

It simply kills me when I see film of the funerals of those young Americans whose lives were thrown away. The patriotic zombies wave their flags, and the parents of the dead choke down the knowledge that their child died for nothing except the false-hearted bravado of the chicken-hawks in Washington, who will not know the taste of blood mixed with tears until, one day in the not too distant future if the American people so decide, it is their own that they taste.

Chapter Twenty-Eight

Detective story

How the 9/11 investigation should really be conducted

If we had a real Attorney General in the United States, instead of a glossolalia-gagged demagogue who takes payoffs from industrialists to advance his religious pathologies, we would have solved the tragic riddle of 9/11 by now.

If we had a real Attorney General who championed the rights of all Americans instead of merely protecting the rich patricians he so obnoxiously serves, we would undoubtedly have hundreds of people — including the top leaders of our country — already indicted and awaiting trials for their roles in the treasonous tragedy of 9/11.

But we don't have such an Attorney General. And we don't have real law enforcement in this country, despite all this cynical blather about Homeland Security. And no one has been apprehended and charged in the most serious crime in American history.

The investigation has been bungled from the start. And the continuing cover-up begins with President George W. Bush, who from day one has covered up the true facts of that dark day, and continues to do so to this very moment.

The official story of 9/11 posits that 19 Arab terrorists hijacked four planes and crashed three of them into well-known American landmarks, costing more than three thousand Americans their lives. Yet no conclusive evidence has ever connected these alleged Arab terrorists to the actual crime. Only a campaign of media hysteria centered-around vague and unproved aspersions from Washington has swayed the American people like some drunken lynch mob into accepting government's story, which amounts to a massive hate crime against Muslims.

A paltry and essentially powerful government-appointed panel frittered away more time dealing with nonessential aspects of the investigation before producing highly suspect evidence before issuing its bland and blame-free conclusions. Public confidence in their deliberations sank day by day as one public official after another — including the President — refused to testify before the panel in public, lest the public got wind of the shallow and self-serving lies they cravenly told.

But if we had a real Attorney General who truly cared about justice for all those dead victims, and we lived in an actual democracy that was genuinely of, by, and for the people, this is what he'd do.

First, instead of locking up every head-scarfed Muslim between Boston and West Covina, he would inquire discreetly about every single financial transaction that was made in the two weeks before 9/11, and quickly determine exactly who made the most significant profits. In a very short time he would discover the names of the investors who made millions from those "put" options purchased on United and American Airlines, and when he had those names, well, that's when the real fun would begin.

Those people would be, as they say in the cop business, brought in for questioning. And I mean questioning. There should be no more important law enforcement goal in the country right now than to identify those people who made that money because of their prior knowledge that 9/11 would happen.

And since these folks are probably such wusses, it wouldn't take much pressure — no more than say a dozen solid punches in the mouth — to get them to spill the beans on where they got their information.

And once that information, and those names, were in the possession of a real Attorney General, well, then the FBI boys and girls — instead of being ordered to sit on their hands as they so often are by high government mucky-mucks who are deftly and crookedly stealing from the American people on a regular basis ... then the FBI and all those other acronym agencies could go out and make some real arrests.

Unfortunately, this could only happen in a legitimate democracy. And you can't possibly imagine it happening in this disgustingly corrupt and prejudiced mess we have called the United States of America, where the rich can commit any crime they want and get away with because they can pay off the judges and lawyers, while the poor don't even really have to commit a crime to get put in jail.

Anyway, in a legitimate democracy — one that actually worked — once the agents made the real arrests that would produce the perps who provided the inside information to investors that 9/11 was coming down and there was money to be made, then we could have some very interesting interrogations, which in a real democracy would definitely be televised. Talk about a ratings boost!

These wheeler dealers would then have to tell the real Attorney General where they got their information. And whom do you think they would finger, hmm?

This would surely lead to a new phase of the investigation.

A real Attorney General would take that information and then deploy a task force to study what influential people had made statements incriminating themselves prior to the perpetration of the crime. You remember — the greatest crime in American history.

In a real democracy without favoritism for the rich or privileges for the powerful, that task force would quickly zero in on a couple of well-connected, powerful politicos who actually had the chutzpah to publish their incriminating statements in book form, making it oh so easy for the real Attorney General's crack task force to bring these individuals in for questioning, and use the same technique that they used on the stock traders to elicit the stories of how these powerful politicos came to utter these statements, these indications used by stock traders to make millions in the first place.

First in line on the hot seat would be Zbigniew Brzezinski, President Carter's former national security adviser, who wrote in a book called "The Grand Chessboard" that "America is too democratic at home to be autocratic abroad. This limits the use of America's power, especially its capacity for military intimidation." Brzezinski then concluded that in order to achieve this goal of increased military intimidation, what was needed was "a sudden threat or challenge to the public's sense of domestic well-being ..."

Hmm, that sounds an awful lot like 9/11.

Since Brzezinski is a member of two high-powered elitist groups, the Council on Foreign Relations and the Trilateral Commission, a real Attorney General would have some interesting choices among the names Brzezinski might cough

217

up as his sources on how that information got to those investors who were savvy enough to make those trades because they knew 9/11 was coming down.

The other bunch of fools who put their prediction in writing and, in the mind of a real Attorney General, automatically qualify as suspects in the conspiracy to pull off the greatest crime in American history were all those so-called neo-cons who put their names in a report produced by a group called Project for a New American Century, known as PNAC, who included such well-known reptilians as Donald Rumsfeld, Dick Cheney, Jeb Bush, Paul Wolfowitz and others of their soulless ilk.

Their PNAC report actually came out and said America's evolution into an unbridled military terror machine would need "some catastrophic and catalyzing event — like a new Pearl Harbor."

Now that really sounds like 9/11, doesn't it?

Just imagine what a real Attorney General, along with his merry band of interrogators who worked in a real democracy and believed in justice for all and not just the super rich ... could do with a line like that.

I'd guess that in short order they'd have the real perpetrators of the greatest crime in American history squarely in their sites, and be frying up the indictments as we speak. Indictments, hundreds of them, for treason, conspiracy to commit mass murder, and obstruction of justice.

Roll the phrase over on your tongue — treason, mass murder, and obstruction of justice. Think of it as the new meme that could save America.

But all of this could only happen with a real Attorney General who worked for all the people and not just the rich. Also, it's important to remember this could only happen in a legitimate democracy.

So it's doubtful it could happen anytime soon in the United States of America.

Chapter Twenty-Nine

Devils from heaven

How religious myths prevent and pervert rational debate

Lately it has been my distinct privilege to be in the middle of a group discussion about the origins of religion. The emphasis has been on debunking, on exposing the fictional roots of allegedly divine events that continue to control so many of world's minds, and complicate so many of the world's problems.

Many of these thinkers have lately focused their perceptual skills on the Machiavellian machinations of the Jews, who claim to espouse an ethical ideology, yet are primarily known in contemporary society as master manipulators, and revealed by their own holy scriptures as murderous maniacs who consider all non-Jews somewhat less than human, rendering their suspect creed profoundly offensive to all compassionate humans who encounter it.

But this is no anti-Jewish rant. The adherents of all other spiritual disciplines suffer from a similar snobbery, even if their claims to exclusivity, divine sanction, and being the only true creeds are somewhat less vicious than the habit of Jews to refer to religious groups other than their own by using the names of lower animals — cockroaches, grasshoppers, and cattle (also known as goyim) being the most frequent insults they typically use.

Still, Catholics have their own negative image, most notably the magical creation of their dogma some 1700 years ago that resulted in a worldwide pogrom against pagans (that, oddly, excluded Jews), which began the process now known as the Dark Ages, and carried out a process of ruthless extermination that decimated the native populations of the New World some six centuries prior to our own.

Catholics also have their own sinister intelligence operatives (Knights of Malta, Opus Dei, and the Jesuits), the scrutiny of which has probably created more conspiracy theorists than anything except those sleuths bent on ferreting out facts about the worldwide Jewish conspiracy or the ever-elusive Illuminati.

But a Catholic friend of mine remains ever eager to point out that it is the Protestants who are always let off the hook in any debate about the negative influences of religion, but shouldn't be, as German Lutherans and English Puritans have been the most eager and efficient killers in world history, if you consider the still-continuing genocide of the natives in North America and the death totals from two World Wars — and numerous other colonialist abuses — in the 20th century.

Arguably the most ancient among the still-existing but ever popular religions in the world today — and the one where real scholars (not those university idiots) will tell you Western Civilization really came from — the Hindus still maintain very high standards for atrocious behavior with the social acceptability of the burning of women (checked out the bride-burning statistics lately?) and the continuing habit of strictly regimenting their society according to race, resulting in the daily persecution and extermination of the poor Dalits, also known as the Untouchables, who are just regular people with a darker skin pigmentation than most. In addition, the Hindu proclivity for burning and raping Muslims, and lately cozying up to cynical Israel on weapons deals, make them as scurrilous as all the rest of those repressive religions whose main objective is to keep their people powerless by focusing on the hereafter and ignoring the here-and-now.

One cache of amazing information I've recently received is from an Odinist, who finds meaning in the historical legends of the Norse deities, and who has learned about a fascinating thread of history from a tome called the Oera Linda book, which details how a Baltic civilization so ancient as not to be remembered by most actually colonized the Mediterranean basin and triggered the ascension of classical Greek culture. (No, I don't know if I believe it, but it's a fascinating thesis.) But he recently ran afoul of Islamic partisans when he bemoaned the influx of African and Arab immigrants into previously all-white northern Europe, with the argument that it is right and proper for ethnic groups to exist among themselves, as long as they harbor no Hitlerian delusions (which the Israelis appear to have copied) that the rest of the world should be stamped out in favor of absolute hegemony by The Chosen Master Race.

The Muslims in our discussion group took him to task for denigrating the presence of immigrants in his part of the world, without perhaps realizing what so many others realize — that the push for diversity in so many previously one-color countries is actually a worldwide plot to diminish the individual, regional ethnic authorities that are generally representative of their local populations.

A worldwide plot? I'll spell this out in more detail in a moment (as if you can't guess who I'm talking about), but first, let's finish with Earth's religious spectrum, or as far as I am able to consider it.

Back to the Muslims, these days the most denigrated and vilified religious group in the American mind, largely because of Jewish control of U.S. media (the Jews want to steal Islamic land and the U.S. wants to continue stealing Islamic oil). To my mind, the Muslims have never attacked America, unless you're one of those dimwitted dupes who still believe the U.S. government's version of 9/11 and all those suspicious terror bombings that bear the unmistakable imprint of CIA Black Ops.

Like Christian dogma, Islamic scriptures generally preach peace, but are commendable in their outlook in that they recognize the right of others to worship as they please, a fact that is not widely known in the West because of all the terror-mongering by Jews. Just read the New York papers, which are guilty of daily hate crimes, if you don't believe me on this.

Yet, as each creed contains its own brand of storm-troopers, so Muslims have theirs, most visibly represented by the strident imams of Iran, who thankfully are losing their grip on that most-ancient of countries to a democratic, secular movement, which may actually succeed if the United States and Israel don't nuke them off the face of the earth first.

If Islamics have something to be ashamed about, it would be that they haven't noticed their countries are all controlled by Western-money whores pretending to be kings and presidents, and if any group is going to aspire toward preaching righteousness, it probably better start by having honest leaders who have not given up the game to their oppressors just for a few dinars. Still, they have nothing on the Western so-called democracies, which are equally corrupt.

In that sense, the Iranian imams are to be congratulated for throwing off the manipulative yoke of Western oppression and at least establishing a government of, by, and for their own people. Their achievement was a rarity in world history, and if they executed a few people for violating a few arcane religious rules, at least they did not murder their own citizens at the behest of some foreign power, as so many truculent Islamic nations polluted by Western influences do now.

Many seemingly wise people think that Buddhism is a creative way to address human spiritual needs, since that philosophy is so self-centered and so nebulous that it can't possibly harm other religious groups, but that is not exactly the case. Just like all the other creeds, Buddhism is based on the principle that somewhere else is more important than here, and as a consequence plays no role in political reality, as vividly evidenced by the Dalai Lama's conspicuous absence from contemporary political discourse, perhaps because he's too busy throwing parties for celebrities in and around Washington, D.C.

We could at this point delve into a few more less-populous creeds practiced in faraway places, but the information would be probably wasted on many TV-lobotomized American minds.

To complete the spectrum of thought about creeds (so we can get to the good stuff), it is worth mentioning just a bit about the division of American Christianity into a gaggle of mostly evil sub-cults.

Did you ever wonder why the nation of Israel bought Jerry Falwell a passenger jet? Or why they won't allow him to talk about Christianity when he's in Israel?

Beyond the Catholic church (which many people say is a watered-down version of its old self since the Vatican II document was approved during the 1960s and masses began to be conducted in English), Christians known as Protestants are divided up into innumerable variations, which can be best generalized into two groups: old-line and evangelical. The old-line churches (Episcopal, Methodist, Congregational, etc.) are generally unobtrusive, not too demanding of their adherents, and almost completely supportive of the governments which permit them to operate.

So too are the evangelical denominations, except for the glaring exceptions that they, like the Jews, consider other creeds the spawn of the devil, and generally support violence against others not of their faith, another very Jewish trait (and Hindu, as well).

So there we have it, except for Quakers, Taoists, Jains, Wiccans, Shintoists and various assorted New Age conglomerations of worshippers — the spectrum of religions in the world, at least as seen from the United States.

And each group argues that only their creed is the right one.

How can any argument possibly be solved using any of these religious perspectives? Answer: it can't.

Let's go at this from a slightly different angle. Imagine a visitor from outer space were to come down and try to discern a viable representation of human religion.

Suppose he listened to George W. Bush first. "God told me to bomb Afghanistan!" Then he watched Pat Robertson on television. Then he read of Abe Foxman talking about Mel Gibson's new movie in the newspapers, especially when Foxman suggests Jews should be allowed to rewrite the Bible.

With all this heated invective being vented over stories that could not be proven — one way or the other — in any rational sense, do you know what this visitor would conclude? He would conclude that the human race is completely insane. And you know what? He would be right.

•••

Now, I said all that to say this, to tell you about some interesting facts I've have heard in Internet conversations, all of which tend to verify my conviction that all religions are false, meant to be used to control restless populations looking for meaning, and trouble humans with infinite imaginations in finite minds looking for a little consolation for the knowledge they will one day, like all living things, be dead.

Most revealing was the piece by M-Theory on Rumor Mill News that Yahweh, the mysterious Old Testament God of both the Jews and Christians, was really a minor Canaanite deity named El Shaddai (a conclusion New Age Sumerian guru Zecharia Sitchin also mentions), and that the name Yahweh was invented in the OT book of Exodus to cover up his real name, because of its embarrassingly shaky Ugaritic pedigree. Further research reveals Psalm 104 to be the Egyptian Hymn to Aten, and the whole compilation of Jewish and Christian myth is little more than a concatenation of mistranslated Egyptian and Sumerian history redacted into a politically advantageous document upon which the passing of the centuries has conferred, for want of rigorous academic analysis, the majestic aura of divinity.

In "The Christ Conspiracy," Acharya writes that many religious precepts Christians assume come from the Bible came from Zorastrianism, including the concepts of heaven and hell; the use of water for baptism; the savior born of a virgin mother; personal immortality and the single life of every human soul; and the final tribulation before the Second Coming.

And thousands of years before the time of the so-called Jesus, there are these interesting facts in the legend of Horus of Egypt: he was born of the virgin Isis-Meri on the winter solstice in a cave/manger with his birth being announced by a star in the East and attended by three wise men; he performed miracles, exorcised demons and raised El-Azarus (El-Osiris) from the dead.

Horus also walked on water and delivered a "Sermon on the Mount." He was crucified between two thieves, buried for three days in a tomb, and resurrected. He was "the Fisher" and was associated with the Fish, Lamb and Lion. Horus was called "the KRST," or the "Anointed One." And these Savior events and stories were attributed to many besides Horus long before the alleged time of Jesus, names such as Buddha, Krishna, Mithra, Prometheus, Apollo, Heracles and Zeus, and many more. The legend of saviors just like Jesus had been around a long, long time before the Jesus we have had pounded into our heads by Bible-thumpers around the world.

Some insist Christianity is a completely plagiarized religion. The first four Gospels which are the sole foundation of Jesus' existence didn't even show up until around the 4th century. And some of the forgery is so bad that they forgot to check their history with such small items like Nazareth not being in existence in Palestine at the time of Jesus.

"The Four Gospels were unknown to the early Christian Fathers. Justin Martyr, the most eminent of the early Fathers, wrote about the middle of the second century. His writings in proof of the divinity of Christ demanded the use of these Gospels, had they existed in his time. He makes more than 300 quotations from the books of the Old Testament, and nearly one hundred from the Apocryphal books of the New Testament, but none from the four Gospels. The very names of the Evangelists, Matthew, Mark, Luke and John are never mentioned by Justin — do not occur once in all his writings," wrote John Remsburg in "The Book Your Church Doesn't Want You To Read.""

One of my correspondents wrote, "Christianity, like most religions, was set up to disempower people and control them. It was set up as a political vehicle. Sell people on their unworthiness and guilt and you can control them."

Another participant in my e-mail discussions wrote harshly about the events during the formal creation of Christianity by the Emperor Constantine in 325 A.D.

"They involved death camps, pogroms, book-burnings, and mass executions. We have all been conditioned to believe that the only people capable of doing such acts were Germans, and the only victims of these acts were Jews.

"In the first several centuries after the Council of Nicea selected the four Gospels out of 80 then in circulation because only these four presented a divine savior, rather than an itinerant mortal Jewish reformer, advocates of the new state-sanctioned revision of the Judaic tradition used all of these tactics and more.

"It would be easy for us to lose sight of the millions of persons executed by Judeo-Christians through a reign of terror that lasted over 500 years and resulted in the burning of the priceless collections of human technology, philosophy, and the humanities as a Judeo-Christian mob burned the Library at Alexandria."

Let me first say something about religious perspective. It has been my observation in reading various tracts about Jews that all too often complaints originate from those espousing a competing religious discipline, most commonly fundamental Christianity. It has always disturbed me that subjective religious favoritism should be used in criticizing another creed, which inevitably leads to biased, partisan judgments, and leaves the writer deservedly eligible for the charge of hate crime.

I have observed this in much literature that could be classified as anti-Semitic, in which hateful terms are clearly the products of jealousies and rivalries with people who simply do things differently, and believe different things.

I trust the summary judgments on the religions noted above will dispel any notion any reader might have that I am advocating some religious alternative to Judaism, and would remind the reader that making observations on the questionable behavior of political entities (which all churches are) is not a hate crime, and is in no way aimed at those who have no valid perspective on the behavior of those who share the same spiritual and philosophical beliefs.

That said, there is definitely a worldwide Jewish conspiracy to control the world. Though Russia slipped from their grasp many decades ago, it is fair to say the United States is definitely controlled by Jewish interests on almost every level.

The worldwide plot to establish diversity everywhere eliminates the very forces that persecuted Jews throughout their history, so when observing a problem such as the relocation of Africans to northern Europe, or the tidal wave of Mexicans into the United States, it helps to see that as a reinforcement of Jewish control. The white Wasp establishment, or what part of it that has not been bought off by Jewish money, will never trouble them again. The problem has been wiped out by the continuing and deliberate flood of immigrants.

The problem for all Americans, however, is the little matter of Talmud, the Jewish holy book that says it's OK for a Jew to kill a non-Jew, or a Jew to rob a non-Jew. Because that's exactly what we're seeing happening all around the world, and especially in America and in the Middle East, where Israel works assiduously every day to exterminate every single one of the indigenous Arab population who dares to stand in its way, while the United States tags along, teaching its sons and daughters to be good killers, just like the Israelis, without really knowing what the real score is.

Is there any doubt about this? Haven't 55 years of no-holds-barred terrorism, plus the undeniable capture of the American political system, proved this beyond the merest penumbra of a doubt?

I would suspect anyone who would oppose this proposition would either be a Jew, or a fake Christian who has been bought off by the Jews, like all those Christian Zionists.

And here, perhaps, we come to sickest of all the phony religious/political deals that have ever been struck on this planet.

Or perhaps just the sickest one since the days of the Roman Empire, when the ascendant Romans gave the Jews special status because they created this fantastic crowd sedative — the Christian religion — that kept the rabble in its place, urged them to turn the other cheek when they were robbed and raped by their betters, and invented a time-tested messiah by stealing bits and pieces of mythological masters from other times and places to keep the peons from rising up against their masters.

What a great invention that was! It didn't last forever, but what does? Nevertheless, it lasted almost a millennium, more or less, but when the Roman aristocracy faded out, so did the Jews' privileged position, despite all the intrigues.

This time around, wouldn't you know, the Christian religion and the Jews are working together again. Evangelicals are doing everything they can to support Israel's monstrous policies because they figure, according to the script featured in the Bible's Book of Revelation that their wished-for messiah will arrive after Armageddon happens in Israel. The U.S. government appears to be following this script, doing everything it can to make sure it happens.

Thus, consider this psychotic religious alliance: evangelical Christians support Israel because Israel is intent on blowing itself up, thereby enabling the Christian messiah — you know, the Horus clone and his father El Shaddai — to return to Earth and choose 144,000 of their most pious followers to come and board and trek off to (ha) God knows where.

The Israelis keep taking money from the evangelicals (as well as all Americans through excessive foreign aid), but prohibit visiting Christians from talking about Jesus while they're there.

The Jews won't make the mistake they made in Rome. Now, they have the nukes. And a time-tested argument is now on their side, instead of working against them.

It goes like this.

Once you can get people to believe things you can definitely prove are not true, you can get them to believe anything.

Are you listening, Baby Jesus? No, I didn't think so. Mythological political constructs don't hear that well.

The claim that Israel has a right to steal all that land in the Middle East because of some Biblical reference is utterly false, for a multitude of reasons, only some of which have been enumerated here.

The human race desperately needs to understand the difference between its need to believe and what it actually believes IN. But by the time we figure that out, it will probably be too late, and the evangelicals will get their wish.

The human race, grasshoppers and all, will get that same wish, too — that death wish.

Chapter Thirty

'No hijackers for 9/11'

Repentant arms dealer reveals disgruntled U.S. military on the verge of revolt

Back in May 2003, a journalist in Portugal reported on a sensational, marathon meeting of a group of U.S. pilots that issued a report concluding that the story told by the U.S. government about what happened on Sept. 11, 2001 was improbable and unlikely.

Except for several notices on the Internet, that story was basically never reported in the U.S., and largely debunked when the reporter flubbed the name of the organizer, creating disbelief in the minds of many readers.

The record was corrected in stunning fashion Feb. 25 on Alex Jones' Prison Planet radio program when former Pentagon arms salesman Donn de Grand-Pre, author of three books that allege 9/11 was an inside job, set the record straight, because he was the man who organized that conference. That 72-hour non-stop symposium by a group of military and civilian pilots concluded the flight crews of the four passenger airliners involved in the 9/11 tragedy had no control over their aircraft.

de Grand Pre, a retired Army colonel, is the author of "A Window on America," "Confessions of an Arms Peddler" and his latest, "Barbarians Inside the Gates." His thesis in the third book "is that the wars we have engaged in for whatever reasons since the end of World War II have not only been unconstitutionally waged, but have caused a net loss in political power. Each war was waged to divert our attention away from the true enemy within, and toward a contrived enemy outside our borders."

de Grand-Pre explained that his third book actually has three parts: "OK, I've got three books out under the title, "Barbarians Inside the Gates." Book 1 was "The Serpent's Sting," Book 2 is "The Viper's Venom," Book 3, which just came out is "The Rattler's Revenge."

"And I'd like to quote from Book 2, which came out October of 2002. There is a very important paragraph there. It says, "The trigger for the 911 activity was the imminent and unstoppable worldwide financial collapse which can only be prevented temporarily by a major war, perhaps to become known as World War III. To bring it off one more time, martial law will probably be imposed in the United States."

de Grand-Pre was the top U.S. arms dealer to the Middle East under the Ford and Carter administrations. What he saw caused him to leave government service and begin investigating the forces he saw warping our nation's future.

In the interview with Jones, de Grand-Pre made several stunning assertions, among them:

• There were no hijackers on the 9/11 killer jets. And he said the chairman of the Joint Chiefs of Staff (Richard Myers) agrees with him.

In response to a caller to Alex Jones' radio show, de Grand-Pre noted: "... the Chairman of the Joint Chiefs himself has agreed, there were no hijackers. There were no cell phone calls. Everybody aboard that aircraft, pilots and crew, were unconscious within 8 to 18 minutes after take-off. And you can take it from there. I've got it covered in books 2 and 3, what actually happened."

"These planes were being piloted by remote control, probably an AWACs aircraft taking over that airplane or airplanes or drones, unmanned drones. And flying them at 5 and 8 G-force that no pilot could withstand. So, in short, and if you read books 2 and 3, you will discover how and why this came about."

• The 9/11 planes that took off full of passengers are now at the bottom of the Atlantic Ocean. "And I'm telling you that we are knowledgeably speculating," said de Grand-Pre in response to another caller. "Those aircraft carrying crew and passengers went over the Atlantic and that was all she wrote."

• Talk of a military coup — to reverse what he calls the administrative coup d'etat that happened on 9/11 — are rife within the corridors of the Pentagon.

In his various interviews and publications, de Grand-Pre has called 9/11 "an administrative coup d'etat." He suggests the only way the neo-cons can be stopped is by a military coup d'etat, and estimates 70 percent of key military personnel are in favor of such a step. But the possibility is complicated, he says, by the large number of key military players who have gone over to the Council on Foreign Relations team. Some of these players, including three- and four-star generals, however, may side with the military while pretending to be on the side of the neo-cons. de Grand-Pre insists he is in personal contact with members of the Joint Chiefs of Staff.

The truly patriotic members of the military have had to sit there and take all these wild schemes by corporate-controlled politicians. de Grand-Pre's prediction? "I think those days are coming to an end. The military ain't going to take it any longer."

In the interview with Jones, de Grand-Pre also asserted:

• It is common knowledge at the Pentagon that Israel fired nuclear weapons at Iraq during the first Gulf War.

• A commercial aircraft did not hit the Pentagon. Most likely it was a cruise missile or a Global Hawk.

• Flight 93, the jetliner that supposedly crashed in Pennsylvania after courageous passengers struggled with armed hijackers, was shot down by the North Dakota Air Guard. "I know the pilot who fired those two missiles to take down 93," de Grand-Pre insisted, adding that the order to shoot down the plane came from the Adjutant General of North Dakota.

• Most likely it was U.S. forces that tried to kill Deputy Defense Secretary Paul Wolfowitz when he visited Iraq recently.

• Military tribunals will try current U.S. public officials when the military decides to take over, de Grand-Pre predicts. "And Cheney, I reiterate, is toast." de Grand-Pre named Cheney as the one man who knows the most about 9/11.

In earlier interviews, de Grand-Pre has recounted that the Chairman of the Joint Chiefs, Gen. Richard Myers, had 500 copies of the 24-page report made and sent out, including, to the White House.

Assessing Myers' reaction, de Grand Pre said, "I'm quite sure that he believed in it. I think that he still believes in it. You can understand the difficulties. The civilian administration, of course, won't recognize it as such.

"There's a definite cleavage between the military of the Pentagon and the civilian hierarchy — and never the twain shall meet."

Jones triggered a response from de Grand Pre when he mentioned a 2002 article in the Washington Times that said morale at the Pentagon had never been lower.

De Grand-Pre responded: "I can verify that from Col. Dick Schultz, who is a friend of mine in the Joint Chiefs. Morale was not only low but he said some of the troops are ready to mutiny. If it wasn't for the fact that the government, the civilian hierarchy, has control over retirements, they would probably be blood in the streets by now."

When other news outlets began checking on this story angle, Jones noted that Pentagon officials were apoplectic. "... they panicked and flew the officers on jets to luxury vacations and had these focus groups. It even talked about a possible mutiny. People were just totally distraught. What would make them become distraught overnight in the Pentagon?"

de Grand-Pre's answer was chilling, and revealed the possibility of a military coup d'etat has been simmering in the corridors of the Pentagon for some time.

"It wasn't an overnight thing. You see, as I outline in book 1, and I carry that on in book 2, as well as book 3, we were on the verge of a military coup d'etat. And this was long in the planning and even after the 78 days of bombing Kosovo, it became critical. And we were close to a coup d'etat at that time. In my survey of the reports and the pilots who worked with that, a coup was a possibility.

"In fact, a coup d'etat was pulled on the morning of September 11th. Only it was an administrative or what we call a cold coup d'etat."

Jones' translation of that was "a counter-revolutionary junta."

de Grand-Pre concurred, and added: "And as we delved into that, we found that the culprits, including Rumsfeld, were part of a neo-con group that had been planning this thing for literally years prior to September 11th."

In a previous interview that appeared on Michael Rivero's What Really Happened website, de Grand-Pre had already outlined his conclusions about 9-11.

"The 9-11 activity and horrific destruction of US property and lives was intentionally meant to trigger a psychological and patriotic reaction on the part of the U.S. citizens, which is paving the way for "combined UN activity" (using the fig leaf of NATO) for striking key targets in both the Middle East/ South Asia and the Balkans. The goal continues to be ultimate destruction of all national sovereignty and establishment of a global government.

"The trigger for the 9-11 activity was the imminent and unstoppable world-wide financial collapse, which can only be prevented (temporarily) by a major war, perhaps to become known as WW III. To bring it off (one more time), martial law will probably be imposed in the United States."

de Grand-Pre had also sounded the same themes on Jackie Patru's Radio Sweet Liberty web-cast.

"The so-called terrorist attack was in fact a superbly executed military operation against the United States, requiring the utmost professional military skill in command, communications and control. It was flawless in timing, in the choice of selected aircraft to be used as guided missiles, and in the coordinated delivery of those missiles to their pre-selected targets.

"As a tactical military exercise against two significant targets (world financial center and the citadel of world strategic military planning), the attack, from a psychological impact on the American public, equaled the Japanese "surprise" attack on Pearl Harbor 7 December 1941."

But the overriding question of that original group of pilots was: If we are at war, who is the enemy?

"The group determined that the enemy is within the gates, that he has infiltrated into the highest policy-making positions at the federal level, and has absolute control, not only of the purse strings, but of the troop buildup and deployment of our military forces, including active, reserve and National Guard units."

Chapter Thirty-One

When the anchor comes loose

What to do when your compass won't work

"What do you think of David Icke?" was the question in the e-mail from Linda.

Icke (rhymes with Mike) is the wildly popular author of a bevy of mind- wrenching books, most recently *Tales from the Time Loop, Alice in Wonderland and the World Trade Center Disaster, Children of the Matrix* and another book subtitled *The Robots' Guide to Freedom.* A former British soccer star turned sociopolitical guru, his most controversial thesis is that the world is ruled by a heartless band of elite lunatics he is predisposed to label as Reptilians.

I must admit for the longest time I dismissed him out of hand as simply another New Age charlatan. Notwithstanding my knowing about the triune brain in humans (and that the inner core is, in fact, the reptilian brain), I simply don't like flip categorizations of human groups, like calling Jews chiselers, Blacks lazy, or Poles light bulb changers.

I first became snagged by his website by the things he reprinted from other sources. What got me was the legendary essay "Report from Iron Mountain," which everyone in the world should read. Then I scoped out some of his works and realized what he was up to. And what he is up to is probably the most important task in the world — how to identify those who control us.

Here's how I responded to that e- mail.

240

I think Icke may be closer to the truth than anybody else, Linda.

At the very least he is metaphorically accurate.

It's undeniable there is a genetic grouping of "relatives" who dominate the elitist group that runs the planet. This is how people can trace the relationship of the Sabah family that runs Kuwait to be cousins, somewhat far removed, of both Queen Elizabeth and President Bush.

That Icke calls them "Reptilian" may be a little unnerving and perhaps melodramatic (although there is nothing melodramatic about how our planet is being destroyed by them), but apparently this genetic link does exist.

Many of these rich psychos believe they are part of the bloodline of Jesus (or Thoth, or Abraham, or Enlil), and even though it's proven that none of these characters were actual human beings, the pseudo-legitimacy of the claims have nevertheless been exploited to accrue great power over the centuries. Oh that supernatural sanction! The main hurdle we now face as a species is to realize that all these gods we've created are merely projected shadows of our own fears, and that cynical manipulators have been using them against us for centuries.

A lot of people regard Icke's synopses of history as spurious pseudo-science, but let me tell you, the official histories used by credentialed academics, who look down their noses at alternative versions, really have no more credibility than Icke's assertions, maybe less.

You only have to consider what mainstream media has told us about the war in Iraq and about 9/11 to realize that if this kind of cynical manipulation of the true story by the powers behind the scenes has been going on throughout history, then we don't really have any idea what happened at any time because we only have the tailored version the power elite used to cover up their various crimes.

When you consider this, Icke becomes credible and prescient. And everything you ever learned about the world becomes open to question. I believe that's the way it is, for real. I believe Icke produces a useful template for understanding events. Nobody ever gets all the little details right.

The top priority for humanity has become how to identify those who are really running things, because the planet is being ruined and they are clearly the reason.

Another e-mail I received that same day, this one from Lucille, took me to task for blaming the Dark Ages on the newly formed Roman church running amok. She rightly pointed out that the Dark Ages occurred because Rome had to that point controlled most of the civilized world, and when Rome fell apart, so did the world it controlled. All the channels of authority disintegrated and chaos ensued. When I read her note, I had an inkling that this is what is about to happen to America and our whole world. A new Dark Ages, ruled by chaos and mass death.

Then my friend Pieter from Holland wrote and said he couldn't cope with his e-mail volume, and even though he loved my essays, he asked me to stop sending them. He also explained he'd had trouble dealing with pronouncements about the formation of Christianity, and while he appreciated my political perspectives, the value he'd gotten from his beliefs and the truths he had read in Christian literature (and Pyramid inscriptions) prevented him from acknowledging the structure of his belief system as false. The proof, as it were, was in the pudding.

I replied:

I know exactly what you mean about the inbox problem. Once a week or so I have to throw away about 500 e-mails I wanted to ponder and respond to simply because I can't deal with the volume, and I spend all day almost every day processing them. In a way, it's a happy problem, but frustrating. I'm sure I offend a lot of people by not answering.

One quick note about those tantalizing historical portents, which can be likened to the warmth of the accepted Christ vs. the flaws in the dogma of established churches. You don't need to give up the former by rejecting the latter. The awesome joy of accepting one's inclusion in the divine plan is in no way nullified by discovering that many priestly scholars are manipulative savages. This is true even if we are merely Nibiruan dog food. The dream is the thing that's real, even if many of the structural directions to get us there are just so many celestial Ponzi schemes.

That's why people who are really solid in their faith don't get upset when I set a match to the fantastic fabrications of religious dogma. They know who their God is, and the validity of their allegiance to goodness and the life force. Sure, they may loosen their collars a bit when I start going into how Jesus the historical character is largely a work of fiction, but academic repartee of that nature is not going to shake the emotional foundations of what they know in their bones to be true, that acknowledging you only work for the higher plan is a far stronger force than some clumsy catechism based on ancient and confabulated fictions.

It's only the poseurs who are NOT sure of their faith who get upset when I start trashing the criminal manipulators who attended the Council of Nicea, or the psychotic propagandists who spasmodically insist exactly six millions Jews died in the German gas chambers. When I say with conviction there were NO German gas chambers, those whose faith is based on a febrile fealty to their ethnic group rather than certainty in the ground of their being instantly go mad, and start arguing that freedom of speech must be curtailed, and we may not talk about this topic.

In this same vein I believe that those who evangelize and desperately try to get others to accept their chosen path are really nonbelievers who are so insecure about their own beliefs that have to put bandages on their own doubts by getting others to accept the very thing they are not sure about.

So I copied this response to Pieter (and the one to Linda) to my friend and beloved Rense columnist Jude Moriarty. She was thankful and replied:

"John...thanks for sending. I had never seen the ICKE site ...its humor is really something. In my many readings of documents/reports from various gatherings of the "elite" it is notable that they really do have this delusional mindset that they are the appointed guardians/gatekeepers/special bloodline: Mad yes, but they believe it ... so remarks like "we have to rid the world of 4 billion people" can be made without any semblance of humanity ... I don't know how many times in conversations with some pretty credentialed astute writers-poets-engineers-etc., that I've heard the same remarks/observations — that so-and-so appears human, has the mannerisms of a human, but something is missing, there's an empty or chaotic nothingness in the eyes (windows to the soul) ... stands to reason if someone is

soulless the eyes have it. But then who would believe — and that's the charm of it ... but one knows madness-inhumanness when in the presence of it. If one has any semblance of discernment that is. Most people don't."
We see the world around us being poisoned, prostituted, and destroyed. Who are the soulless people responsible for such a crime against God? Is it really us, or is someone else? Sure we'd like to blame someone else, but many of us are genuinely doing the best we can to stop the murderous madness. Who are those who don't?

Yesterday morning, the very first e-mail I received, from Greg, contained the excellent recommendation to read a chapter of Carlos Castaneda's *The Active Side of Infinity*, the one called "Mud Shadows." As it happened, I had it in my bookcase. It was an excellent way to start the day.

Carlos the perpetually puzzled student was listening to his guru, the sage Indian nagual don Juan Matus, who told him (and I am condensing greatly):

The ancient sorcerers of Mexico discovered we have a companion for life. "We have a predator that came from the depths of the cosmos and took over the rule of our lives. Human beings are its prisoners." don Juan said this was "the topic of topics."

Sorcerers believe that the predators have given us our system of beliefs, our ideas of good and evil, our social mores. They are the ones who set up our hopes and expectations and dreams of success or failure. Through social customs, the predators superimposed their mind on our own.

Castaneda's whole theory throughout his astonishing series of don Juan books is that humans must resist this predatory mindset that has been imposed on humans by mysterious forces we don't usually notice.

He has don Juan saying: "We are energetic probes created by the universe ... we are the means by which the universe becomes aware of itself."

Now ... this conclusion. Castaneda's mysterious shadows that prey on our minds, and were put there long ago by the creators of social custom, are not that far afield from the mysterious Reptilians whom Icke posits are controlling and savaging our world.

For years in much New Age literature, would-be gurus have been pointing to a moment in time that (to my mind) was first noted by Jose Argüélles in his analyses of the 25,000-year-long Mayan calendar, a calendar which ends — not so incidentally — in the year 2012. Galactic synchronization, he called it. The exponential expansion of consciousness is the way I see it. The hyperbolic acceleration of all human systems all point to it as occurring soon.

When this moment comes, the shameful rhetoric of George W. Bush and all his cynical speechmakers will not stand up to the challenge. All those Democratic luminaries who silently pretend 9/11 was not an inside job, and America's criminal invasion of the rest of the world is an inevitable development of manifest destiny will not stand up to the gut-wrenching test we are all approaching at breakneck speed.

First on the list of challenges we face is to identify the subterranean triggers that makes us kill each other and everything around us. These triggers are both people of great power and ideas that are universally accepted.

Hence the confluence of Icke's Reptilians and Castaneda's predators. The choice is clear. We either send them packing

to rubbish heap of evolution or let them destroy us and
everything we love.

How do we do that?

Stand in your own truth. Never fear what you may not avoid.

You are the reason God exists. Find your job and do it.
We're all depending on you. We're all in this together.
Nobody gets out of here alive. But that's no reason to take
everybody else with us when we go.

Or, as don Juan said, we are the means by which the universe
becomes aware of itself. If we don't do it, no one will, and
that would be the greatest tragedy of all.

Chapter Thirty-Two

No honest Americans

U.S. citizens cheer their criminal nation savaging the whole world

The presidential election, Bush vs. Kerry, what a joke! Two privileged plutocrats, two psychotic perverts from the same demonic college fraternity, neither ever had to hold a job, each advocating continuing crimes against humanity, even against their own people. And to make matters worse, they no longer count the votes honestly. The computer spits out a predetermined total, and the TV whores tell you to believe it. And just like in the election itself, you have no real choice.

Two spoiled children of privilege, born into incomprehensible wealth, constantly gathering more as they go on their immoral ways, devising ever more evil strategies by which to fleece the slaves of the world, preparing to divide America into armed camps, all the while taking their lead from the evil Israelis who build walls against humanity and murder whomever they please. The few people who try to point out the injustice are either prohibited from speaking, thrown into jail without trial, or outright murdered. The new American way is the old Israeli way. But Americans embrace it, as they continue their sleepwalking march toward slavery and oblivion. Cheering with empty eyes as they go.

Does it not strike you as odd — assuming you are a thinking, feeling human being not yet too retarded by fluoride, chemtrails, food additives, antidepressants and demonically engineered food that will eventually poison you to death — that there is not a single principled public figure in America who has pointed out that America's rape of Iraq violates every international law and moral precept that has ever been written by the great minds of the past? That the dispersal of uranium all over Central Asia will kill millions? That the clumsy cover-up of the inside job of mass murder on 9/11 was the ultimate betrayal of all Americans?

What ARE Americans doing? Cowering in their undefendable homes and waiting for the end?

Does it not strike you as odd that no one speaks out about America's crimes against the world? Against poor people everywhere? Against its own citizens?

Now the real deal is on the table. A New Orleans judge has ruled that the cops can invade your own home without a warrant. That's the end of the Fourth Amendment, a citizen's protection against unreasonable search and seizure, the very basis of freedom in America. This is merely the expected verification of the Patriot Act, that Soviet-style law that allows the government to control every aspect of your life. Now, no one is safe from American tyranny. 1984 has finally arrived.

And no one speaks out against it. How dumbed-down we have become. Precious few even paid attention to the recent 9/11 conferences in San Francisco and Toronto, which were sparsely attended. Same with the recent peace marches marking the first anniversary of the American invasion of Iraq. But that may be because participants were afraid to ask the hard questions, intimidated as they were by a choking climate of mindless flag-waving that refuses to consider the real evidence or challenge the lies that are being told every day by our bought-off media.

The 9/11 critics and those who marched with signs merely

nibbled around the edges of the problem, pointing out inconsistencies here and anomalies there. They didn't come out screaming for blood, for retribution, for justice, that America's governmental system is a criminal enterprise that kills innocent people on a daily basis. And as a result, the thugs in power just ignored them and kept telling their same old lies.

There is no evidence Arab hijackers did the dirty deed on 9/11. If there was, don't you think they would have released it, would have trumpeted it to the skies, and said, "Look, here is the proof we were telling the truth." If they had that evidence, you can be sure they would release it. But they haven't released it, which means they don't have it. Forget about all this barking about Richard Clarke and Condoleeza Rice and what Bush knew and when he might have known it. These are all side issues meant to distract you from the real issue.

The real issue is that Arab hijackers DIDN'T do it, or we would have heard the evidence by now, two and a half years later.

So the real question is not about the 9/11 panel, or who said what to whom. The real question is: who did it? And it wasn't Arab hijackers. So who does that leave?

America is a criminal state, flouting international law and laughing about it. Our president makes jokes about the lies he told to enrich his crony corporate accomplices with the scam in Iraq. He makes jokes about the lies he told that cost the lives of hundreds of American service people, not to mention tens of thousands of innocent civilians abroad. He makes jokes about it. And most Americans laugh with him. And wave their flags. And laugh as they break the law.

There is no law in America now. Only tyranny. Only bought-off judges who allow the rich to steal from the poor, and imprison the poor who break no law at all. At the same time they open the borders so hungry immigrants from Third World disaster countries (disasters engineered by oppression from the United States) can stream into the country and lower the standard of living for everyone else. Except the rich patricians who can get away with anything. They are allowed to commit crimes because it's profitable, and they pay off the judges and politicians who allow them to keep doing it.

You should no longer be nursing the delusion that Americans are suddenly going to awaken and rectify the injustices, and America is going to suddenly return to the bastion of peace and freedom it always insisted it was. It's not going to happen. Too much blood, too many toxic substances and greasy lies have passed over the dam, have been vomited all over the floor of public discussion by those who don't tell the truth about anything.

Nobody in the government is telling the truth about anything, and it has been going on for a long time.

Two recent examples have really stuck in my craw. The first was Michel Chossudovsky's story about the three British prisoners released from Guantanamo. Chossudovsky revealed that while we were bombing Afghanistan, the Taliban we were trying to kill were flown out on an American plane with the Pakistani army while gung-ho U.S. gunners continued to kill innocent civilians with their high-tech toys from high in the sky. Rumsfeld, realizing he needed to fill up Guantanamo, so he had the Pakistanis conduct a roundup of innocent civilians from refugee camps and ship them to Cuba, where he has supervised the torture and interrogations of people he knew were innocent, like those unlucky British boys, for more than two years.

That makes me want to vomit. What America has become — poisoned and psychotic — simply makes me want to vomit. And there is not a single soul with any power in Washington who will face these issues. That also makes me want to vomit, and makes me very ashamed of my country.

The other story that threw me over the edge happened yesterday when I was researching various chemtrail material and I happened across Mary Sparrowdancer's magnum opus on fluoride, called "The Battle of Darkness and Light" (everyone should read this at http://www.rense.com/general45/bll.htm). Before she ever got to the really bad part of how the poisonous nuclear waste product called fluoride was put in America's drinking water (can you imagine such a bonehead, suicidal stunt?), she described an episode from the 1980s in which a panel of health experts was commissioned to devise a food chart that would enable Americans to have healthier diets. After they finished their studies and concluded that a healthy diet should be based on plenty of fruits and vegetables, the government bureaucrats shifted all the data and published a document that said healthy diets should be based on heavy consumption of cereals and starches.

The medical results of this prostituted campaign, 20 years later, has resulted in a variety of epidemics: thyroid problems, dental disasters, obesity, and many other maladies that have all reaped trillions in profits for the pharmaceutical industry, which of course is the incestuous first cousin to the petroleum industry. To top it all off, after a long run where gastrointestinal medicine was the leading moneymaker for the establishment drug pushers, a new product has leaped to the top — antidepressants. And it's all traceable back to that cynical decision by the government to change America's eating habits by changing the data that had been produced by health experts.

That's the kind of integrity we get from Washington. Forget about depleted uranium, funky vaccinations, and needless wars that take our sons and daughters from us for no good reason. The government has been poisoning us with its basic medical information for years, so I guess bombing another country for illegitimate reasons should not exactly come as a surprise to us at this late date, I mean, after all the decades of lies that have been told to us about everything.

I mean, if we accept the poisoning of ourselves without much complaint, how could I be getting upset that we're killing people all over the world for reasons that are proven lies? As I said before in a previous essay, we are much farther down the road to hell than I thought.

And I wonder why I write these words, since there is not a single person, either in the Congress or on television, who is currently pointing out that America is doing anything wrong in any area. Only that one rich person is not being very patriotic by criticizing the way another rich person has chosen to kill tens of thousands of people, and that that first rich person would have done the same thing, but he would have done it differently.

Many people get upset when I talk about these things. Yet in the public sphere, I see no one talking honestly. Not a single American public figure talking honestly. About anything.

Chapter Thirty-Three

Hallelujah! In Fallujah

President who talks to God wishes dead innocents a Happy Easter

Happy Easter, 2004, everybody! Praise the Lord! And as you sit in your proper pew this Sunday morning, blubbering out your favorite version of "He is risen," contemplate this.

Americans, just like the Israelis, are now known for killing innocent people as they worship their God in church. Raise your eyes to the heavens you prize so highly and imagine an American B-52 dropping a 500-pound bomb right on your head, splattering you and your beloved family all over your sacred altar. Your finely dressed friends, your fire-breathing pastor, all those beautiful children in their frilly Easter finery, reduced to bloody bits of still-twitching protoplasm dripping from the flaming pages of the Book of Revelation.

See your murmurs of worship become screams of pain. Praise the Lord. Praise Yahweh. He said that's how it should be done. Right in the pages of the Old Testament. And that's how America is doing it today, this very day, Easter Sunday, in Iraq.

Imagine that you're not killed instantly, but your arms have been blown off. Imagine that your daughter's head has been blown off and her body reduced to spasming jelly. You can see her head, eyes wide but sightless, a few feet away. That's how it is today ... in Fallujah, where flies feast on bodies littering the streets.

Do you think this is too graphic? It's nothing compared to what is happening today ... in Fallujah, where American troops prevent medics from tending to the wounded and media from reporting the carnage.

And the reason? There is no reason. You know the reasons for our war against the Iraqi people have been exposed as shallow lies. No weapons of mass destruction. No connection to the terrorists. The dictator is deposed. Yet the killing is rampant, as Iraqis fight for their freedom against the American and Israeli terror-mongers.

In the pitch dark that is the satanic American future, we continue to kill. In the name of democracy. In the name of Jesus. Our president talks to Jesus. He is risen today. Our president says he talks to God every day. God told him to bomb Afghanistan. He told us.

Jesus told him to blast innocent women and children in Fallujah today, and to pile the dead and dying in the football stadium because he won't let medical personnel get to them. Jesus told him to throw away the lives of American adolescents in uniform. Happy Easter.

Praise the Lord! He is risen. Hallelujah! In Fallujah!

•••

Imagine if an all-powerful foreign army invaded the United States of America and began killing Americans at random, gunning down average families at arbitrary checkpoints, spreading the sale of drugs and pornography throughout the land, targeting college professors for assassination, stealing our historic artifacts, making totally innocent people disappear forever without telling their relatives what happened to them, torturing teenagers in ways civilized societies have banned for decades, and spreading an ineradicable radioactive poison across the landscape that guaranteed death sentences to all inhabitants from fatal cancers many centuries into the future.

Imagine if the invaders said the reason they came to obliterate our country was because we had an unstable leader who had used weapons of mass destruction against innocent people, and he had to be removed as a menace to the whole world. (Well, at least that would be an honest assessment of the present situation in the U.S.)

Imagine if this foreign power disregarded everything we held holy and demanded we accept their religion, and declared all the ideas we grew up with to be a terrorist threat. Imagine if they promised us genuine democracy and then refused to let us hold elections and nominate candidates that were not chosen by them. Imagine how you would feel if your entire family was shot to death just for walking down the street to the grocery store.

What would you do? You'd start shooting back, that's what you'd do. You would hate the invaders forever, and spend the rest of your life trying to kill every single one of them. Count on this being a very real part of the darkness of the American future.

This is the situation George W. Bush has produced for the United States, and the situation that John F. Kerry would contentedly continue were he to win the upcoming election. This, my friends, is an even darker part of the American future.

Your vote doesn't count anymore, because of the electronic finagling by fascist corporations.

But worse, both candidates, and every elected representative in Washington, are leading us toward the darkness of the American future, simply by not telling us the truth. And pretending American soldiers are fighting and dying for freedom when they're really throwing their lives away for fatter Halliburton contracts.

America wants war. America has always wanted war. And now we have it. Welcome to the darkness. Imagine your daughter's eyes, gazing sightlessly into the blazing, now-silent dust of that mosque in Fallujah. Hallelujah.

Anybody with a brain and not paid off has to realize that the U.S. invasion of Iraq was not about removing Saddam Hussein. It was about beginning the American invasion of the world, and takeover of all areas deemed to be strategically important in terms of American profits.

U.S. troops have been slaughtering Iraqi civilians for a year, all the while muttering insincere platitudes about democracy and free elections. The aim was to send a message to all in the Arab world that this fate will befall them if they impede U.S. plans to steal everyone's oil in that region.

Put yourself in their place, which all religions urge us to do. Walk a mile in the other fellow's shoes.

What would you do? There is no choice but to conclude America, backed by its behind-the-scenes ideological manipulator Israel, is the real danger to all of humanity. Iraqis know it without a hint of a question; Americans are beginning to learn. But too few. And probably too late.

•••

Fallujah has been a prime target of American abuse, not only since the invasion began a little more than a year ago, but also in the first Gulf War.

Lisa Walsh Thomas recently repeated her report of last year, when the first rounds of killing began, that the people of Fallujah remembered one particularly terrible incident. "Two hundred civilians died in the bombing, with another five hundred injured. A large civilian area of residences was obliterated. Worse, if possible, the coalition (there really was a coalition in the first Gulf War) then polished off the killing by returning to bomb the rescuers who ran to help the injured who had survived the bombings of the market."

Randolph Holhut on the Smirking Chimp website estimated that America employs 15,000 highly paid mercenaries in Iraq, many of whom make $1,000 per day.

Only two days before the high-profile murders of four American hit-men (yes, paid mercenaries who weren't there to escort an oil convoy, but to kill Iraqis), these same "contractors" and other scumbags just like them had machine-gunned women and children in Fallujah, according to a recent report in Counterpunch.

Ghazwan Al-Mukhtar, an Iraqi who was witness to the recent events in Fallujah, told NPR's Democracy Now! the attack on the contractors on Iraq was not unprovoked, but revenge for the massacre of women and children in the city by U.S. mercenary "contractors".

Al-Jazeera reported that two positions being used by its correspondents were bombed by US forces. Al-Jazeera correspondents were targeted and murdered by U.S. troops for accurately portraying the initial war of occupation.

The best line I heard in all the horrible reports about what's happening in Fallujah today was this one from Libertarian Socialist News.

"The U.S. General in charge of propaganda, General Kimmit "the Toad", accused al-Jazeera today of "spreading lies" in claiming the U.S. was being defeated, but then, when asked if he meant al-Jazeera was faking the footage, stated that the footage was correct but their "interpretation" of it — the interpretation that U.S. forces running away and Iraqi resistance fighters dancing on U.S. positions was a U.S. "defeat" — was "wrong". He implied that often U.S. Marines run away from their positions and throw themselves on enemy munitions as a sign of "victory."

The LSN report also said:

"Yesterday, the United States initiated surrender talks with the rebels to save their surrounded and defeated Marine units, but instead of acting in good faith, the U.S. launched two massive bombing raids against the city and bombarded the Golan neighborhood with artillery and mortar fire. In response to the bombing, Iraqi resistance fighters continued to press the surrounded Marines, killing some and taking more prisoners."

And most important of all — something you will not hear on American TV — is that the U.S. appears to be losing control of Baghdad and all the other major Iraqi cities, and the air campaign of killing innocent civilians is a desperate attempt to reverse the trend. Free people everywhere can only pray that the Iraqis will drive the criminal American forces from their land.

• • •

Hallelujah. He is risen. Your pastor, your rabbi, your priest has told you to pray for the safety of American troops in Iraq.

The war in Iraq is based on shameful lies. Now that these lies have been exposed and keep being repeated by the soulless sadists who have led American into war, isn't it time you told your pastor, your rabbi and your priest exactly where they can go? And that would be straight to hell.

America is the evil empire. If you're praying to God for an American victory in Iraq, I hate to be the one to tell you that it's not God you're praying to.

It's that other guy, the one George Bush prays to. It could be time you came to grips with the ugly fact that he is the same one in the Old Testament, the one who urges everyone to just keep on killing and stealing other people's valuables.

As far as the other guy who is supposedly risen? Well, you keep on praying, if you like. Just imagine today - Easter Sunday - that you're sitting in a mosque in Fallujah, and you suddenly hear those American planes overhead. Praying would be the right thing to do.

Pray for the soul — that as an American — you have definitely lost.

Chapter Thirty-Four

Penalty of an ancient fraud

Why killing is the biggest business of all

"And Moses said, Thus saith the Lord God of Israel: Pick up your swords, go from camp to camp, every man shall kill his brother, every man shall kill his companion, every man shall kill his neighbor."
— Exodus 32:27

"Their children shall be dashed to pieces before their eyes; their houses shall be spoiled, and their wives ravished."
— Isaiah 13:16

"And you shall eat the flesh of your sons and daughters."
— Leviticus 26:29

"Their town is all green graves, and blood under the feet of its men."
— Aneirin, Welsh poet, c. A.D. 660

"Who is the third who walks always beside you?
... Gliding wrapt in a brown mantle, hooded ... "
— T.S. Eliot, "What the thunder said," A.D. 1922

When you become aware of a fleeting thought and try to catch it, it always seems to disappear. But if you try to walk away from it, it pursues you like a shadow, an invisible wraith of foreboding that lurks behind your left shoulder. Uneasily, you turn around to face it, and once again it is not there.

They are numbers on a newspaper page. Silhouettes on a TV

screen. Imaginary insects tickling the back of your neck. Objects of hatred targeted by the pastor's pointing finger. Terrorists lurking in your own neighborhood, aiming to blow you up. Who are these people we feel we must kill in order to assure our own safety, to validate and verify our own lives? Who are these faceless savages who give us nightmares, and accelerate the sales of drugs to calm us down?

Yesterday they were the Palestinians. In our minds we were taught to see beasts with dynamite-encased ribcages ready to shatter our lives on a moment's notice. In reality today we see desperate children throwing stones at Apache helicopters; then lying in the street bleeding after Israeli target practice.

Before that there were the niggers coming to rape your white daughters. Subsequent exercises in reason reveal to most of us they were really innocent African abductees dangling from a tree limb in a drunken Southern town.

And before that there were those filthy savages called Indians, on whom white Europeans perfected their genocide techniques that became America's principal export, a social technique which — when combined with the latest style in weaponry — provided those in the United States with their much-admired level of prosperity. Subsequent perspective on these forgotten souls — these Native Americans — has never evolved, and to this day, they are abused and ravished by the local cops.

Today's terrorists du jour are Iraqis (and Arabs in general), the ungrateful recipients of radioactive gifts from that high-tech plantation called America.

Wrapped in tiny shawls and speaking an odd language (as

enemies usually do), they bring us nightmare bombs that manifest the threat we must overcome to stay alive, that give us our reasons for productivity and ingenuity. Funny how it works that way, how civilization evolves responding to threats, whether real or imagined.

Suicide bombers! Splashing the entrails of our own fear all over the front pages of our shrewdly designed existences. Funny how when you see how these creatures of horror evolved, we appear to have invented them ourselves, right in the pages of the Old Testament. You could also call it the Torah, but doing that allows Christians to evade responsibility for this violent horror that grips the world, and it would not be fair to do that, to pin everything on the Jews.

The one good thing about both creeds is that they both stress personal responsibility, and that's what we're trying to define here. That's true, even though they both advocate killing those whose property you covet, as the excerpted quotes at the top of this essay so aptly illustrate.

Few of us ever contemplate that these terrorist threats are works of fiction, crafted by those with an ulterior motive. Usually that motive, if history is any guide, is about stealing someone's land. When you read about so-called villains, the horror is created to achieve the objectives of someone who gains something from creating that threat. As I said, it's usually about land. Or if not, about a very lucrative commodity.

Perhaps it goes back to Cain and Abel, or Abraham and his two sons, one of whom was disinherited and traces directly to the giant wall the erstwhile sons of Isaac are currently building in the West Bank. After all these centuries, still trying to deny the rightful patrimony of their brothers. And murdering their first-cousins at will. And with glee.

There are innumerable instances of righteous killing of those who had something we wanted. Our civilization is built on these lessons. We are still practicing them.

Justice always takes a back seat to avarice because justice is conveniently created and administered by those with power over others.

Those who pretend to be religious are only pretending. The laws of God are contrived to facilitate theft, not forgiveness.

Yet the thought is fleeting. When you turn around to face it it's not there, like a faint but painful memory of some childhood sexual trauma.

Fleeting. And our lives are wasted with murder and mayhem, scarred on our souls like a planet turned to ash by the poisons of our own desires.

Mnemosyne, goddess of memory, what a duplicitous gift you give us. Sweet reverie, how could we kill without you? But we have our Holy Orders!

Somehow our well-being is tied up with having enemies: Palestinian grasshoppers, black rapists, Indian savages. And tied into religion. Defeating death. Repelling the infidel. Planting the flag of Christ in some foreigners' land.

We know who most of yesterday's enemies are. They're still bleeding, those beleaguered few still left alive.

Conject, if you will, on whom tomorrow's enemies may be. And the lies that will be used to condemn them. Chances are good, if history is any guide, it will involve land. And precious commodities of some sort.

Certainly, Bush/Kerry has the Venezuelans in its gun sights. There is simply too much oil there to be left in the hands of people with such dark skin. And Lula's Brazil would be a natural progression once South Guanatamo is established in Caracas, although the Brazilians are reportedly close to perfecting their own nukes, and we all know the United States doesn't pick on countries which can actually fight back.

Which is why – OK, also because of Wal-Mart — that the U.S. will never go after China. Much too tough. Their day is coming. Hell, the U.S. isn't even tough enough to stop the Aztlantics from grabbing San Francisco, Santa Fe and San Antonio, something that will probably happen in the 21st century.

But the Lord says it's cool to kill people for their possessions. And the human race is apparently not ready to distinguish between the spoken words of God and the satanic scribblings of the pederastic priests who interpose their deluded dogma and insist it is the wish of the Messiah. I lately have been deluged by letters from "concerned" Christians for blaming their faith in my "Fallujah" piece. Makes me realize how sick this religion is, in that so many people would be more worried about saving their selfish souls than in the unjust butchery of innocent people. That is not how to save your soul, people, and the principal thing that is absolutely wrong with all religions.

Got another note from a feller in Mississippi who actually bought one of my books but had to send me a little comic book illustrating why it was more important to "keep the Lord's holy word" than it was to do good works. It depicted a couple who had spent their lives feeding the poor meeting a man who had committed murder but who had "accepted" Christ. At the end, when they meet their maker, the wrathful

God welcomes the reformed killer but sends the altruistic old couple straight to hell, pontificating that it doesn't matter what good works you do — it only matters if you follow the word of God.

This may explain why I have such contempt for religion.

I have nothing against God, but religions are pure evil. Simply mind control propaganda meant to assure the serene unconsciousness and political ineffectiveness of the deceived populace.

Why is that bullets and holy men in black cassocks always seem to go together?

In this world we try to find someone to look down our noses at; someone who makes us feel that we are better than. Who is it that declares these infidels evil? How many pagans were slaughtered by the fledging Constantinian church?

I suggest that the true pariahs are the ones who create these distinctions: the Brahmins, the British, the Americans, the Zionists, the white Europeans who propagandize these falsely discriminatory distinctions and teach our children to kill because of the color of someone's skin.

It's all a ruse to begin with. It's not really about lineage; it's about cold hard cash.

The true villains on this earth are those who enslave and exploit; who manipulate and massacre to prove to themselves they are the superior ones, when all they are proving is that they are the weak and evil ones. This concept of elite respectability is a sham anyway, since most fortunes in this world were built on illegal activity, from British drug smugglers to Israeli arms merchants to the American government's drug profiteers.

So it is with Western history. The people who wrote the Bible were the bad guys, who went around killing everyone and then invented noble-sounding reasons for doing so. And we Americans, with our vaunted Western civilization, are their literal heirs, in every sense of the word. We have perfected killing and destruction as the highest art form of human civilization.

All the while marching on subliminal orders from the Old Testament.

In Richard Duncan's very scary piece on the savage world he predicts will develop at the shocking end of the age of oil (http://dieoff.com/page224.htm), he foresees it is the indigenous people who will fare the best, because they are well prepared for living close to the land without canned food and automatic can openers. Said the pessimistic geologist, "If God made the earth for human habitation, then He made it for the Stone Age mode of habitation."

And I am constantly reminded of Becker's maxim: "The greatest evil in human history is material production."

Something to keep in mind when you realize the elite are now trying to kill us all off with biotech food that curdles your insides, with aluminium and barium poisoning from the sky the clogs your lungs with hard mucous, with designer prescription drugs designed to make you more dependent on even more poisonous medications, with brain-numbing fluoride in the water, with gene-shattering aspartame in our soft drinks, with radioactive polonium in our cigarettes ... it's all too clear that the preconscious triggers from all our religions and philosophies are predicated on self-destruction over our obsessive guilt that we die — and that our loved ones must die — and we can do nothing about it.

It's so clear why we are hell-bent to destroy ourselves, and it is best reflected in my favorite Bible quote of all — Deuteronomy 28:56-58:

> *If your mother does not obey all of God's holy laws,*
> *she will be forced to eat her own children!*

Come back to Earth, people, before it's too late. If you cling to your hope of heaven, and forget to heal the wounds of those you have injured because of that hope of heaven, it will surely produce exactly what it is aimed at — the death of us all.

It takes a little more understanding than that to truly live. It takes understanding that the messages in the holy books are only false justifications for killing our brothers and sisters. And it is in that sense that God has truly become the devil.

People are always asking me to stop complaining and suggesting something positive they can do fix the evil in this world. Well, here's an idea.

Boycott your churches. Snub your synagogues. Ignore your mosques. Until those preachers come out foursquare for peace and justice, refuse to accept their pitiful propaganda.

The minute you start worrying about your immortal soul is exactly the point at which you lose it.

Besides, that's not God who resides in most houses of worship anyway. It's Moloch! It's Baal. It's Marduk. It's definitely Mammon. The evil one, posing as your deity, teaching you how to pretend to be good rather than actually teaching you how to be good.

Tell your pastor you have a higher standard of morality than he is able to reach, as long as he keeps preaching that Old Testament bigotry and stays silent about America's mass murder of innocents for reasons that are provable lies. What kind of morality is silence about that? Ask him. Tell him. Stand up for what's right.

Quit worrying about your soul. It will take care of itself. Besides, if you're an American you've already lost your soul anyway. You have almost no chance of getting it back.

The only thing God really cares about is how you treat others.

And bombing innocent people in order to steal their land and their valuable possessions, as that fake God in the Old Testament incessantly recommends, doesn't really cut it, does it?

Chapter Thirty-Five

Fatal flaw in the 9/11 cover-up

Why can no one name the hijackers or prove they flew the planes?

Know how to tell the difference between the truth and lies of 9/11? If they're talking about hijackers having done the dastardly deed, you know they're part of the sinister cover-up extravaganza, wittingly or not.

In order for the people of the world to be convinced that Islamic hijackers were responsible for terrible tragedy of 9/11, we need to see some evidence. Not hearsay, innuendo, aspersion or promises of evidence, but real evidence.

Otherwise, the whole subject is rightly regarded as a ruse, a setup to conceal the identities of the real culprits, the ones who sit smugly in front of the TV cameras and plot their cynical war on terror — otherwise known as the war on the peoples of the world.

As President Bush continues to insist that his word be accepted as truth on numerous questions, time after time his statements have been revealed as blatant falsehoods. Yet he continues to repeat them, and the whorish corporate media continues to accept them.

Why hasn't either the Bush administration or some element of law enforcement in the United States issued a single solid piece of evidence connecting the hijackers to the hijacked airplanes? Why don't the alleged hijackers appear on the airport security videos? Why aren't there credit card records of their ticket purchases?

Why did FBI director Robert Mueller say very publicly to the Commonwealth Club of San Francisco that nothing on paper connected Arab terrorists to 9/11? I mean, two and half years have passed. And the feds produced 19 names within 72 hours of the disaster. Notice a mathematical inconsistency here? All that has happened since is mere vigilante hysteria, hypothetical scenarios trumpeted ad nauseum by America's notoriously brainwashed Zionist press.

Seven or eight of the names on that original list have been found living comfortably in other countries. Why hasn't the FBI made any attempt to correct the errors made on that original list? See for yourself.
http://members.fortunecity.com/911/september-eleven/hijackers-alive.htm and
http://www.welfarestate.com/911/.

And after much hullabaloo about Colin Powell using phony information in his remarks to the United Nations about the reasons for war, why hasn't the U.S. government produced a single conclusive piece of evidence to back up its claim that 9/11 was the work Osama bin Laden and other Islamic terrorists? Not a single piece!

If you disagree, tell me what it is!

There's a simple answer to this, you know. It's because there isn't any evidence. And why is that? Because those pseudo-Muslims revealed to be so publicly incompetent at piloting jerkwater training planes had absolutely zero chance of flying sophisticated jetliners into anything narrower than the Grand Canyon, never mind executing tricky maneuvers with extraordinarily complicated machinery.

The unknown men who played the roles of the so-called Arab terrorist hijackers were really recruited by either

American and/or Israeli intelligence services in a scheme set up as a diversion to inflame dumb Westerners against the Islamic world. The purpose was to divert the world's attention from the Israeli genocide and dispossession of the Palestinians by blaming the attacks on Muslims.

But that was only half the objective. The other half was to enable our despicable cabal of neo-con gang-bangers to fleece the American public with an endless array of no-bid contracts to enrich the conscienceless billionaires who are really driving the war machine.

You know how the Bushista American government uses anything for PR to supposedly authenticate its own evil agenda. If they had any concrete evidence against the hijackers — if they even possessed all their correct names — we would have heard about it by now. There would be an avalanche of TV shows about them, unlike that Jewish claptrap hate crime against Muslims that appeared on NBC the other night.

After two and half years, with the whole world knowing that eight of the 19 names on the hijacker list are fraudulent, the FBI has made no attempt to substitute new names. And why is that? Because the identities of the hijackers were constructed with mostly stolen papers, for some of the patsies designed to take the heat. In any case, and whoever they were, there is no evidence they ever got on the planes.

But nothing. Instead we have one minor player, Mounir El Motassadeq, convicted in Germany; then the conviction was overturned, partly because the Americans refused to help with the prosecution.

We have the so-called 20th hijacker, Zacarias Moussaoui, and assorted other preposterous character actors languishing in jails on specious charges. We have security camera film at the Pentagon, which surely reveal that no jetliner hit that building, locked away in Ashcroft's vault under the phony aegis of national security. We have all the rubble of the World Trade Center, which surely would have revealed the use of nuclear explosives creating shattered beams in odd places, instantly carted away with no forensic investigation. We have transcripts — but no recordings — of these phony cell phone calls, some from people who may not have even existed.

And we have the famous stand-down, in which America's air defenses suddenly evaporated — the only time in our history this has happened.

We have Marvin Bush sitting suspiciously on the board of directors of the security company that had the contract for the Twin Towers. We have Larry Silverstein, who conveniently leased and insured the towers shortly before the big hits, telling officials to "pull" a relatively intact tower, which then fell identically to the two structures that were struck by airplanes, creating the impression that that's the way all three came down.

We have billions of dollars of windfall profits made by savvy investors in the days before 9/11, and an FBI investigation that insists nothing was amiss with these spectacular deals. Of course, we don't get the details. Only "assurances" that the trades were not suspicious, despite patterns and results that were unprecedented in the entire history of financial trading.

We have reports from firemen of explosions at the base of the Twin Towers BEFORE they fell, and the seismographic evidence to back up these assertions.

We have leader after leader saying they didn't know such a thing could happen when the government had been studying the problem for ten years. It had held at least two major drills simulating such a possibility.

And we have a president sitting in a ghetto classroom in Florida, at possibility the most pivotal moment in American history, pretending to listen to children read a story about a pet goat.

Perhaps most tellingly of all, we have the tragic tale of John O'Neill, rabidly honest FBI investigator, prevented from following his leads about Osama bin Laden because he would have discovered the links from Afghanistan back to CIA headquarters. Just review the way he was prevented from conducting his probe of the Cole bombing, and prevented from digging into other leads by the same guys — namely insiders Louis Freeh and Thomas Picard — who prevented significant reports from other FBI agents from seeing the light of day.

So, how does all that make you regard the supposedly impartial government panel that investigated these matters? When they talked about Presidential Daily Briefings months before the event, or chitchat with presidential flunkies who leak out these pseudo-revelations about this and that tidbit of essentially trivial information. And especially when they talk about the dastardly hijackers (without being able to name them) as if there is no question of their guilt. Talk about your misleading urban legends! This one is the champ.

Well, no sense feigning surprise. We knew this commission was a set-up from the get-go. Recycled Watergate investigators, even. Part of the same bunch that has run the country and covered up everything for the past 30 years or more.

Surely you didn't expect a real investigation. Thomas Kean declared at the outset of his hearings that Osama bin Laden was guilty. End of discussion. As soon as he made that statement, there was no way the hearings could be legitimate.

Asserting that genuine Arab hijackers did not carry out the attacks of 9/11 requires analysis of two concomitant categories: the history of American (and Israeli) involvement (and subterfuge) with Arab terrorists, and methods of remote control of aircraft, or other means of piloting the aircraft.

The remote control aspect continues to be a bone of contention among legitimate pilots, with some asserting only real pilots could have made such extemporaneous maneuvers and others insisting only remote control could have accomplished such a feat. An interesting new perspective on this debate can be found here:
http://joevialls.altermedia.info/wtc/radiocontrol.html

A third natural area of study in this regard would be the intimate histories of those whom officials claim to be the hijackers, including putting the microscope on their behavior in the days and weeks before the tragedy.

Many researchers claim the name al-Qaeda was made up in middle '90s by a variety of American functionaries (one of them being none other than Richard Clarke) as an all-purpose villain the U.S. could blame as a convenient reason for its military adventurism. And a group of Israeli provocateurs was recently discovered trying to create their very own chapter of al-Qaeda.

How many more hints do you need? The absence of any relevant arrests or discovery of any clues to the hierarchy of this supposedly worldwide terror group should tell you a lot.

Al-Qaeda doesn't exist except for when they want it to, to blame for any sort of strategic terror they have created themselves for some political reason, like influencing the elections in Spain. Hah, that one really backfired!

Why haven't American intelligence operatives gone to these foreign countries to interview these named hijackers who turned out to be alive? Simple. Because they knew the list was fiction in the first place, and the Arab-types who have been named as terror gurus are mostly their own employees, or people who have been set up by them.

It is a celebrated fact that Mohammed Atta and some of his friends were seen in nightclubs in the hours before 9/11, certainly a fact that argues against them being able to carry out their supposed missions because they were motivated by Islamic religious zeal. So their appearance in strip clubs blows the whole story that they were devout Muslims giving their lives to Allah. Devout Muslims don't drink, never mind cavort with strippers.

If we knew who the hijackers were, we'd know their names, wouldn't we? Or is it now worth bombing other nations and murdering thousands of innocent people because we say we know who the hijackers were, even though we don't know their names? It is the great shame of the American people that they have approved of the murders of thousands of people because of that blatant lie.

Many of the men who were fingered as 9/11 hijackers received preferential treatment from American immigration officials when it came to entering and leaving the U.S. on numerous occasions. Many of these same names reportedly trained at various U.S. military installations.

What has resulted after two and a half years of work by

America's crack intelligence agencies, besides the persecution of Muslims throughout the world?

Well, hundreds of innocent people have been unjustly imprisoned and tortured at Guantanamo. All of them innocent, hapless dupes rounded up in a Rumsfeld-ordered dragnet in Pakistan after U.S. planes had (inadvertently or otherwise) allowed the Taliban fighters to escape with the Pakistani army from Afghanistan.

Two pathetic flunkies have been arrested and held without due process. One of them, the notoriously pathetic shoe bomber who was obviously a deranged personality and not a member of any terror network, was ceremoniously sentenced to life in prison.

Other than that, no al-Qaeda kingpins have been even named, never mind apprehended. No clue about how the 9/11 attacks were engineered has ever emerged. This is simply not consistent with being able to name all 19 hijackers the day after the attacks. It is a case of pretending you have all of the information instantly, and then pretending you have no information for the next two years. What a smell!

In the final two days of the Kean Commission, government officials began talking about Khalid Sheikh Mohammed, supposedly bin Laden's sidekick, who supposedly revealed a years-long timetable of what al-Qaeda supposedly wanted to blow up. Another story on the Internet revealed almost the same day that Mohammed had been subjected to a bizarre form of water torture to get him to talk. Which means, like so many other shenanigans of the Kean Commission, that this evidence is wholly unbelievable, even assuming this cooked-up character is the person U.S government intelligence shills say he is.

It's difficult to avoid coming to two conclusions: that the list of 19 names was a total fabrication, and that the worldwide terror network called al-Qaeda is also a total fabrication, the wet dream brainchild of the CIA and the Mossad to be trotted out as an excuse for a whole string of terror attacks — Madrid, Bali, Riyadh, Istanbul, etc. — that were really carried out by the CIA and the Mossad themselves, cleverly involving designated patsies to give the operations a suitably foreign flavor. Al-Qaeda does not exist except as a bogeyman invented by Western powers to justify their evil agenda. There were no hijackers flying those planes on 9/11. And honest FBI agents have been prevented from publicizing that fact.

If you disagree, prove it! The world knows you can't, though the high-tech mass murder by the United States and Israel spreads around the world because of this falsified version of events.

History will show — and the public will soon realize — that those who are telling these lies not only allowed 9/11 to happen, but planned it for their own personal advantage.

The only question that remains is: will the American public awaken to this murderous, treasonous scam before the perpetrators achieve their objective and bury the whole planet in the flames of their insane perfidy.

Just remember: If they're talking about hijackers, they're part of the cover-up, whether they know it or not.

Much more productive would be analyzing the tiny hole in the Pentagon; how the ejected material in the WTC photos proves there were unexplained explosions, or how those emotional cell phone calls could not possibly have been made as government flunkies have presented them. And the suspicious stock trades.

But you won't hear the official 9/11 commissioners talking about any of that, because they are definitely part of the cover-up. You can obviously tell, because they keep talking about hijackers.

Chapter Thirty-Six

Pick your price:
your blood or your soul

Do you support our killer troops committing genocide in Iraq?

What would you do if your brother — or perhaps your son, father, or husband — was charged with murder? With deliberately taking the life of another human being.

For sure, it would be an agonizing decision — making the choice between practicing what you preach about justice, or standing by your devastated family. A choice no one would envy — defend your blood or obey the laws of God and society.

And then, what if it was a particularly bad murder? Say he shot an old woman in the back, and watched her die — all the while preventing medical personnel from tending to her. Maybe she was already wounded and he finished her off. From a helicopter, even.

It sure would be tough to keep your family — your mind, your heart — together in that situation. Who could blame you, whatever you decided.

Of course, things are different in the middle of a war, even a completely illegal war shamefully based on well-publicized lies such as the situation in Iraq.

I mean, it's easy to say you were just following orders. That's what lots of Nazis did in World War II, but they still were put to death in the trials following the war.

I wonder what will happen when and if Americans find themselves in that situation in the near future.

Being in a military situation means everything is different. Innocent civilians always get killed accidentally when the military's involved. Some are accidental, some are deliberate, but mostly we never get to know the difference. Bodies get thrown in holes and are forgotten, except by some of the living who years later wake up screaming in the middle of the night.

Long after the grisly facts become known, sometimes we get a little tardy justice. Mostly we don't. Remember when former Senator Bob Kerry tried to give back his Vietnam medals, admitting he killed women and children rather than the dangerous enemy gunmen his valor citations described. How did the public react? Hell, we didn't want to hear him. We told him to keep his medals, keep quiet, and forget about the whole thing.

Demonic demagogues like Joseph Farah, Michael Savage and Rush Limbaugh all have recently recommended killing large numbers of innocent Iraqis "to teach them a lesson." The "lesson" being it's not cool to mess with Uncle Sam and mutilate his hired killers, the highly paid mercenaries he hired to assassinate Iraqi intellectuals so when America has that tortured nation sufficiently lobotomized, there will be a minimum of intelligent people around to protest the new "democratic" prison camp that America has created.

The United States, Britain, and Israel have decided to adopt the Pol Pot theory of social engineering — kill everyone with academic credentials. And when the irate Iraqis decide to strike back at this masterpiece of population control, the

U.S. ups the ante on its already-high atrocity level — and bombs a totally defenseless town from the air, no matter who gets killed, and murders all the males under 45. Repeat: murders all the males under 45! That's what's going on right now, my dear American compatriots, in the inferno called Fallujah, Iraq. It is called genocide. No question about it.

This is how your American boys are behaving in a foreign country. Your sons, your husbands, your fathers are committing genocide.

Hey! They were just following orders. Based on lies.

This is what your country is doing to innocent people. Killing them without a second thought, without regard for who they are or what they've done, how many children they might have or how many wonderful things they've done in this life.

Hell, they don't worry about the children because they're killing them, too. Listen to that doctor, forced to set up his clinic in a filthy garage, describe a little boy with a shell of a skull missing its brains. Or the man who was brought to the clinic with burns so bad he will automatically dehydrate to death in 24 hours. How about the boy they threw in the river, and he couldn't swim so he drowned? Or when the fighting first began, the hundred teenagers hooded and kept in the sun, and then shot to death by your beloved Americans boys, one by one.

This was all done by your sons, your husbands, your fathers. Just following orders.

Take a flag-waving break, right about now.

You know, we all ought to be very scared that these killer

punks will be coming home soon, all with the taste of blood on their teeth, ready and willing to tell us all about the wonderful experiences they had in Iraq, or at least the ones who don't immediately get sick and die from the radioactive ammunition they had to handle or the poisonous vaccines they had to endure, at least they'll be able to tell us how they fought the War on Terror in Iraq by shooting defenseless women in the back and bombing residential neighborhoods and splattering body parts all over the tan brick walls of Baghdad.

They were scared. It's OK to kill people when you're scared.

And most of them — y'know, those kids who come to try to return to normal life — they'll be screaming in the middle of the night.

This is the kind of behavior approved by Fox news every night, only they don't tell you about this stuff — they tell you about our tough guy president saying "Bring it on", and how the folks back home are cheering about the lives they are throwing away.

Pretending to be brave and patriotic when they plant their own children in the peaceful soil, saying how proud they are that their children gave their lives for an unjust genocide that was based on lies.

America. What a country. A country gone mad.

And this isn't something new, you know. Don't pretend to be surprised. Don't tell me you didn't know this is the kind of stuff we noble Americans do on a regular basis.

It has been going on — in Iraq, anyway, for FIFTEEN years! But hey, in Palestine it has been going on for FIFTY-FIVE years, at least officially (actually it has been much longer).

I haven't heard the phrase Geneva Conventions lately. The last time I heard it was when Rumsfeld complained about Iraqis taking photos of American POWs being a violation of the Geneva Conventions.

The U.S. uses the phrase Geneva Conventions when it's somebody else they can complain about. Americans forget to use the phrase when it pertains to U.S. behavior in Iraq, Afghanistan, Colombia, Lebanon, Palestine, the Philippines, Colombia, Lebanon, Nicaragua, Vietnam, or any of a hundred other places all related to Fort Benning, Georgia, where they teach courses on how to violate the Geneva Conventions.

At the end of the first Gulf War in 1991, our famous drug czar Barry McCaffrey supervised the slaughter on the Highway of Death which killed thousands of Iraqi soldiers who had already surrendered. This was noted as an egregious violation of the Geneva Conventions — killing soldiers who were trying to surrender.

But Americans cheered. Sons, husbands, fathers.

Then, for nearly 15 more years, the Americans and the Brits — WITHOUT approval of the United Nations — continued to bomb large parts of Iraq, and in direct violation of the Geneva Conventions, bombed water treatment plants, hospitals and other necessary services (all direct violations of the Geneva Conventions), resulting in the deaths of ONE MILLION Iraqi children from birth defects and childhood diseases that could have been easily cured were it not for the embargo of necessary medicines.

Now, the new Iraqi death toll (various American generals

said it wasn't necessary to count Iraqi dead — another endearing American trait) stands at more than 30,000. Ninety percent were innocent civilians.

Obliterated by America's video game weapons, by your sons, your husbands, your fathers.

Worst of all, the whole world now knows America had absolutely no reason to invade Iraq this time around (not that it did before in the era of the April Gillespie sucker punch, either). Iraq had no weapons of mass destruction (just as Scott Ritter, Hans Blix and others said) and Iraq had no connection to al-Qaida (although now reportedly the U.S. is trying to smuggle in WMDs and claim that Saddam had them hidden all the time). No legitimate reason whatsoever to go to war.

The U.S. invasion of Iraq is entirely unjustified, a massive crime against humanity, carried out by your sons, your husbands, your fathers, who murdered innocents on the cynical say-so of the lies our leaders told us, and are still telling us.

And now the opposition presidential candidate, supposedly a war hero himself who only recently found out he was Jewish, says he will continue the same policy of random murders and denial of self-determination should he win the totally-fixed elections of 2004. This means America is destined to be a soulless, killer nation indefinitely into the future. And it is only a matter of time before this kind of thing starts happening here.

Your sons, your husbands, your fathers are murderers. The Geneva Conventions state that when soldiers know their leaders are giving them illegal or immoral orders, it is their duty to disobey them. America used that argument in the post-World War II trials against the Japanese and the Germans, and the whole world damn well better use it against the Americans when it puts America on trial for its illegal genocide against the Iraqis.

Do the world a big favor and think of all these things the next time you hear the Star Spangled Banner, or listen to some pompous ass in a faux military hat say in a drunken stupor, "Support our troops!"

Tip your glass to him, and say, with all sincerity and that American killer smile, "Yes, brother, support our killer troops."

Just don't go to church afterwards. God would puke on you.

Chapter Thirty-Seven

The man in the big white stone

Thoughts on a visit to the Tomb of the Unknown

I received this from Marty Cepielik, publisher of News of Polonia in Pasadena, California:

"I don't know if you saw this in the news but it really impressed me. Funny, our US Senate/House took two days off as they couldn't work.

"On the ABC evening news, it was reported tonight that, because of the dangers from Hurricane Isabelle approaching Washington DC, the military members assigned the duty of guarding the Tomb of the Unknown Soldier were given permission to suspend the assignment.

"They refused. "No way, Sir!"

"Soaked to the skin, marching in the pelting rain of a tropical storm, they said that guarding the Tomb was not just an assignment; it was the highest honor that can be afforded to a serviceperson.

"The tomb has been patrolled continuously, 24/7, since 1930."

•••

Once upon a time, not long ago, I did the monuments tour in Washington. It was the Tomb of the Unknown Soldier that really got me thinking. I lit a cigarette in the gray drizzle, surveying the puddles forming on the august granite quadrangle, in the shadow of the majestic Corinthian pillars of the museum nearby. Gazing at the mammoth cube of Colorado marble, I tried to think about the archetypal spirit of the mythical warrior resting inside it.

In the mist, closing my eyes, with as much compassion and respect as I could muster, I dared to say: "Hey buddy, how's it going?"

And in my reverie, maybe assisted by some helpful spirits nearby, I imagined I heard a raspy response: "Can't complain, man. We all do what we have to do." Then a pause. Then ... "I sure wish I could still smoke though."

The image of a grizzled, unshaven GI, battered helmet askew on his unkempt head, popped into my mind.

"So you were in World War II?" my thoughts guessed in the humid air.

"Hah," the voice shrugged. "I was in all the wars. From Thermopylae to My Lai, I was there. Every time there was a bullet fired in anger, an arrow aimed from ambush, a club bludgeoning the teeth of someone you never met and would never meet again, I was there."

"You know the question everybody asks you," I said in my mind, projecting my thoughts toward the elegantly carved granite. "Was it worth it?"

"No, it's never worth it. At the time it's happening, though, there's really no choice to think whether it's worth it or not. You get caught up in the inevitability of the thing, swept along, as it were. Then it becomes a matter of staying true to your buddies."

"What's it like to kill somebody in combat?"

"It's not a good thing, though for some people it's kind of a drug-induced high. I think the people who like killing don't really like themselves. Killing others is like killing yourself, except you get to walk away, and they don't.

"At that moment you fire the bullet, and someone drops, never to get up again, it makes you feel kind of immortal. I mean, to have that kind of power, to stop someone's life in its tracks, it's kind of like a drug. Or at least until sometime later, days or months or years later, and your mind tricks you and you start seeing the faces of your children on the people you are shooting ... that kind of comes with the package."

"What's it like to be killed in combat?"

"It's funny. There's usually no pain, although sometimes there is and it's beyond anything you ever thought of at the dentist. But usually, unless you're blipped out instantaneously, there is this kind of calm. It's dazzling and boring at the same time. When you know you have about twenty seconds of life left, it's not the wound that you think about. It's where you came from, trivial moments of childhood that somehow foretold the end you are now confronting. And then, for a second or two, it's where you would have gone, what you would have done. And it's about those people who are close to you, that girl, that little boy, or your mom. She'll be so angry, you think. Then the dark shade comes down and you can go anywhere you want. But you can never talk to anybody again."

"Do you get time to ask the question, 'Was I doing the right thing?'"

"Not usually, unless you linger on. It's the wounded who

have to deal with that trip, those with legs blown off or made blind by some explosion in your face. Then you can really work up a case of resentment. The 'what-might-have-beens' are about the most painful injury that can happen in anybody's life. Regret is about the worst thing there is."

"Did you ever realize, in any of all those wars, that what you were doing, was probably an exercise in futility, a pre-arranged deal, a conflict set up by rich men to make money off the sale of armaments or to steal someone else's property. I mean, did you ever realize that the song-and-dance about patriotism or defending your country was just a cover story for some much larger economic crime?"

"Shee-it, every enlisted man who ever served in the military knows that from practically day one. You only need to look around you to see the injustice of the whole system, where rich kid junior officers too timid to poke their eyes out of their tent flaps order rag-tags into harm's way without any thought of what will happen to them. Or how the equipment they give you may or may not work, and superiors don't really care about that, they only care that they don't get their asses kicked by somebody of higher rank. If the enlisted men, the real soldiers, got to run wars, there wouldn't be any wars. The only reason there are wars at all is because the men who decide to make them are never the ones who have to fight them. Can you say Dick Cheney?

"Ha. Well put. Has it always been that way?"

"Yes. Hail Caesar! Onward Zachary Taylor! But at least they got out there and swung their swords on occasion."

"What do you think of all these stories about rapes by Americans in Iraq?

"Pfft. That's war. Happens every time. Nobody remembers the 1.9 million American rapes of German women after WW II. But depravity is not limited to one ethnic group, though it may be limited to the human race. You don't see other animals doing this kind of crap."

"So, you're saying that's normal behavior for any soldier, any warrior in combat?"

"No way. A real soldier is like a wild animal. Totally controlled; utterly savage. He doesn't kill unless he has to. The true soldier is about the most honorable person on the planet, even though he has been hired to kill for wimpy rich men who are afraid to fight. Still, there is the code of honor. A true soldier won't follow an illegal order, but you can tell how many true soldiers there are these days by the paltry number who refuse immoral commands.

"Just like the rest of the country, every country that ever was, people are afraid to stand out, to say what they really believe even though they know it's right to do so. In the service you can't do that either — or not easily anyway — because if your commander tells you to wipe out a village of women and children, and you don't do it, you get thrown in the brig. Maybe you'll get shot. But those who kill unnecessarily or rape women are just the kind of psychopaths who wind up in the military because they can't find a job anywhere else."

"What do you think of our fearless war-making presidential candidates today?"

"Same as every other day. They all think soldiers are little stickmen on a chessboard to be sacrificed for somebody's stock options. Based on what I've heard about Kerry, he did soldiers dirt by opposing what they were doing. They say he has lots of medals, but from the things I've heard, he's lucky he didn't get fragged in 'Nam. And Bush. What a pansy! He's a deserter in time of war. He should have been shot. But he had a rich daddy, so they let him fly planes til his cocaine got in the way.

"And he killed all those people in Texas whether they were innocent or not. Tied them down and killed them, then laughed about it. What he did flying onto that carrier saying the Iraq war was over was a disgrace. I'd like to see him a fistfight with the weakest person in the Iraqi army. Bush'd get his throat torn out, which would be a good thing for the world, though there are plenty of other strutting punks like him ready to take his place."

"As a soldier who fought for your country, you are honored for your sacrifice and your patriotism. Does that make you feel proud in the place you are in now?"

"I wish they would have honored my widow and my orphaned children instead of me. They never had much when I was alive, and now have a lot less. I miss them. And patriotism. There is a difference between patriotism and esprit de corps. The former is used to lure halfwits like me into putting everything on the line for some reason which is never fully explained to us. But esprit de corps is one of the great things in life. You get to know who you real friends are when somebody steps in the way of a bullet meant for you."

"What do you think about the people who come here to visit you?"

"I feel sorry for them, that they venerate a process that is so unnecessary. I appreciate their thoughts, like I appreciate your thoughts, but what happened to me, all those times on the battlefield, was completely unnecessary in all instances, and was caused by those who sought to make a profit by the deliberate manipulation of social forces and public opinion. I would advise people to remember that if they treated me as well in life as they have in death, neither one of us would have ever had to be in this sorry place."

"And kids who want to be soldiers, what would you say to them?"

"Slit your belly open with a knife, just to see how it feels. Then imagine how someone else would feel if you did it to them. Then imagine how your mom would feel if it really happened to you.

"Especially if she found that the war you were fighting in was a total lie, and never had to happen? All wars are lies, you know. None of them ever had to happen."

"So go be a soldier. Go be a fool. Kill somebody over nothing. Watch yourself die. Hell, they might put you in a monument like this one. And no one will ever remember your name."

Chapter Thirty-Eight

Why 'the good war' wasn't so good

Imprisoned poet's long-forgotten words mean more to us now

A slave is one who waits for someone to come and free him.
— Ezra Pound

I have kept repeating one important thought during my rantings over the past two years. It is this — realizing that the tragic attacks of September 11, 2001 were conceived, engineered and then covered up by the powers that be in Washington, D.C. provides us with an open window through which to analyze the misrepresented behavior of American foreign policy during the past two centuries.

Once we acknowledge the political pathology that has us in its grip, we have a realistic chance of rehabilitating our insane society. If we don't, we're about to become fish kill in a permanent red tide of various poisons.

Examining this happy history that has been falsely imbued in our minds by prejudiced corporate media and brainwashed school curricula affords a significant opportunity to reclaim our country from the corporate rapists who have hijacked it in the name of profit. I believe there is no other way to purge America of its destructive dementia and bring the true crooks to justice than to deconstruct the patriotic propaganda that has led us to believe we are a noble nation on the side of truth and beauty.

If we could do this, we could confront our past honestly, and see the devil's smile in the pleasant details of history we have grown up with. The first hurdle is getting Americans to understand about 9/11. The more intelligent among you know for certain something smells. Why else would there have been all these unexplained cover-ups in the name of national security, and all these unanswered questions about what really did happen? But once you have mastered the basic questions, you can't help but see the Arab hijacker fable as a deceptive stratagem to justify future wars and oppression against dark-skinned people from whom we want to steal precious things.

Only then, when you comprehend in your heart the level of cynicism and betrayal necessary to inflict such a grievous wound upon your own countrymen, can you begin to visualize what kind of animalistic society would cloak its policies of constant aggression and mass murder in the righteous euphemisms of fighting for freedom and democracy against dreaded evildoers.

The whole fable that has now come unraveled in the rapes and murders of imprisoned Iraqis now provides us a clear chance to see the true fabric of American behavior, so forgive me if I repeat myself from other essays and again try to make you realize that these recent, twisted exhibitions of heartless sadism are not exceptions to the rule of American behavior, but rather the norm. Wounded Knee. Dresden. My Lai. Fallujah.

It is only through this portal of realization and confession that we may make America into something that can be truly cherished, rather than what it is now, which is justifiably condemned by honest human beings everywhere.

In reviewing the history of America's involvement in foreign wars throughout the 20th century, I observed an uninterrupted series of false excuses — you know the list:

Philippines, Cuba, all of Central America at one time or other, Korea, Vietnam, Grenada, Panama, Iraq, Afghanistan, and Iraq again — used to justify carnage, all of it passed off as defending freedom and democracy, but beneath the surface all of it constructed to maintain financial advantage over a certain commodity or a certain geographical segment of the world. A small percentage of Americans has always known that these involvements have been about protecting the profit-making potential of some corporation which has contributed heavily to the man who made the decision to go shoot up some defenseless, Third World hamlet.

Initially, the only two wars that didn't fit into this pattern of exploitation and invasion were the two big ones, World Wars I and II. Those, we had been taught in schools, were good wars, in which America sacrificed many thousands of its own citizens and millions of lives in other countries to defend "freedom" from evil fascists, nasty Communists, or inscrutable Shintoists.

That always bothered me. I mean, things tend to stay true to form. Tigers don't change their stripes. How could it be, I thought awhile back, could the United States have engaged in all these bad wars, that were predicated upon provable lies, and yet have two good wars in the middle of the string? I reasoned I must be missing something, and I was.

Bits and pieces began to emerge. Worldwide Judea declared all-out war against Germany in the mid-30s. Earlier, the Treaty of Versailles, ram-rodded through by President Wilson's Jewish adviser Colonel House, handicapped Germany with onerous financial entanglements, all but guaranteeing, according to some historians, the inevitability of another war.

And then there was President Roosevelt's apparent

foreknowledge of the strike at Pearl Harbor, and his failure to tell the troops there, in order to aggravate American public opinion into support for war. And even the recent movie "Pearl Harbor" told the tale of how America cut off Japan's oil supply to stir up trouble in the first place.

But the real missing piece came leaping out at me a few days ago, when somebody sent me a story about the poet Ezra Pound, and what happened to him during and after World War II. For those who don't know, Pound — considered by many of those who know to be the greatest poet of the 20th century — was arrested for treason because of the broadcasts he made from Italy during the early 1940s that urged the United States not to get involved in the fighting.

The story was Michael Collins Piper's famous 1997 piece in the Barnes Review (http://www.barnesreview.org/ezrapound.htm).

Unfortunately, given the way histories tend to be written (namely, by the victors), what Pound did and what happened to him because of that are rather widely known, whereas what he actually said that got him in so much trouble is not.

And what he said turns out to be eerily appropriate for the horrible developments happening today. The stories you have been taught about World War II are wrong. Pound spent 13 years in a mental institution (without a trial) for being right.

Consider the way the word "Nazi" has been used in our language as a synonym for depravity. After a lifetime of use, the negative connotation is second-nature to us. But Pound didn't see it that way.

He believed that international bankers were on the side of the

U.S., Britain and the Soviet Union, and they were all arrayed against Germany. He insisted that without the machinations of the banks and their accomplices in the media, there would have been no war — and no wars ever.

Pound saw the American national tradition being perverted by the aggressive new internationalism, the brainchild of Jews who organized Soviet Communism, long had control of British banks, and manipulated the American President Roosevelt.

"Sometime the Anglo-Saxon may awaken to the fact that . . . nations are shoved into wars in order to destroy themselves, to break up their structure, to destroy their social order, to destroy their populations. And no more flaming and flagrant case appears in history than our own American Civil War, said to be an occidental record for size of armies employed and only surpassed by the more recent triumphs of [the Warburg banking family:] the wars of 1914 and the present one."

Although Pound's broadcasts centered on keeping Americans out of World War II, the underlying theme of most of his pieces was money. Free people need to be in control of their money if they are to be actually free, Pound stressed. On the issues of usury and the control of money and economy by private special interests, Pound thundered: "There is no freedom without economic freedom," he said. "Freedom that does not include freedom from debt is plain bunkum."

Pound believed usury was the cause of war throughout history. "The usury system does no nation . . . any good whatsoever. It is an internal peril to him who hath, and it can make no use of nations in the play of international diplomacy save to breed strife between them and use the worst as flails against the best. It is the usurer's game to hurl the savage against the civilized opponent. The game is not pretty; it is not a very safe game. It does no one any credit."

Pound tried to tell everyone that World War II was not an isolated event, and in his words we can hear the warnings that come down to us now in the echoes of Vietnam, Palestine, Afghanistan and Iraq.

"This war did not begin in 1939. It is not a unique result of the infamous Versailles Treaty. It is impossible to understand it without knowing at least a few precedent historic events, which mark the cycle of combat. No man can understand it without knowing at least a few facts and their chronological sequence."

And his words in 1942 ring presciently for the future of America as the U.S. war machine rumbles around the planet in 2004 and threatens every nation on earth.

"This war is part of the age-old struggle between the usurer and the rest of mankind: between the usurer and peasant, the usurer and producer, and finally between the usurer and the merchant, between usurocracy and the mercantilist system . . ."

World War II was not an isolated event. It was part of a deliberate trend spanning centuries, Pound insisted.

"The present war," he said, "dates at least from the founding of the Bank of England at the end of the 17th century, 1694-8. Half a century later, the London usurocracy shut down on the issue of paper money by the Pennsylvania colony, A.D. 1750."

According to Pound, it was the money issue (above all) that

united the Allies during the second 20th-century war against Germany: "Gold. Nothing else uniting the three governments, England, Russia, United States of America. That is the interest — gold, usury, debt, monopoly, class interest, and possibly gross indifference and contempt for humanity."

The real enemy, said Pound, was international capitalism. All people everywhere were victims: "They're working day and night, picking your pockets," he said.

Pound said: "Usury has gnawed into England since the days of Elizabeth. First it was mortgages, mortgages on earls' estates; usury against the feudal nobility. Then there were attacks on the common land, filchings of village common pasture. Then there developed a usury system, an international usury system, from Cromwell's time, ever increasing."

When all was said and done, Pound predicted it would be the big money interests who would really win the war — not any particular nation-state — and the foundation for future wars would be set in place: "The nomadic parasites will shift out of London and into Manhattan. And this will be presented under a camouflage of national slogans. It will be represented as an American victory. It will not be an American victory. The moment is serious. The moment is also confusing. It is confusing because there are two sets of concurrent phenomena, namely, those connected with fighting this war, and those which sow seeds for the next one."

We are clearly in the same spot today.

Pound said one of the major reasons for World War II was the manipulation of the press, particularly in the United

States: "I naturally mistrust newspaper news from America," he declared. "I grope in the mass of lies, knowing most of the sources are wholly untrustworthy."

And now. Same story, different day. Pound tried to warn us, more than 60 years ago, but we threw him into an insane asylum for 13 years, the best poet of the 20th century given his reward by the country he loved for speaking his mind in the land of Freedom of Speech.

A harbinger perhaps of the new Homeland Security laws that ignores all poets and truth-tellers and keep us securely on the road to war for the profits of a precious, pathological few.

Now the entire population of the planet is about to be consigned to a worldwide capitalist insane asylum, in which love and honor are merely interesting advertising strategies useful in the sale of racy consumer goods, while loyalty and patriotism become mere fairy tales at contract time, to be sold by all to the highest bidder seeking to steal parts of the world from someone else.

Now as then, the world's future rests upon those with ears to hear.

Chapter Thirty-Nine

'In the mouth of madness'

As mass insanity grips the world, people of principle remain silent

And if you read between the lines you'd know that I'm just trying to understand the feelings that you lack.
— Gordon Lightfoot

A lot of you have been asking why I haven't written anything lately.

My jaw dropped about three weeks ago and damn few words have come out of my mouth ever since. Mostly I've been asking for food, lots of food. And watching a lot of movies, the black and white ones, film noir, trying to pretend I don't live in this world of 2004. I think this is what many people do when they reach a certain age, when current events overtake them and they can't cope with it, and try to take refuge in the past.

But let's face it. I can't cope with this reality. It's more than I can handle. The best phrase to describe it? Incredulous stupefaction. My head just wags back and forth involuntarily these days.

Some of my friends say I simply read too much bad news. Since the 9/11 deception, there's been anthrax, Afghanistan, Patriot Act, and Iraq, to list the major chapters that go along with perhaps the worst of all the atrocities, that never-ending story about the mass murder of the Palestinians that the world seems so intent on ignoring. And I've been writing about all this ceaselessly for the past couple of years. And I don't mean to demean all those wonderful people who have written to me in appreciative support, but hell, there are six billion people in the world, and most of them are not listening, or doing anything constructive to stop this juggernaut of carnage that is really the world's dominant money-making operation.

Strife makes money for the rich losers who foment it. And it's getting me down to the point of speechlessness.

What hope exists if people who profess to adhere to the principles of the good life remain silent?

For me, this recent paralysis really began with the Abu Ghraib prison revelations. Attaching that poor Iraqi man to electrical wires. That's a photograph that ranks with Jack Ruby plugging Lee Harvey Oswald, with the Challenger explosion, with that little naked Vietnamese girl running screaming from napalm in the ranks of the most famous pictures in American history.

Any American that doesn't feel an overwhelming sense of shame is a complete sociopath. Unfortunately, it would seem that a majority of the American populace — as well as virtually all its leaders — are exactly that: mealy-mouthed chicken-shit perverted immoral sadistic socio-paths. And many of them carry holy books and insist these atrocities are justified.

If the objective of the great Zionist Illuminati Masonic conspiracy is to completely demoralize Americans, the prison scandal was the thing that did it for me. And I'm not one who has exactly tried to hide his head in the sand over time. I've tried to deal with all the facts in a forthright way.

9/11 was an inside job covered up by politicians we elected and media we read every day.

The anthrax attacks came from our own government, but no one was prosecuted.

The Patriot Act was a clearly provable act of treason in which virtually all of our Congress participated.

Afghanistan was target practice on hapless nomads to reestablish the drug trade that is run by the CIA.

And Iraq. Poor Iraq. The American presence in Iraq is what? What do you want to call it?

A deliberate attempt to show the world what will happen to it if it opposes American financial totalitarianism? Your residents will be shot down in cold blood. Those who survive will be stripped naked and raped if they're female, humiliated if they're male. Ghoulish American soldiers will trifle with the corpses of your relatives and make photographs to send home to their friends to prove they're insane.

America robbed Iraq of everything it had, its riches, its dignity, its health, its future. This is the real message America is sending to the world. If the rest of the world doesn't stop America in its tracks, right now, the world has no future. Or, the future it has will be the rubble of the Gaza strip and the makeshift cemeteries of Fallujah.

Imagine. Turning Yankee Stadium into a giant makeshift cemetery. That's what real people — husbands and moms and orphaned children — are contemplating today in Fallujah. The brave people of Fallujah who repulsed the great American war machine.

And then the images of Abu Ghraib and the new American gulag that stretches around the world return. These prisoners have no rights and face torture, even though their captors know they are innocent. This is the new (?) American way, a disgusting reality that most Americans refuse to face.

It is one thing to pretend you don't know American prosperity has been gained by the exploitation of millions of Third World peasants. It is quite another thing to know that the American military practices a policy of torture and indiscriminate murder everywhere in the world.

And so, like me, many Americans turn away from the psychotic spectacle, unable to cope with it.

But we all ought to think twice about doing this, about not facing the reality of what is happening now. Because if we turn away from this, we're only inviting the same sick thugs to do the same wacko stuff, the same demonic perversions, on us.

If we leave George W. Bush in charge — or for that matter, if we elect John Kerry — we guarantee that we all will soon be prisoners in Abu Ghraib prison, in one stark form or another.

The paradigm is, of course, Nick Berg. There are so many questions about that sorry beheading episode that an accurate analysis of the whole event remains impossible. But what is obvious is American involvement. The powers that be had this man killed to create a public relations episode to take the media focus off its appalling torture and murder of imprisoned Iraqi innocents.

Do you realize what this means? It means that it is now OK for the U.S. federal government to come into your home and kill you because they then will tell a story to the public explaining what a threat you were to Homeland Security. If you think this is farfetched, I suggest you watch the Nick Berg carefully video and contemplate your own future. (Hint: you have none.)

Who will be held responsible for this horrific act? We know the policy of emotionally devastating prisoners of the U.S. war machine came from the very top of the organizational chart. We know that this stunt was ordered by the same power freaks who staged 9/11 to cram a state of permanent war down our throats.

And yet we accede to it. What can we DO about it, we ask? We pretend we are powerless.

In my mind, George W. Bush is already guilty of mass murder and treason for what he did — or didn't do — about 9/11. As commander in chief of the war machine, he must also take responsibility for Nick Berg, a deliberate murder for propaganda purposes. I wonder if God told him to do it, just like God told him to invade Afghanistan.

Doesn't it chill you to know that the life of an American citizen can be squandered in this way, so cynically, with all the public facts about it so twisted? Please contemplate the chances that something like this could happen to you.

And continue to ask the question: who is to be held responsible for all these murders, these endless murders? Who do you think?

In my need to escape this bleak news-scape these days, I contemplate a movie made more than a decade ago that, like all good movies do, reflects what is happening now. It was called "In the Mouth of Madness," made by that controversial Grade-B horror movie guru John Carpenter. And it depicts a progressively horrific sequence of inexplicable murders woven into a tale about some psycho and his holy book.

The astonishing punch-line at the end reveals that the people who are watching the movie in horror are actually the same people who are IN the movie committing the bloody murders.

You can imagine the wide-eyed hysterical laughter when the main character realizes he is the person in the movie doing the killing. In fact, if you watch the evening news tonight, and then go into your bathroom and stare into the mirror, you can probably re-create the scene yourself.

Chapter Forty

You can't lie to God

Yet most American Christians and Jews lie about Iraq, Islam, and themselves

The Tibetan Book of the Dead (Evans-Wentz version) is one of my favorite books. It describes how after death our souls pass through a place called the bardo, and after reviewing every event that has happened in our lives through conversations and confrontations with apparitions called the Peaceful and Wrathful Deities, we either evolve into pure light or choose the time and place of our next reappearance on this physical plane.

I am not a believer in reincarnation. So it took me awhile to realize that this ancient ritual prescription is more about life than it is about death. We carry the memories of every bad thing we've ever done in this life with us, and when we die, these thoughtless transgressions are going to come back to bother us, which makes it a lot better to confront those episodes long before we breathe our last. You know, beat the rush! Make those last moments more comfortable, because when you think about it, we really live our lives in order to have our deaths be the best, most enlightening experience of our lives. I mean, nobody has an utterly clean slate after very many years of life, but having confronted one's own faults prior to the moment of big sleep will at least make that last closing of the eyes a lot more peaceful.

It was in this vein I was chatting with a friend the other day about the sundry forms of religion in the world, many of which seem hateful skeletons of what a fully functional, compassionate and healthful human being should be.

Of course it was the vengeful, superficial brand of religion espoused by the current U.S. president that set our tongues to wagging. George W. Bush is fond of saying how he talks to God every day, and God tells him which country to invade, which innocent people to slaughter from the air with his high-tech weaponry, and presumably, which multinational corporations upon whom to bestow his ill-gotten booty.

Bush's brand of religion is endorsed by a larger audience of American evangelical Bible-thumpers, many of whom advocate the death penalty for such human subgroups as homosexuals, peaceniks, and all those who don't accept the fire-and-brimstone version of their Christian holy book.

In our conversation, my friend, shaking her head at all these punitive pronouncements so popular among those who seek to get everyone else to believe the way they do, brought up Catholic confession, and noted that at least Catholics are made to verbally confess their sins on a regular basis to help keep them living honest lives.

But as far as the bizarre belief that some people, including Catholics and George W. Bush (among millions of others), have special insight as to what "God" really said, nothing these days tops for sheer sickness the relationship between the Jews of Israel and the evangelical Christians of the United States, all of whom are collectively known as Zionists.

This special relationship, which is behind what is perhaps the most heartless and destructive political philosophy of all time (the policy of pre-emptive war), links Jews and Christians in a downright pathological bond in which the two pretend to be philosophical allies while underneath the surface each is working and praying for the utter destruction of the other group.

The Christian evangelicals support Israel because it fits their fixated belief that their messiah will only return if Israel is controlled by the Jews. However, when their messiah returns, they believe he will destroy the entire Jewish population, or at least those who don't instantly accept Christ as their savior. The cynical Jews, on the other hand, don't really care what the Zionist Christians think, because they don't believe in Christ at all and are merely contented by the political and financial support brought to them by a group they consider subhuman, but politically important. This is truly a match made in hell, the forging of a powerful coalition of lunatics who together aim to turn the world into a smoldering cinder merely to fulfill their own mutually exclusive and insane desires.

So, getting back to the conversation with my friend, she insisted that some people, when push comes to shove, actually try to lie to God because their egos are so big, and their religion is merely something they use a badge of social status and acceptance. These people, she insisted, merely use the concept of God for their own psychological aggrandizement, and because they are willing to lie to God, they certainly are willing to lie to their families, friends, and everybody to achieve their own selfish objectives.

I let this percolate around in my mind for awhile, and then vehemently (or as strenuously as you can be when you love someone and disagree with them) objected to her characterization that people, in their last moments of life, would actually try to lie to God.

Maybe it's because I've led a somewhat sheltered life. For instance, I've never, like so many Iraqi and Palestinian families, had a loved one shot to death by a soulless enemy right in front my eyes. Or like a Hutu or a Tutsi, I've never seen one of my children hacked to death by someone who can't explain why he's doing what he's doing. Or, like an Afghani or a Serb, I've never seen one of my children born with grotesque external tumors on his face because someone had bombed my neighborhood with poisonous radioactive ammunition. I've led a sheltered, coddled, relatively affluent American life, for which I constantly give thanks to God and many others for my good luck.

But the idea that, at the final moment of death, someone would actually lie to God as they enter the infinite realm of dark shadows is just beyond my comprehension. How could anyone, faced with the freighted moment of their final departure from this life, tell a lie to an all-encompassing being who knows the truth about everything? What kind of delusional indoctrination could make somebody attempt something so ludicrously impossible?

Then I began to re-examine all these hateful things that so-called religious people are constantly saying. I have long held the belief that the people you can trust least are religious people, because they use their divine excuses to refute reason in any and all situations. The current U.S. demolition of Iraq provides a clear example. We are going to bomb these innocent people into submission so they can have freedom. What is wrong with this picture?

It is high time for people of good conscience to ignore the dictates of their so-called spiritual leaders and abandon their churches if they continue to preach divine retribution for what is clearly a case of robbery and mass murder cloaked in noble rhetoric.

And it is time for all Americans to turn on their murderous government and support freedom for the Iraqi people against the shocking sexual perversions of the U.S. government. That's right — only perverts and moral criminals support what the U.S. is doing in Iraq.

What is right is right, and the U.S. attack on Iraq is clearly wrong — immoral, inhumane, ignorant, and against every single word a truly just God would ever utter through those who pretend to be his bewitched human interpreters.

The same goes for Christian and Jewish pronouncements against Islam. Muhammad wrote that worshippers of other religions should be protected against discrimination, and their shrines protected. That makes Islam morally superior to both Christianity and Judaism, whose commonly held holy books (i.e, the Old Testament) endlessly preach destruction, murder, and robbery against all those who won't accept their evil version of ancient events.

To all Christians, I say: how can you accept as your messiah a cynical, figmented construct not verifiable in history who was invented by a Jewish rabbi who changed his name from Saul to Paul?

And to all Jews I say: your God is Moloch, who values money and power over compassion and respect. Anyone who thinks their subgroup is supernaturally superior to all others is bound to be destroyed by the resentful retribution of the masses. It's only a matter of time.

In this respect, both Christians and Jews worship an evil God. All of you will suffer eternal torment when you die for failure to use both your brain and your heart to a minimal extent. If you believe God put us here, it had to be for us to use our brains and our hearts to protect and nurture this wonderful garden he gave us to thrive in.

Getting back to the subject of lying to God, I switch now to another Book of the Dead, the Egyptian one, the actual title of which is "The Book of Going Forth by Day," for a much more intelligent and functional description of what happens to you when you die, and how you should really live your life (if you need to be religious at all, and sooner or later, most of us do).

When you die, you go before the Goddess Ma'at and your soul is put on a scale and weighed against the Feather of Truth. If your unforgiven sins reveal that your soul is no heavier that that single feather, then your soul is allowed to travel blissfully through the Field of Reeds and across the River of Truth to the Island of the Just, where it will repose in peace forever.

But if it is found to be heavier than the Feather of Truth, your soul is fed to Thoth's dog! (Think very big teeth.)

I'm sure you will agree with me that in this sad day and age of war and lies that the gurgling hordes of human souls on this planet — those who believe you can lie to God by using the hateful phrases of warped preachers who are far more interested in property than propriety — are just so much dog food.

Chapter Forty-One

What and why

Because you believe America's lies, you can expect a bullet with your name on it

Ever wake yourself out of a sound sleep because you were screaming at yourself in a dream?

Personally, I've never done that before. Yet I just did exactly that.

WHAT DO YOU NEED TO TELL THEM?
AND WHY DO THEY NEED TO KNOW?!

Over and over I kept berating myself with this manic mantra, tossing and turning, sheets all tangled up in a sweaty knot. All those stories I'd written. This subject and that approach. This example and that phrase. Has it been a waste of time? Most people didn't believe what I was saying. They couldn't see the importance of it. It was like I was stumbling through a darkened town in the middle of the night shouting "FIRE!" and sleepy people rolled over in their beds and muttered, "What the hell is he raving about?" before closing their eyes and going back to sleep. Only the town was America. The year 2004.

WHAT? And WHY?

My message was not getting through. People couldn't see the value of it, the purpose of it. Why would anyone need to know something like that? That their government had a master plan to kill millions, and had already killed tens of thousands.

A conspiracy theory, that's all it was, right?

What importance could this knowledge — that was so important to me! — possibly have for ordinary people just trying to live their lives, just trying to get by. If they kept their heads down and let the power brokers have their way, it would all blow over — right? And America would return to the Elysian vision of the past — right?

Yet my voice wouldn't let me sleep, and my wheezy snore turned into the very clear barking of a drill sergeant in my roiling brain.

"This is very important, John. Wake up. They haven't understood what you've been trying to say. Think clearly about this. Think about what would work. Think about what would really reach them."

On the film, the plane flies serenely, over and over, and slams into the facade of the skyscraper. Over and over we watch the video and try to deduce the truth from slow motion puffs of smoke. From how those towers fell on cue, as if somebody pulled a switch.

"YOU NEED TO TELL PEOPLE DIRECTLY. YOU NEED TO SPEAK TO THEM, FORCEFULLY, SURELY, TRULY. STUFF THE EXOTIC THEORIES. JUST MAKE YOUR POINT."

You know what a harbinger is? A harbinger is a clue that shows that something is going to happen soon, especially something bad. You know when that plane drove into that building? That was a harbinger of what's going to happen to your very own future!

315

"YOU NEED TO BE CLEAR ABOUT IT. MAKE THEM
UNDERSTAND. MAKE THEM REALIZE THE DANGER
THEY ARE IN."

I've said it over and over. The U.S. government planned,
executed, and then covered up the 9/11 caper, covered it up
with layers of clumsy lies and false leads, like pseudo
hijackers with phony names and heart-wrenching cell phone
calls that couldn't have possibly been made. As Barb
Honegger recently wrote on the Conspiracy Planet website,
they covered it up by piggybacking the whole plot on a
military exercise that was being conducted that very day, so
that the air defenses would hesitate intercepting the hijacked
airliners, so that the practice exercise could become real, and
the rich oil pigs could get their way playing hog-in-trough
with all the coins in the U.S. Treasury.

There were so many other reasons: Silverstein's insurance
scam, the fact that the Twin Towers needed to be demolished
anyway because of flawed construction techniques, the
zillions to be made in shrewd investments guaranteed by the
foreknowledge of destruction, and a sure way to defame
Muslims permanently as an excuse to steal their oil.

But mostly it was to terminate American democracy, because
as Zbigniew Brzezinski had warned us, no nation could be
democratic at home and rapacious abroad. And America
needs to be absolutely heartless abroad to please its defense
contractors, to satisfy the international bankers who control
all our money. This was a good way to end democracy once
and for all, and the deed has been done.

"TELL THEM CLEARLY WHAT REALLY HAPPENED."

The fat cats who run everything — how do you spell
Rothschild? — determined that this would be the event to

trigger permanent war, the social state that makes bankers the most money. And since there was no convenient enemy to nurture carefully until it was time to destroy him — like Hitler or Saddam — the natural thing would be to pin the blame on Muslims, and continue the racist crusades that have been going on for a thousand years.

Just like WTC1 and Oklahoma City (where, in the latter, shadowy Muslim puppets were waiting in the background to serve as patsies just in case the phony story about the Patriot wackos in rental truck fell apart — but thanks to corrupt courts, McVeigh was fried and very few smelled the real story that bombs inside the Murrah building meant our government did that job, too), 9/11 was devised in Washington, like all those other events, for the purpose of replacing the unpredictable chaos of liberty with the tightly regimented exploitation of sheer totalitarian profit maximization. That's what NAFTA, the Patriot Act, the FCC consolidation were all about. And 9/11. Mission accomplished. The permanent war is on.

Our whole system of living is based on a lie. The lie that we can pile up enough money so that we don't have to be honest and compassionate, that we can kill anybody we want and take whatever they have and make it our own. That is what the American way has become. And most of the rest of the world, sycophantic cowards all, timidly follows suit.

American prosperity is based on war. And we, the average citizens, get so little of it. Most of it goes to those who get the Bush tax breaks and no-bid contracts. You know how it goes with addictions: the more you have the more you want. So now with the American economy, the plan is to crash it, eliminate most of the population, and resell the real estate that will be taken by default. Great plan. Superior profit potential. For those who have the guns.

WHAT DO YOU NEED TO TELL THEM?
AND WHY DO THEY NEED TO KNOW?!

9/11 was no attack by Islamic malcontents. It was a deliberately scripted terror event to turn America into a police state and simultaneously make billions of dollars for the richest people in the world, some of whom live in this country, many of whom live in Europe, Israel, Arabia and elsewhere. They were the same friends of the Bush family who stole all those treasures from the Iraqi museum. Many members of the Council on Foreign Relations know exactly what happened on 9/11, why it was done, and how it was planned. Some of them are even on the official commission investigating the matter. Some of them also own the giant media conglomerates who ten minutes after the Twin Towers fell declared Osama bin Laden had done it.

The planes flew into the skyscrapers and people died because it served the profit purposes of the richest men in the country. This is what that FBI report into pre-9/11 investments found out; and this is what the infamous Chicago Board of Options report stated. But both documents have been suppressed by the corrupt FBI, which says publicly there was nothing suspicious in the pre-9/11 stock trades.

We must demand that this evidence be released to the public. We must demand it. It will reveal some of the most well-known names in America as exactly the people behind the 9/11 caper. The most well-known names of all.

The FBI's lie about this report is of the magnitude that Iraq possessed weapons of mass destruction when it was invaded, but the American people don't seem to care if their government lies to them, even if it means the ritual sacrifice of their own children in Iraq, or their own countrymen in New York City.

9/11 was a lie, but the American people don't care, even when they realize that the same fate awaits them in our new police state future.

I am awake. JUST TELL THEM WHAT HAPPENED. I understand the facts, the context of American history and the machinations of the international bankers, that Bush is a conveniently positioned sociopath manipulated by rich people with big plans. Big evil plans. And they don't care who they kill. Including you.

I am awake, but the rest of the country continues to slumber. They just won't wake up. It is the sleep of fools.

And why do you need to know? WHY DO YOU NEED TO KNOW? Because our soldiers have been taught to gun down innocent families for no reason. For no reason at all. For the lies their generals tell them. And because one of those doped-up, brain-dead, radiation-laden soldiers is really pissed that he's been lied to, left in harm's way, and ordered to do things he wouldn't have done of his own accord in his worst nightmare.

It's not drug-induced dementia, its policy, devised at the very top of the organizational chart of the U.S. government. The snake that eats its own tail. These soldiers you support and venerate, who have learned to kill women and children without a second thought.

Now his worst nightmare is about to become your worst nightmare. Because one of those sorry soldiers has a bullet with your name on it.

And like the plane that drove into that tall building, which you just can't believe was ordered by your own government, you probably won't believe this story until you feel that bullet enter your body. And then you will believe it.

Stay tuned. It's likely to happen soon. Sooner than you think.

<u>Acknowledgments</u>

It is my great good fortune to have literally thousands of people to thank for the creation of this book, without whose guidance, support, advice, criticism and friendship it would not have been possible.

The widespread exposure of these essays on the Internet was greatly aided by the support of Jeff Rense, James Neff, Dave Patterson, Paul Fearon, Peter Meyer, Victor Thorn and Lisa Guliani, Keith Lampe, David Marvasti, Schantz, Alistair Thompson, Bev Conover, David Cogswell, Graham Jukes, Edna Spennato, Hassan al-Najjar, Jocelyn Braddell, Qasim Khan, John Stadtmiller, Clayton Douglas, Tim Barton, Ingri Cassell and Don Harkins, Brian Salter and Bob Feldman, Tony Graffeo, Michel Chossudovsky, Alice Cherbonnier, Information Clearinghouse Tom, Joe Vialls, Mark Elsis, Shiu M. Hung, Ken Vardon, Vyzygoth IV, Israel Shamir, Michael Rivero, Carol Adler, Meria Heller, Texe Marrs, Peter Kawaja, Carol Brouillet, Blagovesta Doncheva, and Sergius Kislenko, among many others who helped me.

For professional inspiration in their pursuit of the true facts about 9/11 and the operation of the world in general I would like to thank, in addition to those listed above, Ralph Omholt, Jerry Russell, Rick Stanley (both of them), Chris Emery, Don Stacey, Eric Walberg, George Paxinos, Harmon Taylor, Jerry Longspaugh, Jim Kirwan, Judith Moriarty, Maisoon Rice, Richard Wall, Alex, Rick Ensminger, Virginia Raines, J.B. Campbell, and Ernst Zundel

And last but anything but least, I would like to thank my major benefactors without whom this book would definitely not have been possible: Mick Donelan, Dave Bunford, Julie

Boyd, Guido Condosta, Evelyn Goodman, Helen Crowe, Ken Hampshire, Bill Stanish, Mike Djuricich, Michael Brady, Steve Roberts, Michael Lawrence Morton, David Morrison, Leslie Rayland, Carolyn Tester, Mark A. Welch, Cindy Gerber, Bill Stegmeier, Judy Andreas, and Barbra-renée Brighenti.